Visions of
Another World
The Autobiography of a Medium

Visionary and Poet
Stephen O'Brien

Voices

PO Box 8, Swansea, United Kingdom, SA1 1BL

'VISIONS OF ANOTHER WORLD'
A VOICES BOOK
ISBN: 0-9536620-3-9

PRINTING HISTORY:
Aquarian Press edition published 1989
Aquarian Press edition reprinted 1989
Aquarian Press edition reprinted 1990 (three times)
HarperCollins edition reprinted in 1991
HarperCollins edition reprinted 1992 to 1996 (five times)
Voices Books New Revised Edition 2000

Typeset by *Voices*.

Reproduced, printed and bound
in Great Britain by Cox & Wyman Ltd.,
Reading, Berkshire.

For my mother, Beatrice,
and all my friends in both worlds,
in appreciation of your love and friendship.

Acknowledgements

*My thanks to **Psychic News**,
and all the people, from both sides of Life,
who have so willingly contributed accounts
for this volume.*

Contents

Part One
The Spirit Calls

Part Two
The Mission Begins

Part Three
Rays of Spiritual Light

'I have stood on the mountaintops
of the Shining Lands
and experienced countless Visions of Other Worlds
Beyond Death,
and I am not afraid to die;
for Death is the Great Liberator,
the Bright Angel who leads all living things
into an Eternal Life,
which is their natural birthright.'

Stephen O'Brien,
Swansea,
Wales, 1988.

PART ONE

The Spirit Calls

Testament

Let me set this down
  before my lips are stilled
  and my eyes are closed by sleep;
  before my brain can blur events
  into a rushing stream.

Let me carve what I've seen,
  what I've learned
  — so many remarkable things —
  so that generations yet unborn
  may drink from the experiences
  gifted to me
  by the One who is All.

Let me set it down at this point in history;
    while I remember,
      and before I forget...

Stephen O'Brien,
'Willowtrees',
Wales, 2000.

1

The Spirit Calls

Bang! Bang! Bang! Bang! Bang!
I woke up startled and sat bolt upright in the bed.
Bang! Bang! Bang! Bang!
The ghostly hammering on our front door echoed up the stairway. I was ten years old and terrified by the deafeningly loud noise.

Who could be calling on us at two o'clock in the morning?

My brother John slept peacefully beside me and so did Uncle Billy across the room. Why didn't they wake up? Couldn't they hear this unearthly sound?

Bang! Bang! Bang! Bang! Bang!
I shook John frantically but he didn't flinch. The phantom hammering continued. But why didn't mother or father answer the door? Perhaps I was dreaming?

I gripped the skin on my arm and gave it a hard pinch and immediately registered the pain — I was wide awake. But I couldn't get up;

I couldn't move. I was paralysed with fear.

In my childish mind I imagined some hideous monster outside our house trying to get in. He was after *me*, I thought. I shot underneath the bedclothes and hid my face from the night.

I knew if I went to the window and looked down I'd see who it was but I just couldn't do it. I froze in the bed, clutching at my sleeping brother.

The ghostly noise was growing louder now, more insistent on gaining my attention. It seemed to echo through the walls and windows, a hollow, eerie sound. I cuddled up to John and told myself if I ignored it, it would go away — but it didn't. It continued louder than ever.

Bang! Bang! Bang! Bang! Bang!

With my heart pounding in my chest and sweat upon my brow, I began to tremble. Why was this happening?

Then — just as quickly as the phantom hammering had started — it suddenly stopped.

I gasped in fright and waited and listened.

A deafening silence filled the night... calmness fell about the house again and not a sound could be heard.

The ghostly visitor had gone.

I don't know how long I lay there in that dark room before I breathed a heavy sigh of relief; I knew only that I couldn't understand what had happened.

Why hadn't someone got up?

The unearthly noise had been loud enough to wake the dead.

I couldn't figure it out, so I pulled the sheets up over my head, clung onto my brother and decided to ask my mother for an answer tomorrow.

Halfway through the night I eventually settled down and fell into a deep and troubled sleep...

I awoke at dawn. Our small terraced house in Gors Avenue was lit by the early sun. I dressed quickly and went to the window and peered down to see if our phantom caller had left any trace of his presence. But there was nothing: no mysterious footprints or scratchings on the door — nothing but the flowers and the violet dawn lights.

At breakfast everyone said they hadn't heard the hammering in the night. They said I'd imagined it.

'But I *didn't*! I was wide awake and I pinched myself to prove it. *Look!*' And I showed my mother the pinch-mark on my arm.

'Well,' she sighed, glancing at the bruise, 'perhaps someone got the wrong address. It may have been a tramp.'

'Don't you believe me?' I cried. 'The noise shook the air.'

There was no reply, and no more was said about our mystery caller.

But that didn't satisfy me — I wanted an answer and was determined to get one. So that evening I pulled on my winter coat and went to see old Mrs King. She was a Spiritualist who lived just down the terrace and I was fond of her homely manner and kind ways. If anyone could give me an answer *she* could, I reasoned — she knew all about these odd things.

Visiting her was like walking back into Victorian times. Her shabby kitchen was lit only by a few candles and a flickering oil lamp. Everything was gloomy, dark and unkempt on account of her great age and infirmities. I entered the musty kitchen and found Mrs King all huddled up in her usual fireside chair; she was eating a bowl of thick steamy soup. Lit by the orange glow from the fire, she sat like a tiny wax doll; her withered features and pointed nose made her look for all the world like a character from a Dickens novel. She would never let me call her anything else but 'Gran'.

'Well,' she croaked, 'it sounds like *their* work to me.' And she pointed a bony finger towards the ceiling and glared at me over her blue-tinted spectacles. 'It'll be *them* — that's who it is.' Then she mopped up her soup with some stale bread.

Before I could frame my next question there was a loud *thud* on the kitchen door. We turned to see what was happening and the latch lifted up of its own accord and the battered door slowly creaked open wide. But there was nothing outside except the chill night air. Gran and I exchanged furtive glances.

'Oh, here they are again,' she muttered. 'Go and shut it, Stephen.'

I did as she asked but thought to myself: I don't know why I'm bothering, it'll only open again as soon as I sit down. And sure enough, it did. With a strangled creak the door unlatched itself and swung open once more. Gran glowered at me as though it were my fault.

'Well I'll be jiggered!' she said. 'This always happens when you're here. You attract them, Stephen.'

After closing the door again it came as no surprise to see it once more defy all known physical laws and open on its own. As I shut it for the third time Gran's temper suddenly exploded.

'Now listen here, you lot!' she shouted at the spirit people. 'It's got to *stop*, all this opening of doors! It's all right for you — you can't feel the cold like us! Now give it a rest, will you!'

Silence fell in folds around the room.

The pungent oil lamp spluttered in the gloomy kitchen, and the wings of a golden moth fluttered against the windowpane outside, trying to get into the of circle of light where Gran and I sat so cosily.

We waited with bated breath for about a minute, both glaring at the door, but thankfully, it remained shut; so Gran carried on with her soup. 'You see, some folks attract spirit people like moths to a candle,' she said, 'and you're one of them, Stephen.'

I listened to the old lady seated in the shadows, giving her wisdom so freely and with such sincerity that I was captivated. There she sat, spinning tales about a world beyond time and space, a mysterious world of the spirit into which everyone would go one day, no matter what they believed or what they'd done — everyone lived on into eternity according to Gran.

To a ten-year-old boy she seemed like the Oracle at Delphi, a fount of never-ending wisdom.

Her stories seemed to belong to a world of long ago, somewhere in the distant past, but they enthralled me.

Seated in the flickering firelight, which sent strange shadows dancing across the faded wallpaper, I learned about her visits to the little Spiritualist church at the bottom of Oxford Street where she'd sit in what she called 'the open circle'. She spoke with reverence of the times when she felt privileged enough to catch a glimpse of a spirit person there, or to hear a sentence from the so-called 'dead', which was to be delivered to someone in the church.

Gran would then smile as she recalled giving out her 'messages', as she called them, to the congregation.

'I only get bits and pieces,' she'd say, 'but if what I get from the spirit world helps people then that'll do me.'

Then she'd furrow her brow, deepen her voice and announce with gusto to any invisible guests: 'But I only want *the truth*, mind you! I don't want any mischief-makers, nor any fibbers. The truth is all I'll accept and if you can't give me that then you can go and take a running jump!' And I couldn't resist a smile.

'Now,' she said, 'about that knocking on your

front door...' I leaned forward in my seat, eager for an answer. She took a breath then whispered low, 'One day, young Stephen — now mark my words well — one day, you could be a wonderful medium.'

There was silence.

What could I say to that? I returned an innocent look. She took another deep breath and stared over my shoulder. 'There's a North American Indian behind you, telling me this.'

I turned quickly but saw no one; yet *someone* was definitely there because I could feel their electric presence so strongly.

'Yes,' said Gran in her matter-of-fact way, 'you're a medium. They'll be waiting for you' — and quite unperturbed she finished off schlurping her soup.

It was getting late and I hadn't told anyone where I was going, so I fastened my coat and left her in the shadows and dashed out into the cold night.

As I made my way home a million thoughts whirled through my mind: Me? A medium? No: she'd made a mistake. I was only ten years old, how could I be a medium?

But then I felt uneasy. I recalled the strange events of the last few days: those phantom hands, Gran's kitchen door unlatching itself — there seemed to be a link there somewhere.

I pulled up my collar against the sharp wind. My young mind began to perceive some kind of pattern; but I soon dismissed the idea and decided to tell no one at home. I was going to keep this to myself. After all, it's not the sort of thing you could suddenly blurt out.

Very glad to enter our small house and get in from the biting cold, I shouted 'Goodnight!' to everyone and quickly climbed the stairs to bed. But on the way up I had the usual feeling of someone walking behind me: the hairs on the back of my neck had stood on end since I'd left Gran's and they were still bristling now. There was no doubt in my mind.

Someone had followed me home.

I could feel those invisible eyes watching as I swiftly undressed and dived under the cold sheets.

But who was out there in the darkness? Who was it that clamoured for my attention?

I was too frightened to look into the room but my sensitivity told me that there were people there, watching... But why? I dared myself to peer at them but I just couldn't do it. I kept my head firmly covered.

It had all been too much for me, so I tried to relax and get some sleep. Just as I became dozy I felt myself falling down and down. Something strange was happening to me... I was plummeting down into the blackness of nowhere at incredible speed, whirling and twisting... like a parachute-jump into deep space. I spiralled round and round, falling, swirling, dropping at an immense pace yet thoroughly enjoying the whole experience. The lightness and carelessness were marvellous.

Then it ceased abruptly and I realised I was

floating up and away from the bed. Yet how was this possible?

When I glanced back over my shoulder I saw that I'd left my physical form sound asleep beneath me, and in my spirit body I was sailing upwards.

I inspected the ceiling-rose and got so close to it that my spirit eyes crossed. I decided to take a look at the china water jug and bowl on the dresser and before I knew it I was there, instantly placed beside them by my power of thought.

Then all at once I became aware of two invisible people standing nearby and I was swamped by an overwhelming childish fear — and instantly found myself back inside my physical body again. I quickly pulled the sheets up over my head.

But out in the dark room I knew there was a Red Indian and his squaw standing at the foot of the bed: I felt their loving, caring presence, their arms outstretched towards me.

Then everything became heavy and dull and my consciousness slipped away as I fell into a deep and dreamless sleep...

In the days ahead no one mentioned our mystery caller again; everyone seemed to forget about him. But I began to wonder why I was the only person to be woken up by the visitation. And who were those two people in my bedroom? Could it be as Gran had said: they're waiting for me?

Looking back I can see now that other unusual things happened to me in my childhood.

As a young lad I sometimes felt strangely dissociated from my family. I wondered who I really was and what I was doing here on earth: it was an odd sensation of 'being in the world, but not of it'. Once I even asked my mother if I was adopted. 'Don't be silly,' she said, and life moved on as normal. But little did I realise then that this feeling of 'not belonging on earth' was to haunt me many more times in the years ahead.

I now realise that I was the only one to hear those phantom hands because they brought a message for my ears alone. At the tender age of ten, I had experienced the spirit people breaking through from the next world: they'd reached out to me. In my childhood the spirit world had already brought a powerful message: *Behold, we stand at the door and knock.*

The spirit callers knew then, and probably at my birth, that they could communicate with me. With their special vision they could see the years of co-operation and service that lay ahead of us, and how every piece of life's jigsaw would fit into its rightful place at its allotted time. I see now that in my life I was meant to meet certain people who would help to unfold my psychic sensitivity, gifted people whose guidance would set me on a pathway towards a greater understanding of life and self, and of psychic communication between two worlds.

For many years, discarnate minds had been

quietly at work behind the scenes, carefully studying and planning important events.

With their extended vision the invisible people could foresee that together we would join two worlds as one, that through mediumship we would dry the eyes of those who grieve, and give hope to desperate souls seeking spiritual light for their pathways.

They could foresee thousands of people assembling in theatres, city halls, leisure complexes, conference centres and spiritual churches to witness our work. They knew then that the vital message 'Man survives death complete with his character and individuality' would be broadcast to millions on television and radio, and written in the press.

Yet if someone had told me this in those early years I'd have laughed. I couldn't possibly have believed it would happen to me. But truth is sometimes stranger than fiction.

For someone seemingly destined to become well known, my beginnings were very humble. I was born on a typical British winter's night. Heavy rain fell upon our terraced house at number 10 Rock Street in the heart of Swansea town, South Wales. Inside our modest dwelling a few women were fussing around my mother, Beatrice Maude O'Brien, who was lying on a sofa in the small parlour. She was close to the delivery of her second child and secretly she longed for a girl; she already had a five-year-old son called John.

The contractions of labour were more frequent now so it was decided that my father should take John to the cinema while the women did what they had to do. He agreed and they both went off into the downpour.

As torrential rain lashed at the window and lightning lit up the sky, dramatic thunderclaps drowned out my first cries as I entered the world a few weeks early on Friday 28th January 1955 at just after 9 p.m.

Thankful that I was all in one piece, but a little disappointed because I wasn't the daughter she wanted, Beatrice held me close and kissed her second son. They marvelled at my mass of thick black hair; I was extremely slim and 22½ inches long. The women thought I looked like a little rabbit.

Shortly after my birth, Dad and John returned home drenched and my brother, excited by my arrival, proudly proclaimed, 'I'm going up the shop to get him a bottle!' But the shops were closed and it was already past his bedtime — so it was pyjamas for him.

I'm told my mother and father didn't know what to call me. One wanted Stephen, the other liked Neil. So they named me Stephen Neil O'Brien.

By all accounts I was a loveable child but also quite forward and determined. At just nine months old I astounded everyone when I stood up on my own for the very first time, toddled across the room on wobbly legs, collected my wooden train set then tottered back to my place — where I plonked myself down with a triumphant smile. All were stunned by my initiative. 'He's been here before,' they said.

I even outsmarted my parents sometimes. At night I'd lower my cot-gate and grasp the wallpaper then wallow in the delicious ripping sound as I pulled it from the bottom right to the top of the ceiling. Annoyed with me, my parents moved the cot away from the walls and my mother tied dozens of knots on the gate with old stockings. That was me safe for the night, or so they thought. When she came up later there I was with all the knots untied and the cot-gate down, and I was grinning in the bed waving freshly ripped wallpaper!

I was a thin toddler but very quick on my feet. At bedtime when my mother frantically tried to grab us both for a wash, she always caught John but never me: I used to dive through her legs and escape into the street. But I'd eventually give in and come inside because every night was our ritual wash-and-pyjama session.

My mother would yank off our trousers and tops that she'd so painstakingly made from oddments of material and grumble, 'I don't know; you boys can't keep anything in one piece for five minutes.' She'd have found a tear-hole somewhere.

Then we'd be soaped and scrubbed and packed off to bed in warm flannelette pyjamas, and she'd hope for some peace and quiet — but was nearly always disappointed. Hearing us jumping up and down on the squeaky old bedsprings, she'd shout up the stairs, 'What's all that *din*? You'll bring the ceiling through, you two! *Stop fighting*!' But that didn't deter John and me — we'd carry on bashing with our pillows and knocking each other off the bed amid laughter and flying feathers.

We were two healthy boys, yet we differed vastly in temperament and taste: John liked sport and I was a creative child. We loved each other dearly and we worshipped our mother. She was the centre of our lives. If we hurt ourselves, she was the one we ran to for help. She was everything to us: a kind, loving woman — someone very special.

They say that a Welsh 'Mam' is the heart of her family home, and this was certainly the case with my mother. Wherever she went a bright light shone around her. When she entered a room she filled it with warmth; and when she left it the place seemed darker and less hospitable.

It's hard to describe what a child can see in another person's eyes. They say the eyes are the windows of the soul, and I think they're right. My mother's were hazel-green, and behind them I sensed the deep compassion she radiated into the world around her. She was kind and understanding; she took time to listen to people and she was patient above and beyond the call of duty.

I guess my mother spoiled me and John by giving in to our childish whims; and though she tried her best to discipline us we only remember her with the deepest affection.

She was everything to us; someone very special; and I loved her with all my heart.

Her great concern for people often sent her off to somebody's house or other to help wherever she could. She used to 'perm' ladies' hair, wallpaper old people's houses and do all kinds of odd jobs for the old folk in the town. I remember she once took her own dinner to an elderly widower who was feeling poorly; and another time she was almost physically sick after scraping wallpaper off some old lady's walls because there were bugs all over them. Pulling a grimace she told me, 'I pasted them back to the wall.' And then she smiled.

But my father was completely different. I can't remember a single occasion when he picked us up or cuddled us as children. He was a distant figure, an undemonstrative man and we never got along well. If ever I committed the mortal sin of sitting in his fireside armchair he'd command in his booming deep voice, 'Get out of it, boy!' And I did.

Dad was a strange man, not cut out for marriage or fatherhood in my opinion. He would sit and watch television or read is newspaper, wrapped in a wall of impenetrable silence. But if you got him talking about football or politics, or social injustices he'd rant on, 'The rich have always punished the poor: they've done it for centuries and they'll carry on doing it until we stand up and fight them in Unions. That's the only way they'll pay attention to the working man!'

He was right of course.

He was a man of strong opinions and he couldn't be bothered with children getting in his way. But to be fair to him he was a good provider who worked as a steelworks' foreman to feed us.

But I feared my father's quick and explosive temper. In his youth he'd been an amateur boxer and had broken all his knuckles in fights. Whenever I annoyed him, one of his low-voiced growling threats was, 'I'll poke you in the eye!' — and by 'poke' he meant 'punch'.

He had little patience with me and was more closely associated with my brother John.

My green years did not afford me and easy rite of passage.

But many fond memories do flood back when I think of my childhood: like the time when I bought six tins of soapy bubbles and the whole street assembled on a glorious summer's night to watch the air fill with rainbow orbs that the children helped me to blow; and we nicknamed our road 'Bubble Street'.

Rock Street was the kind of place where doors stayed open until way past midnight and women could be found gossiping on their doorsteps about their daily happenings. The only time doors were closed was when families went to bed, and even then they sometimes didn't lock them. It was a close-knit community in far off days when no one feared a stranger or being burgled. There was more neighbourliness and trust around then than there is today. But any street fights or squabbles were public property. People having a fist-fight could expect the whole street to come out and watch.

When two big bruisers called Peter and Jimmy decided to scrap over a skinny woman they gathered quite a crowd. The demented woman got between them to try to stop the fight, flailing her arms and screaming, 'I'm not worth it! Stop punching each other!' and there was blood everywhere. But the more she interfered, the harder they lashed out until someone in the crowd shouted, 'Leave them alone — they might knock some bloody sense into each other!'

That was Rock Street.

Yet in their own way the people of our street loved one another. There was an inner respect for family life and a mutual disgust for immoral activities they heard about; and there was always plenty of laughter. I remember when Florrie, my mother's friend and our next-door neighbour, put a huge tureen of clear soup on the window sill to cool and just as she lowered it a mucky football landed smack in the middle of it, splattering her and the windows all around! Oh, and that's another thing — people spoke their minds: they said *exactly* what they meant and didn't dress it up either:

Florrie was seething with rage.

'You bloody bastards!' she screamed at the laughing kids. 'That was my dinner! I'll wring your scrawny necks if I catch hold of you!'

But the kids laughed all the more.

27

Then I laughed.

And in the end even old Florrie doubled up in hysterics as she poured down the drain what was left of her mucky soup.

Every summer some women hired a coach, knocked on all the doors and collected money for a day out at Caswell Bay beach. Those picnics by the sparkling sea were marvellous: the coach was packed, the singing was loud and raucous and the sandwiches were always full of sand.

We kids would bound out of the bus like gazelles then pull on our 'bathers' behind towels and race along the golden beaches under the Gower clifftops, or bury each other up to our necks in sand. We were bursting with energy and excitement: we squashed seaweed and counted little crabs stranded in rockpools; we built sandcastles and scratched our names next to them with big sticks, then sighed when everything dissolved on the incoming tide.

'*Ice-cream!*' my mother would shout, and hordes of us would belt along the shore to the 'Mr Whippy Ice-cream' van to feast on dripping cones of creamy delight. It was a special treat to have a '99' cornet — thick ice-cream with a chocolate Cadbury's Flake thrust down into it. Heaven on earth!

By sundown we were exhausted, which was probably why they'd taken us there; and John and I would sit on a blanket and lean against my mother (Dad never came on any of these outings) and we'd listen to the seagulls plaintively calling, and marvel at the deep red sunset colouring the sky.

'Soon be going home,' my mother would say with a tired sigh. 'Won't be long now.'

John and I coaxed her into letting us make a final dash around the bay. But trust me to spoil it all when I fell from the top of Caswell Hill and rolled right down to the bottom! I stood up and someone snapped my picture in the fading light, looking dazed — but happy all the same.

John wasn't going to be out-done, so he swam off into an oil slick and the women had to butter him all over to try to remove it.

They were happy times indeed — but then came a shock.

When I was five they packed me off to be educated. I didn't want to go but they made me do it.

I ranted and raved but my anxious mother took me through the big gates and left me there anyway.

Waun Wen School was less than a stone's throw from our house but it might as well have been a million miles outside the universe, for that's how it felt. It seemed so huge and cavernous.

It was a good school though, once I got used to it, with caring staff — all except that ginger-headed, freckled-faced teacher whose name thankfully escapes me. She'd glower down at us in the infants' class, clasping her wooden ruler, then she'd thrash us wildly across the legs if we displeased her.

The swoosh and sting of that ruler remains with me today.

Some people should never take up the teaching profession.

But our headmaster, Mr Allen, was a clever man. Once, when he was teaching our class, he was called away on business, so he took off his spectacles and placed them on the windowsill, facing us five-year-olds.

'Now these are magic glasses,' he said. 'Even though I shan't be in the room I'll still be able to see you through them — so you'd better keep quiet and carry on working until I get back. *Remember now:* I'll be *watching!*' and he pointed at his specs on the window as he left.

We were utterly silent. Furtively we glanced sideways at the transparent orbs and wondered: Could it be true? Then we pressed our lips together in concentration and got on with our sums without a sound until he returned.

I wasn't a difficult child but I was very determined, they say; actions spoke louder than words to me, which got me into several scrapes when I moved up into the Junior Class. I remember one particularly. We ate our lunch in a nearby damp church hall. The food was delivered by van and we were on the end of the tour and as a result our meals were often luke-warm and unappetising.

We'd trudge down the line clutching our plates, dropping with hunger and moaning to the well-fed dinner ladies, 'That doesn't look very hot.' Slopping out mashed potatoes onto plates they'd rattle back: 'Nothing to do with us, love. We only dish it up.'

Toying with our food, we'd often complain to the supervisor. She was tall, thin and mean, with a lightning-quick clip she could deliver at ten paces — and often did.

'Miss,' we'd say, 'our food's —'

'*Quiet!*' she'd snap back. 'Now eat it up! Some children in the world are *starving!*'

Yes, we thought, we know what that feels like.

Well, three of us soon became tired of this and Johnny, Paul and I gathered in the playground and I hatched an inspired plan. We made large cardboard placards and wore them. On them we wrote 'We want hot dinners!' and 'Give us warm food!' Then the three of us stomped around the yard and shouted our chant for a better deal.

We thought it was a smashing idea.

We *wanted* hot food but what we actually *got* was our arms grabbed and we were dragged off and deposited outside the headmaster's study. We stood there, the three of us; a pathetic sight, all pale with hangdog expressions and clasping our hands behind our backs with our eyes lowered.

'Don't feel sorry,' I chirped to the other two. 'We've got a good case.'

Suddenly the study door opened and Paul was summoned in.

Johnny and I looked anxiously at each other, not knowing what to expect. There was a lot of muffled talking behind the closed door and then we heard a resounding *Thwack*! The door opened and a red-faced Paul emerged clutching his behind and he ran out into the yard.

Johnny and I exchanged fearful looks.

Then Johnny went in.

Two minutes later Johnny came out like Paul, with all the dignity smacked out of him.

And then it was my turn.

I stood before our tin god, Mr Allen. He eyed me up and down then raised an educated brow and said, 'So, you're the brains behind this little escapade, I understand.'

Feeling weak at the knees but not showing it, I bravely answered, 'Yes.'

There was an endless pause while he cleaned his spectacles, that infuriating habit he adopted whenever he wanted you to suffer.

'You should have got a petition together, brought it to me and I'd have dealt with this *properly*, instead of all this nonsense!' he admonished.

Suddenly I don't know what came over me and I blurted back, 'Our dinners are *cold*! Would *you* like to eat cold food?'

I guess that took him by surprise. Adults rarely treat children with respect until the moment the child shows defiance, then the adult is shocked. By now I felt I'd stood there thirty years.

'Because you masterminded this plan... you can go,' he said casually. Well I couldn't understand it but I didn't wait for him to change his mind — just as I was closing the door behind me I caught him saying, 'You show qualities of leadership.' But I had gone.

We got our hot lunches.

But I didn't always get my own way. Every two months John and I were given a shilling after school and ordered to get our hair cut. Down we'd go to a small terraced house-cum-shop owned by ancient Willy Woolard. We'd joke, 'We're off to Woolard's to get our wool cut!'

Willy was an amateur barber whose services came very cheap, and looking back it's easy to see why. There we'd sit with a dozen other unfortunate boys, nervously swinging our legs back and forth on the hard wooden seats, trying to look relaxed when we were dreading the prospect of facing his needle-sharp scissors. How we loathed this experience.

Suddenly the door would fling open and Willy would lurch in, dragging his withered leg behind him. His constantly-lit cigarette always had more ash than tobacco on it and you couldn't escape the smoke if you tried. In one hand he clasped a pair of lethal-looking shears and in the other — the dreaded china basin.

The boys' heads shrunk down into their necks.

He'd focus his one beady eye on his first victim in the chair then as quick as a flash he'd flop the basin onto his head and with no skill whatsoever shave right around it. And that was his haircut.

Well, you can imagine how I felt. I used to protest until I got a shaped style. After a few initial battles Willy eventually got the message and he'd ask in a mock refined voice, 'And how would you like it today?'

'Decent, please,' I'd reply.

But if ever I complained about anything, I angered my father and my mother tried to keep the peace by smoothing things over — but Dad wouldn't have any nonsense.

'Stop spoiling him will you, Beattie! He'll grow up soft,' Dad used to shout.

'Oh leave him alone, Ron,' she countered, 'he'll make something of himself one day. Stop picking on him all the time.'

'That boy will grow up dull,' snarled my father, who believed he was always right. 'Let him go and play football like the others.'

'He doesn't like football,' said Mam, 'he's a creative child. For goodness sake stop pestering him all the time. I'm telling you — one day he'll make something of himself. Now leave him alone.' My father would mutter something under his breath and go to the pub.

To say that Dad and I didn't see eye-to-eye would be a gross understatement. If left together for two minutes we'd fight tooth and nail and I've lost count of the times my mother stepped between us to stop the shouting.

Because I was so much closer to my mother I adopted most of her ways. Someone once said that we grow in the image of those we love and this was certainly true in my case.

My mother taught me the value of being valued, the need to have compassion and to take others' feelings into account. She was approachable and kind; and I loved her with all

34

my heart for this. She loved me too, for I remember one gloriously hot sunny day when all the kids went to school in short-sleeved shirts but by the end of the afternoon it was bucketing-down with torrential rain. The raindrops were as big as grapes and the ground was steaming where they smashed onto it.

All the other children just stood and gawped at the heavens opening. They looked from the sky to their short summer clothes and then with disgruntled faces ran screaming into the downpour with no overcoats to keep them dry. But there at the school gate stood my mother, completely drenched; she was waiting with an overcoat to walk me home.

I shall never forget her kindness, and moments like these bring warmly to mind my mother's love for me.

'Can't have you soaked through,' she said, cuddling me up as we ran through curtains of rain, giggling and laughing together. And when we got home she dried me out and made me a bowl of hot soup to warm me up.

My Mam was the best mother in the world.

Slowly I settled into my new routines at school. I made new friends I never dreamed could have existed before. But one morning, something happened to me in the yard that not even my new friends could do anything about. I fell down in pain, clutching my side. 'What's wrong?' they asked. I told them it was nothing, trying to be brave as little boys do. Although I was just eight, I didn't want to be fussed over. But the pain got worse as the day wore on.

'Stephen!' called out a teacher. 'Stop pulling that ridiculous face and get on with your sums!'

'Yes, Miss,' and I soldiered on without complaint.

After school, all the other lads dashed out of the gates as usual, screaming as though their trousers were on fire. But I just crept along the big school walls. I was in dire agony. What was happening to me? I barely had the strength to support myself as I staggered home down the street. The pain cut deeper — twisting inside me like a red-hot knife.

I leaned on our passageway walls. I couldn't go any further. As I called out for my mother, the floor came up to meet me in a frightening blur and I collapsed to the ground.

After that, I don't remember much, just snippets of frantic conversation floating over my head. Then blackness and then more panicky adult talk.

The next thing I knew, my mother had grabbed her handbag and my clean pyjamas and we were in an ambulance shooting through red lights at breakneck speed. In the distance I could hear her urgent voice saying over and over, 'He will be all right, won't he? Please say he'll be all right.'

But that's all I can recall. I was in too much agony to hear the rest; I was slipping in and out of consciousness. I thought I was going to die and I recited the Lord's Prayer over in my mind as they rushed me through the huge swing doors of the hospital and an immediate examination was given. 'God bless you, son,' I dimly heard my mother say as a massive surgeon leaned over me and gave me a painful injection. 'Count to ten, lad,' he said. But before I reached three, I was swamped by the blackness and had gone...

How I hated Swansea Hospital. I was a quiet child but they put me in a children's ward where I was miserable: my natural aversion to loud noise was aggravated by children grizzling and crying all the time.

I prayed for peace and quietness, but I didn't get it.

But I knew I had to tolerate it because the doctors said I'd had acute appendicitis and that if they hadn't operated immediately, the appendix would have burst.

As much as the nurses tried to pacify me, all I wanted was my mother. I looked anxiously across at the small windows in the swing doors. Who was that behind the frosted glass? Was that *her*?

'Why can't they let her in anytime, instead of these silly visiting hours?' I whimpered pathetically to the staff.

After what seemed like a century's wait, a bell rang and my mother came in wreathed in smiles. We hugged each other. I was so pleased that she'd come. But what was that under her arm? A present? It was a Toy-Town Post Office Set! All this and love, too: I felt like a king, despite the aching stitches in my side.

I soon felt safe again but I quarrelled with the nurse when she told me my mother had to leave.

'Sleep well, Stephen,' said Mam as she kissed me and smoothed a lock of hair across my forehead. 'I'll be back again tomorrow to see you.' And then I was at peace. 'Good night, God bless you,' she whispered softly.

But before we parted, I called her back and gave her a token of my love. I presented her with a Toy-Town letter.

'It's a special delivery,' I said, smiling.

And as she read it, her face lit up and her clear eyes misted over with the love of a mother for her son. For on it, I'd written:

Dear Mises O'Brien. I love you.

2

Silent Watchers

When I was ten, we moved house. We had to —
our street was being demolished under a slum-
clearance scheme; so we ended up in Gors
Avenue about a mile away. But we couldn't
persuade our beloved cat, Tibby, to join us. After
all, why should she? She'd ruled the house from
the moment we'd taken her in as a tiny scrap,
wobbling on weak legs. No, Tibby wasn't having
any of this silly moving nonsense! Besides, she
had countless gentleman-friends in the district,
as her frequent litters proved.

In the end she had to be manhandled in two
thick overcoats, shrieking and flaying her claws
as we carried her off to our new home. But she
soon settled in like the rest of us — blessing the
new place with yet another fluffy litter.

After all the hustle and bustle of the move had
passed I sat on a empty tea-chest and,
prompted by the insecurity of the wrench away
from familiar surroundings to somewhere new,
asked my mother, 'Mam, what happens when

people die? What'll happen to us when we all go?'

After a moment's uncertainty she answered, 'Don't think about such things, Stephen; you're far too young to worry over subjects like that.'

'But I'd like to know about it,' I persisted.

She pondered... 'Well, I believe we'll go on living, somewhere,' she said. But I could tell she wasn't sure.

Number 22 was a nice place as terraced houses go, but it was much smaller than our Rock Street home; and (with apologies to Tibby) you couldn't swing a cat in the living-room. It was a two-up and two-down affair, which meant that John and I shared a room with Uncle Billy, one of my father's brothers who lived with us, and Mam and Dad had the other room. Trying to sleep at night was an absolute impossibility — positively *everyone* snored, rattled and wheezed; how the windows stayed in their frames I can't imagine.

Yet, on the night when those phantom hands hammered on our front door in the early hours, the air was uncannily still and everyone was strangely silent.

After that spirit visitation I guess I became more and more aware of old Gran King's words, 'You attract spirit people like moths to a candle, Stephen'. Glancing back at my childhood I can see now that my invisible friends were often with me, and sometimes may have protected me from harm — like the time when I climbed over the school wall after hours with some of the boys, for a dare.

Everyone else made the wall but when my turn came I reached up to grasp a hand-hold and a huge boulder loosed itself. I saw it come crashing down towards me but there was nothing I could do — I was suspended off the ground and couldn't run. I closed my eyes and hunched my shoulders waiting for impact. The stone hurtled down onto my head but simply bounced off as if the blow had been cushioned. This could have been the work of spirit guardians eager I should come to no harm. Even though I carry the dent on my head to this day I felt no pain and no damage was done by this blow, which might have sent many young boys into concussion.

I think the spirit people were also close to me when I was thrown from a twelve-foot high wall and landed directly on my skull. There was a loud crack and old Mr Williams nearby came rushing over, panting for breath and white as a sheet with shock, expecting to find me bleeding and unconscious with a broken neck. But I simply got up, dusted myself down and walked away totally unharmed. 'I'm all right,' I said.

'Well, I'll go to Hell!' said Mr Williams. 'There's not a mark on him!' And he stood there completely amazed.

Some people believe that a blow to the head can instigate psychic vision. I don't think that's true but on occasions I did see the spirit people as a child. I remember one morning when I glanced through the living-room window and saw a small girl sitting on our garden wall. She wore a white party frock and as I idly admired it she suddenly stood up and jumped from the wall. I shot out of my chair, fearful that such a small child would injure herself with the six-foot drop. But before she reached the ground, she vanished. I was quite taken aback because she'd looked so very real to me.

At other times on hot and sultry summer afternoons I'd sit at the bedroom window, twisting my hair and watching the people strolling past our house, just ambling along with their shopping bags or their children, their heads ringed with sunlight. But when they got to the brow of the hill, sometimes they disappeared.

None of these visions struck me as odd, so I never felt the need to discuss them with others; I guess children take things at their face value and accept psychic happenings without question. There was never any need for alarm anyway, my spirit people were always quite friendly and smiling folk.

I think the most startling clairvoyant vision I experienced was what I now know to be called a 'phantasm of the living'. I was visiting old Mrs King when it happened, trying to gain more knowledge about these peculiar events. It was a steamy-hot July day, the kind of weather that makes the pavements shimmer with rising heat. We were chatting away in her kitchen, awaiting the arrival of her grandson when I happened to glance across the room and saw him walk past the big window; he was as large as life, bouncing along and making for the side of the house.

'Here he is!' I cried and I got up and opened the door for him.

Mrs King looked at me bewildered.

'But there's no one there,' she said, appearing a little worried about my strengthening powers.

We waited for another ten minutes, then I couldn't resist it any more — I went outside into the sunshine to sort him out! But Gran had been right; her grandson was nowhere to be seen.

'But I definitely saw him,' I said, and I described what he was wearing. Her face changed as she realised what had happened.

'Oh, I expect he's been *thinking* of coming home,' she replied, hidden wisdom prompting her words.

Over a half an hour later her grandson arrived, happily whistling in the bright air. *But he was not wearing the clothes I'd seen him in when his phantasm had passed by the window.*

'Your gifts are getting stronger,' Gran warned.

I've had strange experiences like this several times since and I now believe our thoughts are living things and, if powerfully projected — even on an unconscious level — they can be seen by sensitive people.

Time moved onward in the hazy, slow way it does when you're a child, and it took with it many happy memories I shall treasure for ever. The days of youth were so carefree and full of enthusiasm that even the bad times seem better now, when I recall them through the mist of recollection.

One of the happiest moments my mother and I shared was when I slipped home from school early one day and fell into her embrace. I'd passed my 'eleven-plus' examinations, which meant that I'd qualified for a Grammar School education. 'I'm so very proud of you,' smiled my mother warmly, and the family nicknamed me 'Brains'. It was no mean feat to win this scholarship, coming as I did from a home where education was largely left to schoolteachers.

According to Dad I was to go to the best place in the area: Bishop Gore Grammar School for boys, in the Sketty district. We received official notification and my mother took borrowed money and came home loaded with the clothes they said I should have. She'd spent her last penny on them.

'We must have you looking fine,' she smiled. 'It's not every day someone gets an opportunity like this. Bishop Gore's a school cap-and-tie place.'

I tried everything on but she confessed there was one item she couldn't afford to buy — the school status symbol: a splendid all wool maroon blazer with an embroidered yellow crest on the pocket.

'Don't worry,' she said, 'no one else will have one on the first day, Stephen. They're very

expensive. I'll get you one when I can.' And with
that she produced a shiny brown raincoat that
she'd gone into debt to buy. The sleeves had to
be tucked well up and the hem was shortened. I
was eleven years old but quite small and
terribly thin: I was four feet 10½ inches tall,
according to my school report. Everything had
to be altered to fit me, and for days my mother
did this work until late into the night.

Finally, the big day arrived.

I travelled on the number 40 bus then got off
and approached the awesome red brick
buildings. They looked terrifyingly big to such a
small lad. I gulped some air, steeled myself to
face the ordeal, and self-consciously entered the
gates — and was nearly bowled over by a wall of
noise: boys of all ages were shouting and
bustling about everywhere.

Suddenly a bell rang out and the masters
appeared, some of them dressed in black caps
and gowns. Whistles were blown and roll-call
was taken and we were shepherded into a
quadrangle and made to stand in line, in strict
order of initial.

There were 150 new boys on that day. I looked
around me at them all, and I had never felt
more humiliated in all my life — 149 boys wore
their splendid maroon blazers and I stood there
in my outsize, hemmed-up shiny brown
raincoat. I just felt I wanted to die. The
experience of going there had been bad enough
without this added shame. My face burned hot
and I was in no mood to embrace school life.

Furthermore, I hated the place: it felt like a concentration camp; they made us march up and down and then into a massive assembly hall where they told us that discipline was the making of a young man. It was awful and I couldn't wait to be released, and when I got home I could feel my throat tighten as I belted in through the front door, threw down my raincoat and shouted and raved at my mother about the blazer then dashed upstairs, fell onto the bed and sobbed and sobbed my heart out. I hated that place.

My mother softly climbed the stairs and sat beside me. 'I'm sorry,' she whispered gently. 'I'll get you a blazer first thing on Monday morning, Stephen.' She gently wiped away my tears with a finger. 'Look, it'll be all right. I'll borrow some more money.'

I rolled away from her. 'I don't want to go back there,' I whimpered; then more defiantly, 'I never want to go near that school again!'

She put her hand on my shoulder and squeezed it softly. 'Give yourself a chance, son. Don't be too hasty about this. You'll see. I'm always telling your father you'll make something of yourself one day; and I know you can make it.'

I cried in disbelief.

She smoothed a lock of damp hair from my forehead and assured me that I'd soon fit in and would learn to like the new life very much; and, despite my doubts, she was absolutely right.

After a few teething troubles I *did* settle in

well, and I learned to love the old school. The masters and boys, who came from privileged backgrounds, excited in me vistas of thought and opened up fascinating new worlds of mental stimulation.

Slowly, the Grammar School 'grew' on me and it gradually occupied a special place in my heart. I have many happy and amusing memories of my days there: like the way my friend Mark and I ducked out of a compulsory cross-country run through Singleton Park. We hid behind some bushes, completely shattered and breathless, then caught the lads up on their second circuit — and we still managed to get in last!

I remember when our class was queuing outside the chemistry labs awaiting the tetchy master. That big red fire-hose wheel had always fascinated me. One of the boys started waving it around amid laughter and I got it off him and pulled the lever and — *Whoooosh!* Water gushed out everywhere, soaking the lads, who scattered and yelped all the way down the corridor. Then Mr Leyshon appeared.

'*Who made this ridiculous mess*?!' he raved. Everyone turned and pointed. '*He did!*' they chorused, and I got the usual punishment — six wallops across my backside from a springy gym-shoe.

The boys played a marvellous trick on the French Mistress once. A quiet lad called Henderson had his trousers stolen and the poor boy couldn't persuade anyone to tell him where they were. He was so retiring and shy that the rowdier lads lifted him up and sat him on top of the cupboard behind the teacher's desk before she arrived. He stayed there all through the French lesson. She must have known but she didn't react; but we chuckled throughout the class.

Our poor Science master was an aged absent-minded professor type. We called him 'Tommy Test-tube'. He forgot things so easily that we often wondered how he'd managed to live this long. One afternoon he turned the Bunsen burner onto its invisible flame and completely forgot about it and rambled on incoherently and put his sleeve right through the burner. It immediately caught alight amid gales of uncontrollable laughter.

'Boys! *Boys!*' he screamed. 'Cease this merriment! Cease it *at once*! *It isn't funny!*'

But we thought it was.

I remember I also had a few difficult encounters with the staff. I disliked the Welsh lessons very much; it was such a hard language to learn and to me it seemed 'dead' and 'useless' because at that time hardly anyone in Wales spoke it — English was the first language.

I suppose that's why I daydreamed in this compulsory twice-a-week class. During the mistress's confusion I raised my hand, a thought having occurred to me. 'Miss, have you marked our test papers yet?' I queried. She turned instantly blue. I thought she was going to explode.

I was right.

'Get *out!*' she screamed like a virago. '*Get out!*
Get out of my class you *ignorant* little boy! Get
out *this minute!*' Well I got the message and
sloped off into the corridor, wondering what on
earth I'd done. Later, she confronted me.

'Well, O'Brien?' she exclaimed in a rising tone,
her body towering over me. 'Haven't you
something to say to me?'

After a few thoughts, it struck me that she
wanted an apology. Another thought hit me
too — I'd done nothing to warrant such
unkindness.

'Well; come on!' she sneered. 'What have you
got to say to me?'

Facing her square-on I replied, 'Nothing... I
have nothing to say to you.'

I shall never forget her face.

She drew in a sharp breath then ordered me to
report to the headmaster immediately. But
when I explained my case he simply shook his
head and said, 'Don't do it again.'

I've always rallied against authoritative
people, particularly if they try to take advantage
of someone younger or more vulnerable. I guess
that's why this next memory is so painful to
recall.

Mr Walters tried to teach us mathematics and
set us impossible problems for homework. He
was a stocky man who sported dark wavy hair
and an Adolf Hitler moustache. One day in an
exceptionally foul mood, he demanded to view
our geometry sums. But Lear, one of the class

who sat in front of me, admitted he hadn't done them. Mr Walters strode purposefully towards the boy and gave him such a resounding smack across the head that the rest of the class gasped in horror.

Lear began to cry.

A fearful silence pressed in around us.

When it was my turn to be questioned, my face was already red. 'You haven't done it, have you O'Brien?' said Mr Walters with a rising sneer, no doubt gloating over the prospect of another attack.

'Oh, yes I did, Sir,' I gabbled, frantically flicking through the pages of my jotter-pad. 'It's in here somewhere,' I said; and I became more and more flustered. The bulk of Mr Walters leaned over me in disbelief, waiting while I pathetically searched for the homework I hadn't done. I lied to him; and to this day I recall the dreadful sense of guilt and fear I experienced, especially as he gave me the benefit of the doubt and didn't punish me. Yet, looking back now, who could condemn a small boy's lie in these circumstances? And what right had he to strike Lear so fiercely?

None whatsoever.

Another school incident shines out in my memory, though for very different reasons; it occurred when I was thirteen and I now believe it presaged my platform work as a medium in later years.

I was approached by the Head of the English Department to read a Bible lesson at the morning assembly. Nothing wonderful in that you might think, but there was.

Our school was a grand old institution: it even had its own orchestra that played the morning hymns, and the lessons were usually given by the masters themselves, or else by a small elite of hand-picked Prefects. Young boys like me were never invited to read.

'If you want me to do it, Sir, I will,' I said.

The morning arrived and once the hymns concluded I stood up and approached the huge lectern and stepped up onto a box. When I gazed out into the hall I was confronted by a sea of young faces, expressions as still as tombstones, all eyes staring directly at me.

But what struck me most was their absolute silence: it was unheard of — there wasn't even a whisper in the ranks. The boys usually shuffled their feet; but on that day they didn't.

They sat quietly and waited... and listened attentively while I read the lesson. My voice was as clear as a bell and it carried to the back of the vast hall.

When I finished and stepped down, if someone had dropped a pin it would have sounded like a gunshot.

It was an altogether strange experience.

(Years later a noted public speaker was to say to me, 'You're not much to look at but when you open your mouth, people sit up and listen.')

In my teens I was good at languages — French, German, English and Latin — and gave more time to these than to other subjects. But as I got older I was forced into thinking about what I wanted to get out of my life. I didn't have a clue about what I wanted to be in the future: it was as much as I could do to cope with life in the present because school workloads and pressures at home from my father were building up. In my teens my relationship with Dad was even worse than before. I was an adolescent now and determined to be counted as at least 'living', even if I didn't matter to the dull adult world around me.

Dad and I would hotly disagree on practically anything and if I dared to speak my thoughts he'd shout angrily at me, 'And what do *you* know about it? You're only a *kid*! You don't have an opinion.' That usually started another tirade, which would end with my dashing out of the house, slamming doors loudly behind me.

I wouldn't go back to my adolescent years for anything.

Back at school we were marched in to see the Careers Officer. One by one, very reluctantly, we fifteen-year-olds trudged into his small office, like lambs going to the slaughter.

'You're a clown, O'Brien,' he said to me. I don't know exactly what he meant by that to this day. 'Well lad. What are you going to do with yourself?' he asked.

'I don't know,' I said.

When I told him I rather fancied being a pilot or even being involved in space flight, he laughed right at me and I couldn't help thinking: Who's the clown now?

He detailed a few opportunities, none of which appealed or made me want to fly out of the room screaming 'Look out world, here I come!'

Then he sighed and gave me permission to leave; but before I did, he launched a surprising remark.

'Well,' he said, 'There's hope for you yet, O'Brien.' I lifted my chin. 'Out of the hundred boys that I've interviewed so far, you're the only one who's had the courage to look me in the eye right through it.'

The stress at school and at home was increasing all the time but I found some relief in joining the school choir, which gave excellent concerts and allowed me the chance of pursuing one of the great loves in my life — music. I loved to sing and I still have a good voice to this day. How I craved and yearned for a piano to accompany it.

'But Stephen,' said my dismayed mother, 'I can't afford a piano stool at the moment, let alone a piano; I'm still trying to pay off the loan for this year's new school clothes.'

So I was left with a song in my heart and nothing to play it on.

I can see now that we were quite poor really, just scraping a living from day to day...

At sixteen I was about to face sitting my major examinations but I couldn't be bothered with studying: I wanted to enjoy life and living; I wanted to run free and feel the great pulse of life in my veins. So it wasn't difficult to accept my friend Mark's offer of coffee at his home one evening, rather than to read up on history. But little did I realise that this was to herald my next contact with the spirit world, one that would leave a vivid impression upon my mind for the rest of my life.

I arrived at his plush home in the west of the town and took off my shoes so that the carpets wouldn't be marked. We chatted cordially until his mother went out. 'Behave yourselves now, you two,' she said with a smile. The door closed behind her and suddenly Mark became conspiratorial.

'Check the coast and get two kitchen chairs,' he whispered. I obeyed but didn't know what he was going to do. He pulled the curtains and dimmed the light in the room. I placed the chairs opposite each other, as directed, and from a brown paper bag he produced a ouija board — a board with the letters of the alphabet all around it.

'I've just got this,' he said. 'Let's have a go.'

We placed it on our knees just as the instructions said; and then a thought struck me. 'What if your mother comes back and catches us?' I rattled out.

'*Shh!* Just concentrate on it,' rebuked Mark. Hesitantly, our fingers moved towards the pointer... the room seemed to become still, as though it were wrapped in a blanket of peace.

Our fingers lightly touched the wooden pointer and it astonished us by immediately speeding around the polished board. It quickly spelled out something and we could hardly contain our excitement.

S-T-E-P-H

'Stephen!' I called out — and it shot across to the 'YES' and then made fast, thrilling sweeps around the board again.

'Well, what do you want?' I gasped, holding my throat with my free hand. The pointer seemed just as excited as we were: it was buzzing with some kind of invisible energy as it whizzed past all the letters, as if it were getting used to the experience and thoroughly enjoying it.

'Just look at it go!' cried Mark. 'That's amazing!'

'We only touched it and it started straight away,' I said.

Then all at once, the pointer stopped.

There was a brief pause.

'Is it me you want to speak with?'

YES

In disbelief we watched the pointer moving to the letters and we were tense with anticipation, awaiting its message. What on earth was it going to say?

I AM A FRIEND...
I BELONG TO STEPHEN

Mark and I looked at each other, lost for words. 'Well ask it something, Stephen,' he cried. 'Don't just sit there with your mouth open — talk!'

So I spoke the first words that came into my head.

'How many exam passes will I get?'

SIX, said the spirit people.

'And what about Mark?' I continued.

SIX, said the board again.

Well neither of us could believe it; we hadn't studied hard enough so we knew this prediction was absolute nonsense. But before we could question the other side further, Mark's mother walked up the drive unexpectedly and we dashed about setting the room to rights so that she was none the wiser about our activities.

'We'll never get six passes each, Mark,' I laughed. 'We're much too daft for that!'

Or were we? We would have to wait and see...

Soon, the telling moments arrived. Mark and I sat among the 150 boys taking the General Certificate of Education 'O Level' examinations in the huge assembly hall. This was to be the first of nine three-hour papers. The thought of that ouija board séance was furthest from my mind — I was far too busy scratching my head and trying to recall facts and figures to even remember the prediction. The nervous tension in hall mounted, then we turned over our papers and got down to it...

Several weeks later the results were posted to our homes. Straight after the summer holidays Mark and I got together on the first day back at school and I was bursting with curiosity.

'Well, how many passes did you get?' I questioned. Mark pulled a face and rather shamefully admitted, 'Just one — how about you?'

'Three,' I said and we both exploded with

laughter because the ouija board had been completely wrong, which caused further amusement on that day.

But the spirit people had the last laugh.

When Mark and I re-sat the examinations, he obtained a further five passes and I added three more to mine. This meant that we both had gained six passes each.

Six — just as my unseen 'friend' had accurately foretold.

But how on earth could the other side have known the results before the examinations had been taken? How could *anyone* have known?

Yet, there was no doubt about it, they had been right. As strange as it seemed, somehow:

they knew my pathway,

they were watching,

they were waiting...

And I couldn't help remembering those ghostly hands hammering on our front door at two o'clock in the morning six years earlier. And over and over in my mind, one phrase kept tumbling round and around:

Behold,
We Stand at the Door and Knock

Unseen, we may be.

Unknown, we're not.

   Yet we're watching the path that all souls tread;

   We once walked there on the Earth ourselves:

And now

We're far from dead.

So listen,
Carefully,
And be aware, my friend:
 For we are near;
 Sweeping the face of your life's clock:
Behold, we stand at the door and knock.

3

Whispering Voices

The insides of the dark bedroom windows were ringed with ice and swirling snows covered gardens and streets outside in the black velvet night. But I was snug and warm in bed when the sun shone through the blueness and woke me up on Christmas morning. Even though I was sixteen, there at the foot of the bed was my usual stocking full of fruit and nuts and an old pillowcase containing new clothes. Little did I appreciate then that Mam and Dad had spent their last pennies on those gifts.

It's only now, in later years, that I realise just how deeply my mother loved us children. She worked very hard indeed and went without to keep us clean and fed; her compassionate mind always put us first if there wasn't enough to go around.

I shall always be grateful for the privilege of having such a wonderful person for my mother. And through her powerful mother-love, I'm convinced she also had a special kind of healing power. Once, when I crushed my thumb in a school accident, she gently held it and in a soft voice said, 'Here, let me kiss it better for you.' Her hands seemed to soothe the throbbing pain, and my new thumbnail grew quite quickly.

'Mam I do love you,' I said, in the awkward way adolescents express their feelings. We were kneeling before a blazing coal fire at the time, decorating a fir tree with glittering tinsel and baubles. 'Really...'

'I know you do,' she smiled warmly, 'and I love you too. And God knows, Stephen, no matter where life takes us in the years ahead I'll always help you whenever I can; don't forget that.'

'Oh, I won't,' I promised.

'I only hope that I'll live long enough to see you two boys settled down. That's my dearest wish.'

I thought that was an odd thing to say but I shrugged off the remark.

Time rolled by and we moved house again, returning to the same area where I'd been born, only now the council had built a brand new estate on the slum-clearance site.

Number 27 Lion Street, back in the Waun Wen district, was a neat three-bedroomed tidy-sized house with the luxury of central heating but paper-thin walls, which conducted the noise from neighbours' television sets right through into our rooms. But we had a little patch of garden at the back and in the front, and we even had a brick shed, which we soon filled with all the rubbish we couldn't bear to throw out.

Our cat, Tibby, was again manhandled in two overcoats and taken back to her glorious roots. She wasted no time in renewing her amorous friendships with her gentlemen-friends. But soon, she went missing.

I searched the streets high and low for her, but couldn't find my beloved friend anywhere.

Then my mother learned that the caretaker from Waun Wen School opposite had found the body of a cat in the busy road.

My childhood friend had been killed by a hit-and-run driver. We didn't even have the opportunity to bury her ourselves, and for a while I was inconsolable.

But then Christmas arrived again, and this meant putting on a brave face and visiting relatives we didn't even think about for the rest of the year.

Dad's father had died before I was old enough to have known him, but by all accounts he was a good and honest man, having educated himself and got on in life through book learning and hard work. I did, however, know my father's mother quite well. She was Mary-Jane but everyone called her Polly. She was a short and tubby, fussy little woman with a high squeaky voice; and every Christmas Eve my father reluctantly dragged me and John along to see her.

Polly's main problem was that she was mean with her money. She'd had five sons — one of them being my father — but she had so much trouble getting two of them to work and bring in money that she padlocked the food cabinet to prevent them eating. 'If you don't put money *into* the house, you don't take anything *out!*' she screamed at them. And she meant it.

As we stood on her doorstep and Dad knocked on her door, my tummy rumbled and I wondered if she'd give me a dry biscuit or a cup of tea. My father must have read my thoughts.

'She's as mean as dirt,' he said. 'Now don't touch anything and keep your big mouth shut.'

Her home was sparsely furnished and dark and depressing.

Polly was rather pitiful really, as I remember her. She'd had no end of bother trying to keep her sons in order and because of the endless bickering and fighting, my Dad had run away from home at fourteen to join the Navy. He told me in later life that he just couldn't stand the atmosphere any longer. Poor Polly was distraught. When she was widowed and left with five men her endless worries drove her further and further into her usual state of, 'Oh God, I don't know what I'm going to do, really I don't!'

These Christmas visits were a duty and not a pleasure.

Her greeting was always the same: she would wipe her plump hands on her pinafore then throw her arms around me and squeeze and cuddle me with all her might; and then she'd cry buckets of tears as she exclaimed, 'Oh, you're wonderful. If only your poor grandfather could see you now. You're so smart; you're a real swank. Your grandfather would be so proud of you.' And she'd hoot and howl away for a good few minutes.

After she and Dad had exchanged family chit-chat and discussed the welfare of one of his brothers — who was ill and undergoing constant treatment — we'd give her the Christmas card (written by my mother) then rise to leave.

She'd shuffle us towards the door and make a grab for her coat.

We didn't get our tea and biscuits.

Polly would pull on her Salvation Army bonnet and cloak and then off she'd go to her beloved 'meeting'. She used to sing the Temple down and join in the gossip between the hymns.

(Many years later I heard that at her funeral someone mentioned to the boys her favourite hymn was something to do with 'hidden in the cleft of a rock'; so the next day two of Dad's brothers practically took her garden wall apart, searching for concealed money. I don't know whether that's true, but that's what I heard.)

The O'Briens were a funny lot altogether.

But my mother's parents were much closer to me and I recall them both with great and deep affection. Mary-Ann and Albert Price were two of the most sincerely lovely people a soul could ever wish to meet. They had been childhood sweethearts, having met at school in Tredegar — the small Welsh valley town where they lived — and married quite young. They were very good-looking too, in their younger days.

Mary-Ann was a kindly soul with smiling eyes, a hard-working woman who bore Albert eight children, seven of whom survived. There were several sittings at their terraced house for each meal of the day, especially when all their children brought their offspring on flying visits.

Albert, my grandfather, was a gentle, loveable man. He was just like my mother. In fact they were like two peas in a pod, and when people say I have his nature and his ways I consider this the highest of compliments.

He was a good soul who used to walk on the Welsh mountains and hills, humming little tunes that he'd made up himself. He would plod along through lush green fields, not letting anything worry him or disturb his inner peace. On long walks down country lanes and flowered slopes he'd contemplate all manner of things. He was a simple man with simple needs and his great gentleness truly marked him out as a gentleman.

I was over the moon whenever my mother took me and John on the bus to spend a week at Nana and Grancha's, as they were known. Mind you, the three-hour bus journey was not a pleasant experience because we travelled over half-finished country roads and always seemed to get Dr Death as a bus-driver: you know the one — the madcap speed-lover who hits every bump in the road.

Nana and Grancha lived near to a disused viaduct that towered up to the heavens close to the back of their small house: it had nine incredibly huge arches supporting it; and under 'The Nine Arches', as they were called, a clear mountain stream bubbled along. My cousins and I would go fishing for 'tiddlers' there, which we put into jam-jars then later returned to their deep cool homes.

Further downstream there was a weir and on boiling-hot spring days we children would swim like fish in the water, splashing and dancing about in it. Those memories fill my mind with happiness. 'Have a good splash!' my mother would shout. And we did.

It was after such a swim that a group of my cousins and I trundled back home across the fields to Nana's house, dragging our weary legs through the long grasses while a relentless sun beat down upon our bare backs. We crossed the stiles and I fell — my foot caught on a stone and I tumbled headlong into a three-foot high patch of stinging nettles. I yelped in pain and the others half-dragged me out as if I had leprosy. I was stung from head to foot: I had stings in places where other people didn't even have places. When I got home the women covered me with 'blue-bag', an old-fashioned remedy for all complaints. I must say that by the end of the exercise I looked like 'The Thing from Outer Space'.

But that wasn't the end of my misfortunes on that hot afternoon: I later topped this by falling fully-clothed into the river.

Happy days!

When we visited Nana and Grancha we would often take a short bus trip to see one of their son's families — my Uncle Clifford and Auntie Charlotte and their six children. I guess I thought of them as the brothers and sisters I would have liked at home.

Aunt Charlotte was a small German woman, wiry and full of life, and she had a most peculiar accent I loved to hear. Her jet black hair was arranged in the 1940s style of straight down at the back and fluffed-up on the top of her head.

'Zey used to say I voz an old vitch,' she burred. 'Back in Germany, in ze War, I read my sister's cards and told her if ze soldier she'd arranged to meet zat night vos going to turn up or no. Zey didn't believe I could do it, so zey checked me out — and every time, ze cards voz right.'

Fascinated by her tales, I asked if she'd read the playing cards for me. She agreed and spread out the shuffled deck — and she was remarkably accurate. What's more, she showed me how to do it.

'You've got a funny kind of power viz you,' she said and instructed me on her methods. I was only young and thought I'd master this new ability to show my friends in an idle moment. But little did I realise that this skill would turn out to be so popular and frighteningly accurate that it would herald another contact with my unseen 'friend'.

Back home in Swansea I soon discovered that when people were seated in front of me I didn't need to 'read' the cards at all. I'd mysteriously receive strong mental impressions: thoughts, phrases and mind-pictures occurred to me, and sometimes I'd sense presences moving around the room.

It was only done for fun and there was no payment made but people began talking about these strange sessions and the word quickly spread.

I told one young woman she was expecting a child.

'I most definitely am *not!*' she protested.

'Check with your doctor,' I heard myself reply — and I was right. The following morning her pregnancy test proved positive.

How on earth had this private information popped into my mind?

What was supposed to be fun suddenly took on serious overtones. Nevertheless, being just sixteen I carried on, unaware at the time of the deeper implications.

One bright day I told an elderly Scotswoman such extremely personal details about her family's secrets that she exclaimed, 'Jesus, Mary and Joseph — *no one* knows about those things; not even my husband! Son, you've gobsmacked me.'

I added, 'You chose your husband from three men who were "possibilities for marriage" at that time.'

Her jaw dropped open.

'Furthermore, some days you've wondered if you made the right choice.'

The next thing I knew I was whisked off to

Glasgow to be put on display at her private home.

I fancied a holiday, so I didn't mind helping a few people along the way.

She paid my fare and I went on the coach from Wales to Scotland. I don't think I'd ever experienced such a gruelling trip in all my years: it was eighteen hours long and I just shivered and shook all the way there. I'm such a bad traveller that when I got off the coach I had to be helped to stand: my insides felt like jelly.

My first lesson in 'sacrifice in order to serve' had been well and truly driven home.

From her private house, news soon spread about the young Welsh lad who was 'gifted' and people came from miles away for a reading. But the hostess warned them all, 'If you don't like the truth then stay out of there because that's all he gives.' Even boys from the roughest, toughest districts in Glasgow astonished their families by scrubbing themselves clean, donning suits and paying a visit — but they couldn't get in; I was fully booked.

In the end I placed the cards down simply as a focal point. I didn't consult them at all: I just worked from my feelings and impressions. I got strong sensations of invisible presences at my elbow or moving around me; hands gently touched me; and unseen people whispered their thoughts into my mind.

Was the spirit world in touch again?

I supposed that it was, and decided I wanted nothing more to do with it; so as quickly as reading the cards had come into my life I let them slip out again — not understanding that they'd been another bridge-head consolidated by the other side, in preparation for our partnership in the years ahead.

When I next visited Aunt Charlotte and told her about my experiences she said, 'If you don't feel right about zeese things, Stephen, zen best leave zem alone until you're older.'

Sound advice, which I was happy to take. The only trouble was that the people on the other side weren't listening to it; or if they were then they certainly weren't paying attention because they planned another psychic 'event' while I was staying at my Aunt's home.

I can see now that with the onset of puberty my psychic powers were increasing, and the people in the Beyond intended to make the most of this burst of supernormal energy.

Late one night my cousin Ilona and I were sitting up gossiping and, although this sounds like a scene from a thriller movie, the next psychic 'happening' occurred as the clock struck midnight.

We'd been discussing spooky stories, so our minds were already firmly directed towards the next world, which must have given them the opportunity they needed.

Ilona was sitting on an old-fashioned three-seater sofa; it was a heavy and cumbersome piece of furniture that would need a good deal of strength to move it. Yet, although she was perched right on the edge of the seat, it suddenly swung right around into the middle of the room, completely on its own. Ilona went with it and was shocked.

'What does it mean?' she asked in a frightened voice.

I was speechless. A few moments ago we'd been chatting calmly and the next second this weighty sofa had come lurching across the room directly towards me.

Just then, we heard the sound of footsteps outside, clicking up the cold garden path.

Ilona and I locked eyes and held our breath.

A key turned in the lock... the front door swung wide open and we nearly died on the spot.

But it was only her father, my Uncle Clifford! Words couldn't describe our great relief. Uncle Cliff had just finished his night shift at the steel furnaces where he worked. We didn't mention anything to him but we both related the experience privately to Aunt Charlotte the next day.

'Zey don't interfere wiz this world vizout a reason,' she wisely educated us; and Aunt Charlotte was quite correct — this was a paranormal warning.

Shortly after this, Uncle Cliff was blown up in an accident at the furnaces and put in a private hospital room to die. His burns were so horrific the doctors didn't think he could possibly survive.

But against all odds he made a miraculous recovery.

I can only assume that my invisible 'friend'

had foreseen this terrible event and used it to prove his presence to me once again.

Back at school in Swansea, I felt that if I studied another book or attended another lecture my head would split wide open and my brains would come gushing out; so I left at seventeen.

But the following day the Head of the English Department called at the house to persuade me to return. 'You're worthy of a University education,' he said.

Weakly, I gave in and dragged myself back on the next day; but after this my mind was firmly made up and I gladly danced home out of the school. But Dad ordered me to get a job. 'If *I've* got to work, *everybody* works!' he bellowed.

My mother intervened.

'Find yourself a decent position, Stephen,' she cautioned. 'I'm sure you'll get something if you walk the town.'

So, to keep the peace and much against my wishes, I agreed and reluctantly dragged my heels behind me as I trudged the town — and I got a position in a swish jeweller's shop. Forty hours a week for a pittance, and it was slave labour in my eyes. We were all dressed up to serve the rich but *we* were practically on the poverty line.

It was a place full of plastic smiles.

To say I was bored there would be the understatement of the century. I was out of my mind with the wearisome tasks.

However, there were one or two lighter

moments that eased the insipid atmosphere. Maisie, a scatterbrained and wrinkled middle-aged assistant with dyed blonde hair and a red lipstick gash across her mouth, took me by the arm and said, 'Observe.'

I was supposed to be learning how to deal with the public. She approached a fur-coated customer who was dripping with jewels and whose make-up was as thick as plaster layered over every available space. The woman handed Maisie a diamond ring and imperiously demanded that it be cleaned.

'Certainly, *Madam*,' said Maisie with an eye-crunching smile. I thought her face was going to crack.

'Come on,' she said to me in her normal voice; and downstairs we went, Maisie telling me that she would now demonstrate how to clean a valuable diamond ring.

We arrived in the tiny kitchen used by the staff — it wasn't plush and carpeted with good-quality pile as the public areas were. Deftly, she popped the ring into a glass of hot water drawn from the tap. 'There,' she said. 'Now, give it a minute to soak and I'll show you what to do.' With that, she took some green washing-up liquid and squirted it onto a toothbrush and scrubbed the diamonds willy-nilly.

I was *agog*!

It's a good job 'Madam' hadn't seen the proceedings!

One day at the shop there was an electric thunderstorm and a lightning bolt struck the roof just as I was making my way outside with a customer to view a watch in the window. I jumped out of my skin and yelled then ran back into the store. The management were *not* pleased. But there was no time for a scolding because the shop's basement had flooded and raw sewage was pouring up through the toilets and covering the cellar floors.

The manager 'Creepy' Morgan appeared from nowhere — that's why they called him 'Creepy' — and ordered me to go downstairs with a bucket.

'Clean it up!' he said. Then he pulled a most astonished look: I think he saw my face when he'd given the order. Anyway, down I went to start this filthy job. There was sewage everywhere and the stench was vile. With my hand over my mouth and gagging for air, I collected two buckets and poured them back down the toilets; then I suddenly thought: I'm a sales-assistant, not a plumber. So I climbed back up the stairs and confronted 'Creepy'.

'I don't want to do this,' I announced; and I handed a very surprised man a dirty bucket.

'Oh, *don't* you?' He said, raising his eyebrows off the top of his head.

'No, I don't,' I said.

So *he* took the bucket and *I* got the sack.

'Thank God for that,' I said as I walked out into freedom, happy to be out of an establishment that was so full of hypocrisy.

I couldn't understand why everyone was so upset about my being out of work. They wanted to pressure me into slavery but all I wanted was to be free. I'd been cooped up in school for twelve years and now I wanted to be as free as a bird; I wanted to go wherever the breeze took me — and that's exactly what I did.

In the evenings I joined an amateur drama group in the YMCA and got involved in various shows and had a marvellous time. I loved the 'Am-Drams', as they were known; and I wrote plays and pantomimes for them, directed revues and other shows too. At last I'd discovered a powerful outlet through which I could channel my creative talents; and the people were lovely and it was great fun.

One season I played 'Buttons' in the pantomime *Cinderella* to a packed hall of 300 screaming children who were thoroughly enjoying a matinee performance, when all at once I realised the 'Ugly Sisters' hadn't arrived on stage. They'd missed their cue. What on earth could I do now?

In the wings I could hear frantic people scampering about and whispering. 'Where *are* they? They're supposed to be *on*! *Get them quick*!' ordered someone. To make matters worse there was no prompter in the wings.

I was facing a waiting audience: what should I do?

Then quite out of the blue a small voice right inside my head spoke clearly to me. 'Tell them that joke about the supermarket,' it said. I instantly recalled the long joke and delivered it to the audience, who fell about laughing. They were still roaring a minute later when two partially clothed 'Ugly Sisters' were flung on stage, red-faced and abashed. If it hadn't been for that paranormal voice the show would have come to a standstill.

In the dressing-rooms everyone patted my back and congratulated me on my quick thinking; but I didn't tell them what had really happened — they wouldn't have believed me anyway.

Soon afterwards, I was elected Chairman of the Swansea Youth Theatre, becoming responsible for running it, and my first decision was to entertain handicapped people. We got in a pianist, who hit more cracks than notes, and rehearsed lots of old-time Music-Hall numbers for weeks until we were ready. Then we visited a local society.

The handicapped people there ranged from about six years upwards to adulthood and they were delighted to welcome us. They gathered around the stage while some of us watched from the wings and we were immensely moved by their courage and fortitude in bearing their grave disabilities.

Nurses wheeled people into position; some wore callipers, others were carried to their seats. Some sat themselves down, eager to hear the concert but they were unable to speak; others were blind.

Watching from the tiny wings, I found myself quietly uttering, 'Dear God.' And Linda close by said, 'It must be awful for them, Stephen.' I couldn't find the words to express how I felt. 'Heart-breaking,' was all I could say.

But we pulled ourselves together, roused the cast, and with no scenery but plenty of flat notes and bags of youthful enthusiasm, started the show.

It was a lively production that was only half-produced really. Nevertheless, after many successful chorus numbers, duets and solos we were overwhelmed by the cheers and clapping we received. They'd thoroughly enjoyed themselves — especially during the *Alexander's Rag-Time Band* number, in which we all played imaginary instruments and everyone joined in. We had to do that one twice!

A nurse stepped forward amid the cheering and said, 'Thank you for coming, so many people forget about us.'

Moved to an encore, we sang more happy numbers and the audience loved them: they stamped their feet and clapped and sang along and even pulled us out to dance an enthusiastic Conga all around the hall.

It was a night full of laughter, happy faces and cries of delight.

When the show finished we could barely leave the building. There was a mad dash to thank us. Our hands were shaken, our coats were pulled and there were cries of 'Please don't go!'

Suddenly a small dark-haired lad of about eight, who could barely stand, was thrust forward by the crush and he clasped me firmly around my chest, smiling and chuckling, obviously grateful for our visit. His hug was so tight I could scarcely breathe. 'God bless you,' I said. But there was no reply.

I looked into his young eyes. There was a most wonderful light in them; and to this day I swear he was a great and noble soul, trapped in a tired and unresponsive body.

'It's been a lovely night,' I said, meeting his smile with mine. 'What's the matter, cat got your tongue?'

A nurse touched my arm. 'He can't speak,' she whispered. 'Hugging you is the only way he can say "I love you".'

I held him tightly, and tears welled in my eyes. I couldn't speak a word; if I'd tried to say something it wouldn't have made sense.

After more handshakes we said our goodbyes and, deeply moved, made our way homeward.

My mother was sitting by the fireside reading her newspaper.

'How did it go then, Stephen?'

'Oh, fine,' I said; but my face gave away the story and I was soon telling her all about the evening's soul-stirring events.

'I'm proud of you,' she said. 'If you can help someone less fortunate than yourself then that's what life's all about.'

Her loving words echoed through my mind as I lay in bed that night, pondering over the show and its effect on those souls. It was then that I decided to help people in need: I didn't know exactly what I would do, I just knew I'd do something in the future.

The next day at Linda's we discussed the concert. 'Fantastic work,' she said, 'and everyone was pleased.' I heartily agreed and we joked about all the songs that had gone wrong and the people who'd missed their cues and left the stage embarrassingly empty, much to the delight of the audience.

As we chatted, something strange happened. I suddenly felt as though a blow had struck my head: it wasn't a pain but the sensation of an electric shock sweeping over the left side of my brain — and in that instant I knew someone had been hurt. I clasped my head and cowered down in my seat. Linda looked bewildered. I quickly glanced at the time and noted it was three o'clock.

'Somebody's been hit,' I said, 'struck on the head.'

Linda glared at me in disbelief. 'Have you gone mad?'

But later that day I felt I had to check out this psychic experience. I questioned my mother first.

'Don't start all that again, Stephen,' she said. But undeterred I did the same with Dad and then Uncle Billy, but I drew blanks in each case. Then I asked my brother John.

'How did *you* know that?' he barked at me, very much the young man. But my explanation fell onto deaf ears. Nevertheless, at three o'clock that afternoon he'd been loading heavy crates onto a lorry when an iron girder had fallen and struck him a glancing blow to the left side of his head.

'Someone *told* you about it!' he said, not wanting to believe me.

But by now I'd learned not to argue. The world could dismiss me as much as it liked — I knew what had happened and no one could take that experience away from me.

I didn't understand the mechanics of the event then, but now I realise we have a psychic link to all those we love, whether they're living in this world or in the next. It's a kind of spiritual/ magnetic energy-line that can never be broken, a thread of awareness that connects us to each other. Whenever loved ones are distressed, sensitive relatives can register their feelings, and distance is no obstacle to these psychic powers.

So: had John mentally called out to me? Did he think of me the instant that blow struck? He wouldn't say; but whatever had happened this impression certainly reached me — the millisecond it occurred.

But this wasn't the only strange psychic happening that lay in store for me in my teenage years.

One of the theatre group members was a young girl called Marie who was tired of living at home. She decided to branch out and get a flat. When she found one several of us trouped along to give it a clean and help her to settle in. It was an old building, full of dilapidated furniture in faded rooms, which had been built in Victorian times. She rented some downstairs rooms that were in poor condition, so I painted the woodwork for her.

During our chats Marie told me that she thought she was being 'pursued by something inexplicable'. She made the hair on the back of my neck stand up with her tales of frightening psychic experiences, which we group of friends neither fully accepted nor rejected. We didn't know what to make of it.

I kept an open mind. At seventeen, what else could I do? What did I know of hauntings and such like? I was certainly no authority on them. So we comforted her and told her to forget all about it; and that was the end of that — or so we thought. Again, I'd failed to realise that my psychic powers were beginning to flower, and in this case they would burgeon.

In the early hours of the morning I awoke suddenly: it was pitch black in my bedroom (for some reason the street lamps had gone out). But what was that noise? Who was crying so pitifully? It sounded like Marie — but she lived five miles away in her flat. How could this sobbing possibly be coming from her?

The sound seemed to be registering in the middle of my brow, between my eyes.

I was thrown into confusion until I realised that it was 2.20 a.m. Then I knew why Marie was screaming out, 'I'm frightened! It's back in the room again!'

She was being 'haunted'.

I didn't understand how we could communicate telepathically, nevertheless I tried to transmit my voice back to her. When I spoke a few comforting words they seemed to echo down a void, down through a black tunnel or some kind of hollow cavern — I can't really explain it.

'Don't worry... Go to sleep,' I said. 'Its all over now.' And after this, Marie's crying faded out. But had the spirit entity departed? Had Marie received my thought-response in that early morning? Could she have heard me as clearly as I had heard her? I hoped so; but I'd certainly find out the next day.

As I drifted back to sleep my mind filled with Marie's incredible story: how, at a quarter past two each morning, the doorknob of her bedroom began to twist and rattle; how she was then terrified by the appearance of a spirit woman who seemed to want to 'possess' her body and her soul — this was what she feared.

I was determined to visit her to investigate; and the next sunny afternoon I was startled when Marie reported back — word for word — *exactly* what I'd transmitted telepathically on the previous night. The five miles that separated us had been no barrier to the psychic emanations we'd sent out.

We had experienced a pure mind-to-mind contact.

While we sat and discussed the whys and wherefores, suddenly Marie screamed out: she'd felt the presence of the spirit woman approaching again; and with that my spine prickled and I too sensed the entity moving along the outside wall. All at once the electric presence of the form glided into the room and transfixed our gaze.

We froze.

There in the doorway stood a tall woman dressed in long grey draperies: her straight white hair was parted in the centre and tumbled down to below her knees. She stood six feet tall and oozed pure selfishness and enmity. Her black eyes took in the room, darting quickly from side to side as she weighed up the situation. She paid particular attention to me and then — quite suddenly — she glided towards an alcove and sent a burst of hatred into the psychic atmosphere as she disappeared through the recess.

Neither of us knew what to do next.

We'd both seen her so clearly and guessed there must have been a doorway in that alcove when the house had been built.

We regained our composure slowly.

When emotional balance returned I found the strength to make myself audible. 'I believe you,' I said.

There was no doubt about it — action had to be taken.

That night, Marie and six friends and I trundled into her apartment laden with pillows, blankets and thermos flasks. None of us had told our parents what we were going to do but we intended to spend the night in the haunted flat. Looking back now, we must have had some pluck; many adults wouldn't have been so

brave. We were determined to sit up, absolutely
alert, and keep a sharp look-out, especially at
about 2.15 a.m.

Thoughts of meeting the apparition face to face
generated nervous and spooky conversation
before we settled down at about a quarter to
two.

Everything was peaceful and quiet but we
were so uncomfortably hot — none of us had
undressed in case we had to make a speedy
getaway. But would anything happen?

We didn't have long to wait.

At 2.15 exactly the room became icy cold as I
registered the tall spirit woman floating along
the hallway outside. Marie gasped, 'She's
coming!'

The others didn't sense anything and thought
we were playing a game, but we were far too
frightened for that — we were deadly serious.

The entity quickly moved into the room. She
wasn't visible this time but her presence was
incredibly strong. Marie screamed and began
flaying her arms about as if trying to push
someone away.

'She's moving around me!' she yelled, her voice
fraught with fear. 'Go away! Get her away from
me! *Tell her to go away!*'

I rushed over to her as fast as I could, but no
one else moved: they were petrified.

When I tried to protect Marie the apparition
emitted a feeling of intense hatred. I enclosed
Marie's body in my two arms, forming a circle of
psychic light about her, and the spirit went wild.

She circled round and round us with ever-increasing speed but she couldn't get near to her victim.

The tighter I gripped Marie, the faster the spirit went: she was furious I'd interfered with her plans. Marie was hysterical and shaking with fear, perspiring profusely, tears streaming down her face.

'Get her *away* from me! *Get her away!*' she kept screaming out.

The others were stunned into silence, totally unaware of what we two could sense, yet terribly afraid just the same.

Angered and frustrated, the spirit rushed out through the alcove again — so we took our chance to make a quick getaway. We ran like the wind out into the street, our blankets flapping, and eight of us we piled into a freezing-cold car, where we spent the remainder of the night — wide awake.

As we gradually returned to normality, Marie and I cast a quick glance at each other: we had both received an identical picture in our minds. Someone on the other side had obviously taken command of the situation and we were both shown the spirit woman being removed from the premises — and we knew everyone was now safe.

But what a frightening experience it had been.

Looking back with maturity on my side, I can see that Marie's highly-strung nature, coupled with her unconstrained fear and innate psychic abilities, allowed this mischievous entity the pleasure of provoking a young girl into hysterical behaviour.

This distasteful spirit produced terror and tears purely for morbid pleasure. This episode highlights that mediums and sensitives don't always find love and light in the Beyond. *Everyone* survives death and there are places in the next world to hold all kinds of people in all manner of conditions.

The golden rule is *Like Attracts Like*: broadly speaking, those of a similar nature inhabit in the same spheres of existence.

I've also learned that no one can 'possess' someone else: we are individuals who are spiritually 'in charge' of our bodies and minds; they can belong *only* to us.

This malicious earth-bound entity — a soul bound to the earth conditions by its jealous and vengeful nature — had been taken away by unseen friends; but not before spiritual lessons had been learned by all.

As soon as Marie regained her composure and became emotionally and mentally quietened, she stopped emitting the violent psychic energies that had allowed this 'haunting' to take place.

The moment she disciplined herself to be peaceful, instead of being fearful, she naturally prevented any further unpleasant visitations.

And Marie never had another sleepless night after that.

4

The Angel of Death

Unemployment was high and work was difficult
to get in those economic depression years of the
1970s. By now, I'd had a selection of really
mindless jobs. I'd walked the town as a kind of
Council Planning Department 'spy', checking on
people's gardens, roofs and sheds to see if they'd
had permission to build; and I'd been in the
Personnel Department at the British Steel
Corporation, too. I was so unbelievably bored
there that I complained to the manager of the
whole multi-million pound complex.

'Just bring a book in to read,' he said. Little
wonder this country's on the floor, I thought to
myself. There were other jobs too, all terribly
unfulfilling and lacking in job satisfaction; and,
to be frank, I simply didn't want any of them.

I guess that was when I decided to apply for a
place at Drama College. I reasoned this was
preferable to being unemployed and I'd
thoroughly enjoyed all the plays and concerts I'd
written and performed in at the amateur

theatre groups at the YMCA.

So I knuckled down to memorising a few speeches, one from Shakespeare — 'Romeo' no less — and wrote away for an audition to the Welsh College of Music and Drama in Cardiff, Wales' capital city. This was the *only* place I applied for and I got the interview. But on the morning of it I lost my way through the city, having been misdirected by several people, so I was late arriving at the Principal's office inside Cardiff Castle.

I forgot some of my words, too — my mind just went completely blank. It was a disaster really, yet as I was opening his study door to leave, the Principal called out, 'I'm prepared to accept you as a student; not on what I've seen here today but on what I've heard about you from references people have sent.' I suppose I should have been pleased but I wasn't impressed by the announcement.

College life was very active and full of stress. But there was one snag — I wasn't offered a Mandatory grant; instead the council had given me a Gratuity grant, which amounted to little money and I was for ever left short. My mother knew this and came speedily to the rescue; she'd slip me back a few pounds out of the weekly 'keep' money that Dad had ordered me to give her, which was taken from my grant allowance.

'Don't let him know,' she'd whisper. 'Put it in your pocket quickly.'

Dad most certainly did *not* approve of my attending college. But being there helped me to brush up on a number of skills: how to exercise and project my voice correctly, how to move well; how to command and hold an audience's attention; above all it helped me to gain greater confidence and professionalism when appearing before large audiences — something I would be grateful for in later years.

Although I enjoyed the work I was struck by the unreality of it all: it was purely make-believe, illusory, transient; and it had little connection with everyday life. I was also struck by the sudden shock of learning to be a daily commuter, travelling for two hours every day, 700 miles a week on dear old British Rail. I couldn't begin to count the number of times I heard over their tannoy systems: 'British Rail regrets the late arrival of...' As I stood on their freezing-cold platforms surrounded by winter ice I often wondered: Do they really *mean* it?

But unknown to me then, this was all training in preparation for some greater purpose lying ahead of me...

Life moved along slowly but smoothly, until one day our front door burst open. 'Quick!' snapped by brother. 'The baby's on the way!'

Breathless, we dashed out into the car and sped through the town to Mount Pleasant Hospital, where my sister-in-law gave birth to Claire, my niece.

My mother was over the moon! At last she had the little daughter she'd always wanted. The fact that she was a *grand*daughter made no difference to her at all. She was overjoyed.

Within eighteen months we were back at the hospital again, but this time the powerful screaming lungs belonged to my nephew, Jonathan.

My mother revelled in the new arrivals. She pampered them and nursed them in the family Welsh shawl that John and I had been wrapped in as babies. She completely spoiled them — as all good Nanas do.

Every weekend we'd see the children at our home or we'd visit them at theirs. My mother was particularly close to Claire, the firstborn; and when Claire began to cut her teeth by rubbing her gums wildly on the bridge of my mother's nose she nicknamed her 'Mad Maggie'.

It was such a joy to see them playing together.

As soon as the weather broke, all of us except Dad drove up to Tredegar where my mother's parents lived, and four family generations were united under one roof: Nana and Grancha Price, their children, their grandchildren and their great-grandchildren. What a smashing day that was, seeing all those happy smiling faces. And my mother couldn't get enough of her little angels. She worshipped them. Somehow, they'd brought a glow back into her eyes and a new purpose into her life.

Everything seemed wonderful with the arrival of the babies; but life has its own unusual way turning and changing; and soon there was to be a dark cloud hanging over our family — a cloud that would abruptly end my childhood and catapult me into the adult world.

I'm not given to superstition but one winter's night Uncle Billy and I were both reading quietly in the living-room when a landscape picture loosed itself from the wall and crashed down onto a shelf. The nail that held it bounced off the shelf and landed right in my lap.

Uncle Billy and I exchanged looks. He drew in a sharp breath. 'Who put that picture up?'

'My mother did.'

'Well, there's trouble coming when a picture falls,' he said darkly.

'Oh, don't be so superstitious,' I admonished, 'that's just an old wives' tale.'

'You listen to me, brother... the same thing happened not long before my own mother took ill.'

I shrugged him off and clicked my disapproval. But indeed, those invisible hands which released that picture knew what they were doing, for shortly afterwards my mother became unwell.

For years she'd had a good deal of trouble with her stomach in the mornings, and frequently she'd felt sickly. But this was something else.

She went for medical tests because she was in such discomfort; her energy was ebbing away and she was losing weight. We were all quite worried about her.

As soon as the results came through she was rushed to Singleton Hospital to undergo major stomach surgery; it was scheduled for the next day and there was nothing we could do until the following evening when the operation would be over.

It was such bad news to receive, just before Christmas, too.

'We'll all be thinking of you, Mam,' I assured her with a kiss.

'I know you will, Stephen,' she drowsily whispered as the medication took effect. 'You're a good lad... a good lad...' and she drifted into sleep.

The next morning my friend Jayne suggested visiting a fortune-teller she'd heard of — 'just for a laugh'. I agreed; but at the appointed time Jayne backed out and I was left standing on the woman's doorstep. Nevertheless, something told me I should go in; and so, against my better judgement, I did.

A plump old lady in a wrap-around pinafore and faded slippers led me through a dark passageway into a small dirty kitchen. The place felt oppressive and claustrophobic and I remember thinking how similar it was to old Gran King's house, all those years ago when I was a boy. Everything was awry and the smell of the coal fire filled the room. The mats were worn through and as for the fortune-teller — well, she was about sixty with greasy skin that resembled a freshly ploughed field. But there was some kind of goodness about her, which checked my desire to leave. I didn't know why I was there anyway.

'Take no notice of the place, dear,' she croaked. 'Cut the cards.' I obeyed and watched her crinkled hands as they shuffled the deck. Then followed a string of confusing questions and she was so incredibly wrong I felt like getting up and leaving — until she paused and said, 'Someone isn't very well. Am I right?'

My ears pricked up but I was careful not to feed her any information.

'Well, love, whoever it is, you'll remember this year as their last one — the year when they began to crack up.'

I walked out into the cold December night, troubled by that last statement.

And it wasn't long before my father revealed to me my mother's true condition, as told him by the surgeons.

'Your mother has cancer,' he said.

When I could find the words, I broke the awesome silence with, 'She must have no pain, Dad... she mustn't have any pain.'

After this, I visited the hospital every day. The surgeons had discovered widespread cancer tissue throughout her body and she'd been cut almost in two to check the growths; but nothing could be done for her: they removed two-thirds of her stomach and sewed her body back together again.

On the night of her operation I'd wanted to go and see her at the hospital, but my father wouldn't drive me there.

'She'll be asleep, you fool — under medication. They won't let you in there; how many more times must I tell you?'

'They *will* let us in,' I fought back. 'We're family.'

'No!' he insisted.

But I was not deterred.

In the end, I went to the hospital alone: all the buses had stopped because of the Christmas holidays so I walked the three miles in pouring rain just to see her.

When I arrived the Sister-in-Charge refused me permission to enter Mam's small side-room; but when she was called away I crept quietly unseen to my mother's bedside. I moved apprehensively towards the bed. She was propped up on one side with her back facing me. She lay there absolutely still, looking so frail that my eyes filled up with emotion. I slowly approached her and I kissed her shoulder, as a kind of healing gesture I guess; but she didn't sense anything: she was unconscious to avoid the desperate pain.

While she recovered on the following day, my friend Jayne and I went knocking on doors to collect money for cancer research. When I told my mother that same night, she agreed it was a good cause and gave a sad knowing smile.

In the new year the doctors released her from hospital but she was still very weak and painfully thin. The operation had been so extensive that she couldn't stand up straight: she walked slowly and hesitatingly, with her shoulders bowed over because the scar tissue was pulling at her stomach and back.

It was agony to watch her suffering, this woman who was the centre of our lives. We all wondered how on earth she could manage to place one foot in front of the other. I used to hug her and help her to walk around the house.

Of an evening, when we were alone together by the fireside, I would sit by her feet while she read her newspaper and completed the crosswords she loved. I asked her at such a time, 'Mam, what ambitions do you have?' Her answer was as touching as her look.

'I've lived out all my ambitions, Stephen. I wanted a family and a comfortable home. I've got two fine boys and my life is now complete.'

I couldn't answer her, for I was aware in that moment, beyond any doubt, that she knew her life was coming to a close.

As the days passed she became weaker and weaker. Yet despite this, one morning I found her carrying two heavy shopping bags up the hill towards home. That was my mother — a fighter, a determined and loving woman who never mentioned or grumbled about the agony she bore without complaint.

As the weeks moved forward she had to take to her bed. Unable to walk now, she could barely move without pain. One night she asked me for a pair of socks to keep her feet warm, so I found the thickest pair I had and pulled back the sheets to put them on her feet. It was all I could manage not to show my shock: she'd lost so much weight that the bones of her feet were stick-like and protruding. And when she asked me to rub her back to relieve the pain, I knew she wanted me to realise she was dying: the bones of her spine were like white knuckles on a hand.

In the afternoons she would sit on the side of the bed and count the hours on the floor with her fingers to the next time the nurse would deliver a pain-killing injection.

Then she decided not to take any more medication because it was blurring her last precious memories of us all. Although this was a brave and noble step to take, she soon had to reverse it because the suffering was too great.

At night I'd lie awake for hours in the next bedroom, listening for any sound of distress that might come from her. But the house was filled with an ominous silence. Secretly I'd cry and pray. 'Please God, give me the cancer and make her well again. *I'll* die,' I said, 'but please let her live. She's a good woman, a wonderful person. Please take me instead,' I would silently plead. But of course, I didn't realise in my youth that the Great Spirit of Life doesn't work in that way.

Neither did I know that my father had been found crying at work. Poor Dad just couldn't understand why this was happening to his wife. My brother was also deeply hurt but avoided speaking about his feelings. 'There's nothing we can do,' he'd say sadly.

As for me, I'd managed to contain my emotions until one evening at college when a brass band played Christmas carols: the music reached down inside me and stirred my soul; tears began to stream down my face. I hurriedly left the crowded hall of students, all of whom stared at me. Sally knocked at the cloakroom door.

'Are you all right, Stephen?' she asked. I couldn't find any words; I was sobbing uncontrollably; I was going to lose my mother. Knocking again, Sally called out, 'Stephen, is there anything I can do?'

'There's nothing anyone can do,' I said. 'That's the trouble.'

Now my mother's last days were approaching. Her family drove down from Tredegar to be with her: she'd held my father and called out for them in delirium, knowing her time was almost spent.

It was a cold Saturday evening in March when her breathing became very irregular. You could count the pauses between the breaths she took; and as the night progressed it became obvious the lapses were getting longer.

On Sunday morning I instinctively knew this would be her last day. Outside, brilliant sunshine flooded the sky and I remember thinking: Why is the sun shining so brightly when my mother is dying?

Inside, there was heaviness all about the house; it was filled with silent moments when no one really felt like saying much. We didn't know what to say anyway.

At about two o'clock I climbed the stairs for the hundredth time to see her. She was lying motionless in the bed, eyes half closed, breathing whenever she could find the strength. I stood by the bedside and leaned over her and kissed her on the forehead.

'Good night, God bless you,' I said, even though

it was daytime. 'This is Stephen, Mam. Never forget: I love you with all my heart.'

And in a whispering, almost inaudible, voice she replied, 'Stephen... I'm dying.'

I couldn't speak a word...

In a timeless daze I pulled on my coat and walked down the hill to my mother's dearest friend and neighbour, Florrie. I entered Florrie's open door but my vision was blurred by a wall of tears. I could barely form a sentence but somehow managed to whisper, 'Mam's dying... if you want to see her... please come up with me now... I don't think she'll last the hour...'

In the stillness, Florrie put on her coat and together we walked up the hill. I don't know if we spoke much at all. Through tears I think Florrie said she was sorry but I'm not altogether sure. I only knew I was numb and silent.

I climbed the stairs and Florrie sat down by the fire, content just to be there with some of my mother's close friends who had gathered for the end. Up in the bedroom, my brother and I closed in around the bed. My sister-in-law came inside and we stood silently and watched my mother's last few moments of life. We never said a word. My father, too upset to face the end, had gone next door to a neighbour.

The seconds ticked away and memories flooded into my mind; thoughts of our childhood filled my vision: those happy picnics by the sea, the loving kindness my mother had shown to all the elderly folk in our street. I could see the time she'd collected me at the school when I was just a boy, but the other children had been soaked in the rain because their mothers were nowhere in sight. I recalled the wonderful moments we'd shared through our lives: her gentle voice as she sat me on her knee when I was a toddler and said, 'Stephen, I love you, son.' A million thoughts occurred at once; a million kindnesses, thousands of loving moments. Then the bedroom came back into focus.

Her breathing was now very spasmodic. There were long pauses of utter silence.

And then — my sister-in-law suddenly burst into tears and my brother joined her. She'd been counting the seconds between the pauses and the last breath had gone.

It was all over.

My mother was dead.

John left, wiping the tears from his eyes, and I followed him to the bathroom where we held each other tightly and cried from the very depths of our beings. A great dark cloud filled every corner of my mind as John and I cried and clasped each other, heavy with grief and total despair. The sound of our tears echoed around the walls as the devastating fact of my mother's death struck home, right to the heart.

When my failing strength returned, I wandered through to the bedroom again — still unable to comprehend why we'd suffered such a tragic loss — and I found Mary, one of my mother's friends, with some rosary beads in her hands, praying for her soul in a whispered, hushed voice that turned the room into the hallowed ground of a thousand souls in reverent prayer.

'May God keep you safe, my friend, safe in His eternal kingdom...'

Unable to watch any more, I slowly turned and wiped my eyes and descended the stairs.

It was three o'clock.

Florrie joined our tears; Mrs Ross could find no words to express her grief; then Nora from next door came through. The women wept quietly into their handkerchiefs and wiped their eyes.

'She was wonderful person...'

'It's not fair that someone as kind as Mrs O'Brien should die in so much pain...'

I just sat by the fireside, deep in my solemn thoughts.

All our lives had now come to an end. The light of my mother's smile had gone. The centre of our family had been taken from among us; the woman I loved had died.

How could life go on without her?

We'd lost our first, our last, our everything.

We'd lost our best friend.

We had lost our mother.

5

Revelation

On the morning after my mother passed, I was the first to rise. Drowsily, I crept into her room where her body lay motionless in death. I kissed her on the forehead and said, 'You were a marvellous person and a wonderful mother.' Then I left the room as silently as I'd entered it...

On the day of the funeral, I answered the door to the florist who delivered many wreaths and moving tributes. Only when the flowers were arriving did I fully realise that my mother had died. I suppose it was some kind of delayed shock, and I was quiet for most of those early hours. This was the first time I'd witnessed death so close at hand and it was a great and devastating blow to us all.

One by one, people began to gather in our small living-room. Some were crying, others were downcast and very solemn. They'd come to pay their respects to a much-loved woman.

The door opened and a clergyman arrived. I didn't know him; I don't think any of us did, for we were not at all religiously minded as a family and followed no particular faith. If I'd had my own way I wouldn't have had any outsiders to conduct this service — as young as I was, I'd have taken it myself. But that wasn't the 'proper' way and so they hired a clergyman to preside.

He started speaking empty and meaningless words: he'd never even known my mother, so how could he possibly appreciate the loss she was to this world? My mother's sisters started to weep, so I placed my hand on one of their shoulders and squeezed it gently. Her tears moved me and my eyes filled up; and then a small voice somewhere inside my head said, 'Be brave... Try to be brave.'

The tributes were loaded into the hearse outside. There was one from all the children of our estate, another from the children of the school where Mam had worked as a playground supervisor. Soon the hearse was so full of flowers that the coffin could barely be seen. But right on the top of it was my own special tribute to her — a single red rose, placed in a see-through box. The card inside read: '*As long as I live, you'll never die.*'

At Morriston Crematorium I dimly recall that clergyman speaking more uncomforting and hollow words while I kept my eye on the coffin as it slowly sank down at the side of his pulpit. He looked at me as I stared at it; and I remember thinking: That's the last I'll ever see of her now.

The service concluded and we sadly filed outside.

Someone asked me where I'd like the ashes to be scattered, and I pointed out a small tree.

From this moment on, our family seemed to break apart. My brother got on with his life, my father immersed himself in work, and I tried not to think about what had happened. I dashed about filling my time with anything and everything to obliterate the sense of loss, not wanting to face the fact I'd never see my mother again. I comforted myself by thinking she was now at peace in 'heaven', although I didn't really understand what that meant. I knew she was out of pain, and I was grateful for that.

Dad and I were now under great emotional stress and our relationship had quickly broken down. We were both exceptionally tense and terse, both missing Mam and neither of us mentioning it. The rift between us got so bad that one night his temper exploded and I got the worst of it when he hit me then slammed the door and went to bed in a rage. I sat alone, crying and thinking to myself: He never would have done this if she were alive.

I was a deeply sensitive twenty-year-old.

Life went on aimlessly from day to day — but it seemed meaningless.

Birth; life; death; what was the point of it all? I couldn't fathom any answers and nothing could soothe my spirit.

To make matters worse my college grant had run out and I was now penniless. There were three weeks of graduation term left and I couldn't attend unless I could pay the £15 rail fare. Even if I *could* raise it I still wouldn't have any money for daily food. I was at my wit's end.

One afternoon I found myself spilling the whole tale out to my brother. He couldn't help me because he was in financial difficulties himself, but he mentioned an endowment policy my mother had taken out for me years previously. 'It matures soon,' he informed me. 'Why not cash it in now? You'll get about £16.'

That was the answer! After all, it's what my mother would have done. But when I approached Dad he refused point-blank to release the policy. Desperate, I sought out the insurance company, clutching my identification details, and explained my precarious position.

'I'm sorry,' they said grimly, 'but we can't pay it out without your father's signature.' My heart sank. Now I'd have to go back and confront my father. Swallowing my pride, I did; but he wouldn't sign and I was left completely in limbo.

The next day Florrie's daughter, Marion, approached me stealthily. 'Look, I want you to take this £15,' she said, handing me a sealed envelope. 'Never mind how I borrowed it. Now get yourself to college: it would be your mother's last wish.'

I was speechless, but from somewhere I got the words to say 'Thank you' and assure her that I'd pay it back whenever I could.

So I continued my final studies and graduated with my College Diploma; but it was no great joy to receive it, not the way I'd been feeling.

Even when the children came to call I was melancholy because nothing was the same without their Nana in the house to greet them. Although Claire was only two years old she missed my mother greatly. She'd suddenly stop giggling in the garden and ask quite seriously, 'Uncle Stephen, where's Nanny O'Brien?' I hoped she hadn't seen my reaction. What could I say? What could I tell this little girl whom she'd loved so much?

I framed my words gently.

'Nanny O'Brien's in heaven,' I told her.

Claire became pensive for a few moments then followed up with, 'Is God looking after her, Uncle Stephen?'

'Oh yes,' I said, 'God loved her so much, He's taken her to be near Him.'

Then in the innocence of childhood she wanted to know, 'Will I ever see her again?'

I took her hand. 'Oh, yes,' I said. 'One day I'm sure we'll all be back together again.' At least that was what I'd hoped, but I didn't really know.

Children have a strange way of putting their fingers right on the pulse of things.

Then, one morning, something odd happened. Deep inside myself I knew I should visit my grandparents — it was as though somewhere in my soul they were calling out to me, thinking of me. Perhaps the three of us were united in our grief, I don't know. I only knew I must go to them. So I packed a bag and made for Tredegar, where Nana and Grancha lived.

As the bus chugged and spluttered up the winding hills, I couldn't help hearing my brother's laughter as we both joked and played childish games of 'I spy' with my mother on the same journey we'd made so many times before. But now the seats beside me were empty and another bump in the road broke my reverie.

Outside, the sun was shining like a bright ball of fire but the cold March air took my breath away as I approached my grandparents' home. Everything looked just the same from the outside: the creaky garden gate, the lace curtains at the window, the warmth that seemed to radiate around the very walls themselves.

As I walked up the path to the door, I saw the yellow goldenrods and remembered collecting bunches of them when I was no bigger than a sparrow, to present to my mother one Eastertime. Deep in my memories, I moved to the back of the house and knocked at the kitchen door.

How would they be feeling now, so soon after the funeral? And what on earth could I say to them? I was so young... and secretly I hoped they wouldn't be shocked to see me because I hadn't told them I was coming.

But there was nothing to worry about: the door opened and I fell into my grandmother's arms. 'What a lovely surprise,' she said, smoothing the back of my hair and holding me tight. 'It's so good to see you, Stephen.' Grancha gave me a hug too, but he was still so deeply hurt. I could see it in his solemn eyes.

Nana and Grancha were both in their seventies and were utterly devastated by their eldest daughter's death. Quietly, we sat and talked together.

'God knows, it shouldn't have happened,' said my grandmother. 'We never expected one of our own to go first. It should have been one of us,' she said, stricken with grief. Grancha remained silent. Not a man of many words at the best of times, now he was walking around in a daze, like someone lost in a waking nightmare. I dimly recollect him saying, 'She was only forty-nine.' Then he heaved a sigh of bitter regret.

As I listened, my eyes took in the humble room. Their house was just as I'd always remembered it, and the memories that came flooding back brought a lump to my throat. Then 'something' urged me to help Nana and Grancha in some way. I wondered what my mother would have done had she been there on that day — and my mind was made up.

I rolled up my sleeves, got a mop and bucket and a Hoover and cleaned the house from top to bottom until it shone like a new pin. You could see the reflection of your face in the lino after I'd finished this mammoth job. My mother had often done this cleaning for them and now it was my turn. Grancha kept saying, 'You needn't bother you know, Stephen.' But I think he knew why I did it.

After tea I strolled out onto the mountains, those lovely hills and vales in the Welsh Valley. The grass was strong, the air was crisp and clear and I was totally alone with my thoughts. In the distance I could see the Nine Arches where we'd all picnicked when I was a lad. I walked past the weir and in my mind's eye I could still see the children splashing happily in the waters.

All around me were the scenes of my mother's childhood, the things that made her the good person she was.

But I couldn't remain on the hills, as much as I wanted to. The sun was sinking and I ended my daydream and went to collect my travelling bag, my mind still full of those days of long ago.

As I bid my grandparents goodbye at the bus station I said, 'I'll still come and see you both.'

'We know you will,' replied Grancha, blinking back his tears. 'You do your best to get on with your father, Stephen. You've only got each other now, you know.'

He hugged me. I got aboard the bus as he said, 'And never forget: we loved your mother more than words can say.'

The big bus pulled out of the station as I watched my grandparents disappearing from view through the back window.

I was going home; but I didn't want to go...

My nights were long and sleepless; my days were empty and devoid of all love and kindness. People felt awkward in my presence, not quite knowing what to say or do; and Dad and I just couldn't communicate at all. Whenever we spoke we started another pointless argument. I didn't want to be harassed and condemned by every other word but that's what was happening; so, when he came in, I went out — and in this way much difficulty was avoided — though when I couldn't time my departure properly another awful session of being criticised would get underway.

What terrible memories I have of these, my darkest hours.

Seeking some solace I decided to sort through my mother's things. I felt impressed to do so and it's a good job I did because soon afterwards items started 'walking' out of the house. Bit by bit our home was being taken away, until my father shouted and put a stop to it.

Up in the bedroom I sifted through all the papers, photographs and jewellery my mother had collected over the years. There was nothing of any value there; it was all inexpensive and sparkly — we never had much money to waste on the so-called finer things of life. I did come across my mother's wedding ring though, and decided to keep it in memory of her.

I also found snapshots of us when we were younger. Those days seemed so far away now, somewhere in a distant past. Amongst the bundles I discovered birthday cards sent by my mother to John and I when we were infants. I sat on the bed fondling these treasured memories and was greatly moved when I read upon a card: *To my darling Stephen on your first birthday*. There were kisses all along the bottom of it and under them were the words: *With all our love, Mammy and Daddy*. But Dad never sent us cards and the writing was my mother's.

That old feeling began haunting me again — that strange sensation of 'being in the world, but not of it'. Coupled with this, I felt so alone.

But my soul was moved when I came across a small heart locket. I'd never seen it before. When I opened it there was a picture of me on one side and my brother on the other, both as small boys. I still have it today.

The days rolled onwards and I began to feel unwell. I was losing weight. I wasn't eating properly and my nervous system couldn't cope with the added stress: it was a tough job for me to climb the hill to our house and I couldn't manage it without a few rests on the way. Mrs Walker from next-door asked me what was wrong when she found me sitting on the wall. 'Oh, nothing,' I returned. 'I just need to catch my breath.'

My appearance was slowly changing: I'd lost such a lot of weight that my face began to look sunken and drawn. Florrie told me to take better care of myself and to eat at least one decent meal a day. I don't think Dad paid much attention, and probably didn't even notice; but I just couldn't be bothered to buy food or prepare it.

This new way of life thrust upon us had taken its toll of the whole family. The dark cloud it formed around us filled our lives with uncertainty and a nagging grief that pulled us all down into despair.

But somewhere out in the worlds of light beyond this grey little planet a soul was stirring. Through the mists of death, beyond the veil, the mighty power of love was planning to claim its own...

One evening, about three months after my mother died, I returned home on a late summer's night. Realising that the house was empty I opened the door and suddenly heard my name called from above. I swung around, startled — and there in a brilliant blaze of light at the top of our stairs I saw my mother. She was beckoning and calling to me.

'Stephen! Stephen!' she cried out anxiously, 'Come up! Come up!' — and she waved her hand for me to join her. Spellbound and light-headed, I turned on the hall light. I couldn't believe what I was seeing. How could this be?

'Stephen! Come up!' she called out once more and she turned and moved out of sight around the landing.

Dumbfounded and bewildered, I climbed the stairs at her command, looking around excitedly to see her, and when I reached the top of the landing I heard her call to me again: '*Stephen*!' Her voice was full of urgency.

I quickly swivelled to face the direction of the sound — and there was my mother again, standing outside my bedroom door as large as life, and bathed in glowing light. I stepped backwards and braced myself against the wall. I didn't know what to make of this. I wasn't frightened, she was my mother. How could any son fear his mother's love? But how could she be here? She was dead. I'd been there when she'd taken her last breath.

Yet here she was, standing before me, wearing a hospital robe and leaning on a walking stick for support. She was still bowed over as I remembered her in her last days.

But those eyes, that face: it was my mother.

Slowly she moved towards me, still smiling, then she leaned forward and kissed me on the left side of my face; just as I'd often done to her when she lay dying from cancer, when I'd said 'Goodnight, God bless you' to her.

Then she laughed — it was that special laugh that only she could make. A laugh that said, 'I'm alive, what are you all worrying about?'

As I stared fixedly at her, mystified by it all, she quickly faded from my sight. The landing suddenly lost its radiance and I stood there totally alone.

I don't know how long I stayed anchored to that spot. I just remember feeling dazed and perplexed as I eventually moved down the stairs, one step at a time, supporting myself on the walls as I went. I made my way to the living-room and sat on our settee and gazed across at my mother's chair... it was empty now — but I had just seen her. She'd spoken to me, called out my name from beyond death.

Slowly, gradually, my astonishment was

replaced by a dawning realisation. Somehow, through the power of our love, she had returned. She had bridged that Great Divide and spoken to her son. She wasn't dead — *she was alive*! I had *seen* her!

But what should I do now? Should I tell the rest of the family? Surely they had a right to know?

But how could I approach them with this news?

The excitement made me dizzy but I made up my mind that I *would* tell them. I'd have to pick the right moment though. But right now, I just felt like dancing and shouting from the hilltops. I kept thinking to myself: If *she's* alive then *everyone* lives; I must tell the world.

When my brother called for coffee, the time was right.

'She's alive in another world,' I said.

John was confused and a little angry.

'She's dead, Steve. You *want* to see these things. Face the facts — she's gone. Our mother's dead.'

I protested, but it was just no use. Yet, for her sake, I had to tell them all. That's what she would want me to do.

I shall never forget my father's face and the strange, fiery look in his eyes when I told him.

'Why *you*?' he snarled at me. 'If your mother came back she'd come to *me* — not you. You're only her son; I'm her husband.'

'But I've told you the truth, Dad,' I said. 'I saw her.'

'She's dead, son,' he said through clenched teeth. 'You were at the crematorium. She's gone and she'll never come back. Your mother's *dead.*'

No one would believe me. Did they think I was lying? Why didn't they believe me?

Sad and angry, I walked out through the fine rain and eventually wandered into an old Catholic church. It was completely empty so I approached the altar, still deep in thought and consternation. The atmosphere was so peaceful, so tangible you could almost grasp the tranquillity.

Moving towards the altar I noticed a candle-stand and upon it was the inscription:

I have suffered.

I don't know why I did it but I took a nearby candle and lit it and placed it in the centre of the stand, for my mother.

Wrapped in the sweet smell of incense, I sent out a prayer. Quietly I whispered, 'I tried to tell them, Mam. I tried but they wouldn't believe me. *I* know you're alive, even if no one else wants to accept that. I did my best for you,' I said.

Noiselessly, I sat at one of the front pews and became very still, thinking of how wonderful she had been to us all in life, and how saddened she must be to think that no one but me accepted her existence beyond death.

Just then, a hand touched my shoulder. Beside me stood a pleasant young priest in full ceremonial garb.

'Are you all right, son?' he asked. 'Do you need

any help?'

'Oh, no thank you,' I said. 'I just thought I'd sit here quietly and meditate, if that's all right.'

'Of course,' he smiled. 'You take as long as you like.'

And he turned to go back up the aisle, fading away into thin air as he went...

* * *

PART TWO

The Mission Begins

6

The Mission Begins

Although no one believed that my mother had
visited me from beyond death, I knew what I'd
experienced. Somehow, somewhere, she was
still alive, still existing as herself. I never once
doubted my sanity — I'm a practical man. So I
now resolved to keep quiet about the whole
episode and do my best to get on with building a
new life.

I got a job as an Assistant Stage-Manager at a
theatre but the contract only lasted for eight
weeks and it was unstimulating work. However,
there were some memorable moments, like the
time I authorised the curtain to be raised too
early during a deadly serious drama, only to
reveal a workman clutching a vase of flowers as
he dashed panic-stricken off the set! The
audience hooted at my mistake; but I guess I
just wasn't concentrating, having lost someone I
so dearly loved.

There were more laughs in store though: the
cast held a comedy football match in aid of a

local charity and they cajoled me into dressing up as a frightened goalkeeper. Every time the ball came near the nets I ran behind them and cowered on the ground while the opposition scored another goal! All the players wore fancy-dress costumes 'borrowed' from the theatre wardrobe department and one of our team was hilariously funny: she'd dressed as a tipsy Christmas Fairy, complete with highly-stiffened tutu and a sparkly wand. Whenever she kicked the ball she collapsed exhausted to the ground and lay there spread-eagled and unconscious until she was stretchered off the field by two circus clowns. The crowd really *loved* her.

Back at the theatre, at odd moments during the performances while I stood in the dark wings, my mind filled again with visions of my mother's spirit-return. Quietly, I shrugged my shoulders then got on with the job: I didn't want to make more silly mistakes.

After the contract ran out I forced myself into travelling to a few auditions — something I didn't want to do. I went hither and thither at great expense, mostly to London, and had no luck whatsoever. Being auditioned was such a degrading experience: they lined people up like 'prize cows' to be paraded and judged, then — nine times out of ten — rejected.

Then something happened.

As with most of the important events in my life, a sudden change occurred literally overnight. One morning I woke up, stretched and yawned, then announced to the fresh air,

'That's the *end* of that!' — and I said it with vigour and really meant it. With positive determination I knew my days with the theatre were over; I was tired of make-believe and now I wanted to be *me*, Stephen O'Brien, the real person inside. I threw off an old overcoat and set out on a new tack. I wanted to move into a new way of life — into reality — and quite unknown to me that's exactly what was about to happen.

One evening while ambling through the town I realised I was close to a Spiritualist church: it was old Gran King's church — the one she'd spoken of all those years ago when I was a boy of ten. I turned the corner and saw the painted sign:

Lower Oxford Street
Spiritualist National Union Church.

As I approached it I had a most remarkable experience: I felt as light as a feather and as if I were floating six inches above the pavement. It was an incredible feeling of levitation and I remember thinking to myself: Someone wants me to go in here. So I did.

Carefully, I tiptoed up the twenty steps to the inner door, behind which Gran King said there was some kind of upper room; I could hear muffled conversation.

I stopped for a moment.

Should I enter or not? What would I find inside?

A thousand thoughts clamoured for my attention. Little did I know, but I was standing on the threshold of a completely new life. Once I passed through that doorway, my whole world would change — but I had no idea of it then.

What were the people in there whispering about?

I took a deep breath, pushed open the door and went inside... and was rather surprised to find a small horseshoe of chairs neatly arranged around a portable gas fire, and all heads turned and smiled at me. The people seemed quite 'normal'.

The ceiling was high, the walls were painted light blue, and the whole place seemed to radiate friendliness.

Then an elderly lady beckoned to me as I stood hesitantly in the doorway. 'Good evening,' she said in a warm, smiling voice. 'Come and sit down. You're very welcome.'

Gingerly, I took my seat opposite her.

'Been here before?" she asked.

'No,' I said, not even sure why I was there now.

At seven o'clock precisely, this elderly woman, whom everyone called Mrs Palmer, stood up and announced that the Open Circle was going to begin. Oh, I thought, this is what Gran King used to talk about, where she gave out her spirit messages; and that note of familiarity helped me to settle in.

The twenty people trembled their way through a hymn, unaccompanied, then Mrs Palmer delivered a beautiful spontaneous prayer, sincerely given from the heart; it was very moving. She called for peace to come into the world through each individual soul and asked that brother should love brother. She embraced the whole of humanity with her thoughts, which made me feel quite at home, for these were my sentiments too.

Gradually all tensions ebbed away and without any hesitation Mrs Palmer began speaking to invisible people and she passed on accurate messages from them.

I was completely enthralled.

She saw 'dead' relatives and named them; and the people she singled out gratefully accepted their communications, delighted that she could even tell them where their loved ones had lived when they were alive. Personal messages, factual messages and snippets of information flowed out to them through this lovely old lady, as I sat captivated. I couldn't take it all in at first; it seemed too marvellous for words.

But then something odd happened. I became uneasy. All at once I felt my unseen 'friend' of long ago drawing close to me. I could psychically sense his strong electric presence: he was standing at my left-hand side. The hairs on the back of my neck rose. For a few panicky moments I lost touch with my surroundings. I rubbed my eyes then opened them wider to watch the rest of the meeting.

Mrs Palmer's voice brought me smartly back into the room. 'There's an Indian healing your back. Have you hurt it?' she asked.

I nodded.

'Yes,' I replied, thinking that she could 'see' the invisible person I was 'sensing'. Then I wondered if my mother would communicate. Was she even present in this humble church? Would she be able to get a word through to me at all...?

But she didn't.

The medium mentioned the fireworks at home with Dad, detailing facts with pinpoint accuracy, then thanked me for my attention and promptly started a message for someone else. A wave of disappointment swept over me. But then:

'Oh, a strange thing's occurred here; I'll come back to that young man, please. As I was going to leave you I saw a woman's hand placing one red rose across your lap.'

I went numb.

What did Mrs Palmer just say? One red rose? But I'd only ever given a red rose to one person in my whole life — that special rose in its own transparent box, which I'd presented to my mother at her funeral.

'Can you understand that?' she asked. But there was a pause. My mind was momentarily stunned. 'Does that mean anything to you?'

'Oh, yes,' I replied. 'It means a great deal to me.' And in that moment I knew my mother was with me.

After the meeting I walked out of that church fully realising why I'd danced on air when I'd approached it an hour earlier. Death's silence had once again been broken. My mother had communicated *again* and my joy was indescribable. I felt the whole world should know that a mother had returned from the eternal realms beyond the grave to reach her son.

All week, I couldn't get that message out of my mind: I couldn't concentrate on a thing. My thoughts kept slipping back to Mrs Palmer and her vision. Through this complete stranger my mother had lovingly returned the flower I'd given her; and those other accurate messages the medium had given had made such a powerful impression upon me. The moment I left that church I knew I would return again — but unfortunately commitments didn't permit this for a few weeks.

Those weeks were endless and I didn't tell a living soul about my visit to the church. I remembered their reaction the last time.

Every fibre of my being drew me back to witness Mrs Palmer's mediumship again. When I was at last able to make another visit Mrs Palmer asked, 'Would you like to say an opening prayer for us?' I don't know why I said it but I just said 'Yes' and was quite calm about the whole thing. I couldn't to this day tell you why, because I'd never prayed in public before and I hadn't a clue what to say.

Don't ask me where the words came from but they certainly didn't come from me: they flowed as though some external intelligence had used my mind, somehow blended with me to express itself. I didn't recognise the phrasing or the vocabulary, yet I couldn't stop the words flowing out. It was an unnerving experience.

But Mrs Palmer was obviously impressed by the invocation, judging by her subdued comments of 'Bless him' as it was delivered.

After the congregation had bravely trembled their way through another hymn, the service got underway. But as much as I wanted to listen, I couldn't quite register anything properly. My mind kept performing quiet little spins and I found it impossible to keep my eyes open for very long. Pulling myself together and hoping that no one had seen my head tilting slightly to one side, I caught Mrs Palmer's voice saying curiously, 'Have you anything to give out?'

I was going to say 'No' but before I could form the word, five lightning-quick spirit messages rushed from my lips at incredible speed, and they were accepted by open-mouthed watchers.

When I'd finished I felt rather embarrassed, for there was a deathly hush in the room.

Why were they all looking at me like that? I hadn't known what was going to be said and, what's more, I hadn't known I was going to say it! Had I done something wrong?

I didn't think so, for when I turned I saw Mrs Palmer was positively beaming.

The people seemed delighted with their evidence. All of them were pleased except one lady who'd received a prediction concerning an emotional shock that was about to happen. She was warned to brace herself in readiness because her feet were about to be knocked from underneath her, emotionally. She couldn't understand it and neither could I. After all, *I* didn't supply the information, I'd simply had it passed through me.

The following week, when I entered the church eager to do more mediumship, this highly-nervous woman whisked me off into a corner and gabbled her profuse thanks for the spirit warning. She and her husband were buying a dream-house, she said: it was the most wonderful home she'd ever seen and she'd envisaged a bright new life there for her family. For them, it was literally a dream come true, and as far as she was concerned the finances had all been settled. She'd set her heart and soul on purchasing it, but two days after the spirit prediction she'd been gazumped: someone made a higher bid and they lost their dream home.

'If you hadn't given me that message,' she gabbled emotionally, 'I think I'd have had a nervous breakdown.'

I was shocked.

And so the first visible threads of the pattern began to appear.

Behind those earliest communications, no doubt delivered by my invisible 'friend', there was a hidden world at work.

Behind the words that had rushed from my young and inexperienced lips, an intelligence outside of my own was making its presence felt — and serving because it loved.

For twenty years they'd stood at the doorway and knocked. At odd times, they'd peered through the portal known as 'death' and had either reassured me or realigned my footsteps back onto the pathway that led me to discover the reality of an eternal life.

Now that door had been unlocked and flung wide open.

At long last the connections had been made.

I was now a medium.

7

The Coming of White Owl

Without doubt the messages were reaching me
from an external source, but I didn't know who
was sending them.

Walking along the fresh seafront and kicking
up the sand between my toes, I sent out mental
requests asking who was responsible for my
work; so far, it had been a puzzle I couldn't
solve. Then one evening a young medium at the
church informed me, 'Your guides want to speak
with you. They say they can write through your
hand. Take up the pen.' Well, anything's worth
a try; so I set a time for the next day and did as I
was advised.

After a short period of silence, all at once I felt
a powerful urge to write. I put the pen to the
paper and the words came flooding through my
mind and out through my hand. The speed at
which I wrote amazed me; some of the words
merged into a blur on the page. But the other
side wasted no time in making itself known.

The writings were being given under the

direction of someone who claimed to be my main Spirit Control or Guardian Soul. Could this be my 'friend' of long ago, I wondered? Avidly, I scanned the pages and read:

> I am your guiding soul. I am a part of you and you are a part of me. Through all your trials and difficulties, I have travelled with you. Every tear you have shed, I have shed also.
>
> My love for you is higher than the mountains, deeper than the oceans. I am your Guardian Spirit. I am your Friend.
>
> My name is White Owl.

I was deeply moved and eager to learn more of this man:

> When on Earth I was a Red Indian but I died at twenty-one: my life was taken by a jealous man; he struck me with a tomahawk at the base of my skull and I fell lifeless into the river.

His gripping story unfolded and stirred my soul. He described his life as a boy in his tribe and how at fourteen he had passed his man-task. The elders had sent him alone into the forests with no weapons or food and somehow he had to survive; and when he returned to his people, he was proclaimed a man.

He recalled his great love for his woman, Running Deer, whom he cherished deeply. He spoke about his days of courage and youth when he rode like the wind on his white stallion,

Silver Cloud.

This remarkable 'dead' man had been my companion before my birth, he claimed, when he was approached by Higher Minds to guide my footsteps along a spiritual pathway:

> I was told that there was much work to do back in the dark earth-world. I was approached by those who know and asked to return to guide a spirit on Earth who would be a medium between Two Worlds.
>
> That spirit is you, the soul. I was told where you would be born, who your parents would be; and I was given all the necessary information about one hundred years — as you would gauge time — before these events took place.
>
> I prepared for my mission, which I undertook gladly to help mankind towards a greater understanding of the Truth.

My breath was taken away. Slowly but surely, everything began to crystallise: those strange events of my childhood at last held some meaning — a thread of purpose was now visibly moving through them. The visions, the pathway, the predictions — they all seemed to fit into place as part of some great Scheme which had been worked out and set down before my birth, according to 'White Owl'.

He also told me that much work lay before us and that I would have to prepare myself for hardship and disappointment, as well as for the great satisfaction of knowing that fallen souls would be lifted back into the light:

> There is much darkness in your world. It is the darkness of ignorance of which I speak; that all-engulfing blackness that is keeping mankind from the great freedom which knowledge brings.
>
> Together we can help to dissipate that darkness and replace it with light. But I cannot do this alone; I need your help. In the Earth-world you could be my voice, my hands and ears.
>
> If you can help me to achieve my mission, then when your day comes to join me here in the realms of light you will look back upon your life on Earth and be well satisfied that you and I both will have helped to pave the way for greater peace on your small planet.
>
> I do not work alone in these tasks. Just as I am in touch with you, so there are those much more evolved than myself in touch with me. This chain of minds links high into the realms of spirit; and down these connections teachings can pour into your world. But only if you are willing to co-operate with us.
>
> The pathway will not be easy; in fact, it will be difficult. But at the end of the road it will have been worth while. This I can promise you.

He was asking for my unswerving co-operation.

What on earth could I say?

I was still young, still inexperienced as a medium. I was twenty years old: I didn't have a vast knowledge of anything, least of all life and its meaning. So I whispered out to him, 'Please give me some time to think about it. I'll give you an answer soon.'

His thanks were quick to be rendered. 'You will not regret it,' he said.

Several days passed by.

Down on the hot seafront I wandered along the shore and gazed out at the waves crashing in on the rocks. With each breaking wave I pondered on this 'mission' he'd mentioned and wondered why I was the person he'd chosen to achieve it. My young mind wasn't capable then of perceiving the greater events that were to follow in the years lying, as yet, ahead. Still, I reasoned that if he'd followed my progress through life for so long then he must know me well; and on the strength of this I knew he'd fully realise that when I give my word on something the pact is sealed.

Seagulls cried overhead and the sun sank gently beneath the ocean waters as I climbed the rocks overlooking the bay and gazed out over the rippling sands. This invisible friend of mine must have known me when I was a child, I thought, when I used to run around these beaches chasing oyster-catchers and playing in the bright sunshine with my brother. And I wondered if he'd sat on these same rocks and watched over me, as I was now watching the deep orange sky.

Quietly, I closed everything earthly out of my mind. Listening to the soft breeze and the waves lapping far beneath me, I sent out my thoughts to this man who claimed the guardianship of my spiritual work. And in those quiet moments he heard me say, 'Very well. I'll help you, my friend.'

'I am so grateful,' he returned, 'for now my mission begins.'

At every service after this, White Owl entranced me to deliver to the public an inspired talk which lasted from fifteen to forty-five minutes; its length and content varied with their needs. I couldn't remember all that he'd said through me, but I taped the talks and learned much from listening to them over and again. In this way our relationship was cemented, and soon we shared the same philosophical ideas and moral codes. After a while our use of language also showed similarities; and as each psychic link took us forward, so our attunement became stronger.

Usually at my public meetings a song was sung and I'd close my eyes and become quite relaxed. Then I'd start to feel light-headed... my eyes would roll upwards as though to view the inside of my dark head — that's how it felt anyway. The sound of the singing would become blurred and distant, then my voice box would begin to move: it was an odd kind of pulling sensation as though someone was testing the mechanisms.

At this point I'd feel as though I was someone else. I can't express this sensation any more clearly than that, except to say that I felt overshadowed by an older person, a much wiser soul who was more experienced about the vital things of life. White Owl describes this unique psychic link with me thus:

It is a subtle blending of two minds, so closely joined that they appear to be one. Indeed, for those moments of attunement it is as though two personalities are functioning through one individual.

Imagine two tuning-forks both set at the same musical pitch. If you strike one of them it begins to resonate and vibrate the surrounding atmosphere, creating its own unique sound. But move it closely alongside its counterpart and you will find that the unstruck tuning fork will also begin to sing at the same pitch: it responds to the vibrations of its neighbour — both singing together because they are both naturally attuned to one another.

So it is with mediumship.

The Spirit Control has to attune himself with his medium and vice versa. Upon the precision of this at-one-ness rests the success of the experiment in communication.

He also gives an explanation of how he and I can blend our minds:

The medium has fields of energy about him; these are seen by us as pulsating light. I, too, have 'auras' such as these.

We in Spirit exist at a much higher frequency or rate of vibration than you do on Earth. When I wish to be beside my medium I have to think myself close to him. By this act of concentrated and purposeful will I descend from my higher world, lowering the frequency of my spirit body to approximate to the frequency of the auras about my medium.

When our two wavelengths are closely vibrating at roughly the same rate, attunement has taken place.

After this, it sometimes can prove very difficult to retain this at-one-ness. There are many factors involved which can prevent attunement being held.

Communicating from my side of life is not an easy process. It may look easy when it is working proficiently but I can assure you it is not a simple matter.

When I am attuned to my medium a great many of my thoughts can pass through his mind, and thus I make myself heard in your world.

Although White Owl's trance talks were most impressive, especially as at many of them he began by delivering a blessing in his own tongue, I still had some doubts as to the separateness of his identity. I was not an ignorant student of the paranormal. By now I was well read and I possess a most analytical mind. I was concerned about whether or not the trance talks had originated in the mind of a separate personality known as 'White Owl', or in some deeper part of my own consciousness.

Could they be springing from what psychic

researchers call 'a secondary personality', another portion of the medium's character, which assumes a guide's identity?

The largest obstacle against these theories was the content of the talks my guide delivered. Afterwards, I had to look up some of the words he'd used to find out their meaning. Also, he spoke about matters which had hitherto not entered my thinking; and if I was ignorant of them, how on earth could I have spoken so fluently about, and made such good common sense of, subjects that were unknown to me?

Nevertheless, I'm not a gullible person and I required further evidence, irrefutable proof. He must have been aware of my feelings, because it wasn't long in coming.

I possess that rare quality of losing touch with the room I'm in; I can then experience my mind filling with scenes of the past as well as with events which might have been — it's a day-dreaming quality that comes naturally to visually-active minds. This was to prove beneficial, for on a number of occasions I was taken from my physical body and made to astral-project. My mind dissociated from its environment and in my spirit body I travelled to locations in the spirit realms. Such experiences are perfectly real and overwhelmingly convincing to anyone who has tasted them. And I was about to do just that.

One day while quietly meditating, I suddenly found myself loosed from the earth and I arrived in a plush, verdant valley. The colours were bright and intensely vibrant, far more alive than any we have here on earth. The very air about me was filled with life; and a few yards away I could see and hear a cascading waterfall, just like the one White Owl had described to me in his writings. He'd told me that he'd often bathed there with Running Deer, his woman. The water was gushing down and splashing with an unearthly musical sound.

Just a few feet away from the stream stood my guide's white stallion, Silver Cloud. He was a magnificent horse; and there he was in all his beauty, champing at the grasses. His slim fetlocks looked as though they might hardly hold him erect and yet I knew instinctively that with them he could race the wind.

Suddenly, he pricked up his ears and raised his quizzical eyes until he was staring right at me. *The horse noticed that I had 'arrived'.*

Then all at once, the scenes shifted rapidly and I was caught up in the embrace of White Owl and we stood together against a backdrop of purple-headed mountains.

His deep tanned skin, his well-shaped handsome features and his hair — raven-black and billowing in the fresh mountain breeze — this was such a real excursion. For the first time in my memory I looked into the eyes of this man who had been my unseen 'friend' all along my pathway — and in that moment I knew I was loved and cared for, not only by him but also by many others associated with him.

'It is I,' he said; and he smiled at me.

In the next instant I was sitting back in my armchair, feeling heavy and dull once again, with the cold grey earth all about me, so slow and uninteresting.

It was an experience I would never forget.

However, as wonderful as that excursion was, I was the only one to experience it; it was a subjective happening. White Owl must have known my thoughts on this too, for he soon corrected them.

Quite by chance (?) I was unexpectedly invited to attend a Transfiguration meeting with the well-known medium Mrs Queenie Nixon. A seat became available with a group who were driving to the event. I bought the ticket and took the opportunity, not even realising what a Transfiguration meeting was. But all was soon made clear by Mrs Nixon's celebrated spirit guides, who deeply entranced her.

Her two main spirit controls, Paul and Sister Edith, explained the whole procedure to the capacity crowd as we sat and listened in the blacked-out hall, lit only by a small ruby-coloured lamp that was directed at Mrs Nixon's face.

Her spirit guides said that from the people gathered in the hall they were going to withdraw a special substance called ectoplasm, which they would then condense around the medium's head. They would use this psychic 'fluid' to make themselves visible, they said: they would materialise their features by placing upon the medium's bone structure their own 'ectoplasmic mask'. (I've since seen many mediums claiming this rare ability of physical mediumship but none has equalled the spiritual gifts of Mrs Nixon.)

In the middle of the séance in the blacked-out room she called out an evidential message for me, which was acceptable and quite correct. Then, as her guide Sister Edith put it, 'We're now going to bring your people to you.'

As we watched, the transformation was remarkable: Mrs Nixon did not pull her features and distort them as some charlatans or deluded folk would do, *she actually transfigured*.

The crowd was astonished.

First to arrive was my grandmother — Dad's mother — and without doubt it was most certainly her: the little snub nose, the half-closed eye, the grey hair and the heavy jowls — beyond any doubt I was looking at Mary-Jane's face. Then she quickly disappeared by dematerialising.

Next came my mother, but she wasn't as successful as Mary-Jane in making her features visible. Nevertheless Mrs Nixon's hairstyle did change, her cheekbones heightened and my mother was reasonably recognisable. (Paul, the other spirit guide, had already explained to the crowd that it wasn't easy for newcomers to the spirit world to achieve success.)

But to clinch it all, my mother managed to whisper through a few words; not many, but they were very evidential. 'Thank you for the flower,' she said — reference again to the special rose I'd given to her at her funeral. Without a doubt she was present.

And *everyone* saw these changes occurring around the medium. We'd already been treated to witnessing Mrs Nixon's thick mop of jet-black hair receding as a bald gentleman transfigured for his daughter in the hall. His daughter called out enthusiastically to him as the medium's hair gradually disappeared, 'Come on Dad, boy! I know what you're doing! Yes, that's right! You were as bald as a coot!'

And we'd marvelled at a little girl who contacted her mother and at the way the medium had changed from an elderly lady into a bright youngster, complete with visible plaits in bows. So my mother's attempts were sympathetically received by all. In fact, a woman next to me said to her companion, 'Well, just look at that — it's a completely different person.'

My mother quietly said, 'Watch... watch...' And when she dematerialised, there was a short pause.

We all waited to see what was coming next. By now I was breathless, the whole experience having stunned me, yet I was quite able to hear the gasps from the audience as Mrs Nixon changed from an old lady into a healthy, bronze-skinned young man. The features were exceptionally clear; the dignity shone from every pore.

This spirit had the countenance of a highly compassionate soul.

There, in that dark hall, I was gazing again at the materialised face of my Guardian Spirit, White Owl.

Without any doubt, here was the same man who had recently caught me in his embrace on the mountaintops in the spirit spheres. He was noble and finely featured.

I called out a greeting to him and he turned and looked me right in the eyes, picking out my exact location from amongst the 200 people present in the blackness.

He didn't speak, he simply smiled — a dignified, happy smile of knowing. He had achieved his goal. From beyond the veil he'd used another human being's exceptional mediumistic talents to prove beyond doubt his separate identity.

'Say something to him,' said a woman next to me. 'Speak to him.'

For a few uncertain moments I remained quiet; but when next his compassionate deep brown eyes met mine, I called out to him, 'It's lovely to see you again... I believe in you.'

And he smiled right back at me, and dematerialised.

8

Communications
and Spiritual Healing
from the Beyond

There were plenty of opportunities for service. I worked as a jeweller's assistant by day and as a medium by night; and every Saturday evening I was at the Open Circle to unfold my psychic powers under the expert tuition of Mrs Palmer.

In those early days I couldn't get enough contact with the spirit people to satisfy me; and each time I worked my abilities they strengthened — and the mediumship proved itself genuine. People kept coming back time and again to tell me the information they'd received had been verified.

Of course, there were quite a few 'misses' as well as 'hits', but gradually I got more and more proficient.

Then one day Mrs Palmer said, 'Stephen, you're ready to take a meeting on your own now. How do you feel about that?'

Without any hesitation I replied, 'Fine.'

'You'll be all right,' she said. 'My guide told me you're capable and I've watched you working. You can do it.'

As the big day drew near, the announcement in the local paper advertised an appearance at the church by Mrs Palmer but only we knew that it was I who would actually take the meeting in her place on that coming Wednesday night.

All heads turned as I arrived at the church and there were positive gasps as I went behind the curtain into the medium's rest area. Mrs Palmer straightened my tie — she was to chair for me — and we took the platform. To the astonishment of many, I was announced as 'Young Stephen, a new medium.'

While the second hymn was being sung, all at once I felt extremely nervous: I reached for a glass of water and I could see my hand shaking uncontrollably. I couldn't stop it — then suddenly the most unearthly peace descended upon me: I felt as though a soft warm blanket of tranquillity had wrapped itself around my spirit, as though some wiser, elder being had blended with my mind. All nervousness ceased immediately; the shaking stopped and I felt utterly calm.

In that moment I had some conception of what the peace that passes all understanding may be like.

I rose to my feet, overshadowed by my inspirer who began to speak to the people. I lost consciousness of where I was, of the crowd, of everything: all I could hear was this deep resonant voice speaking inside me, through me, seemingly at a distance. To this day, I can't recall what was said.

The next thing I knew: I was sitting down again and opening my eyes. Realising I was now seated, I was just about to stand quickly but Mrs Palmer beat me to my feet and announced, 'Out of the mouths of babes has come forth wisdom.'

I guess she meant the trance-talk had been meaningful.

Then the spirit messages flowed *to* me and *through* me, and were gratefully acknowledged; the words were precise and the visions were crystal clear — I can remember them today.

Before I knew I'd started I was being called to time and had to sit down again. I'd spoken for an hour and a quarter and it seemed like just a few moments. Time, as we know it, was meaningless — it passed so swiftly when I was attuned to the Greater World and working with it.

After the service people came up to the platform to shake my hand and express their thanks for the service. I couldn't register it fully, their words came at me in a blur... 'Thank you for a lovely evening'... 'Very evidential, Mr O'Brien'...

They'd obviously enjoyed the meeting, and it was nice to know I'd helped people.

Afterwards, over a much-needed cup of tea, I

sat awaiting Mrs Palmer's verdict: hers was the opinion that mattered the most. Her eyes smiled and she congratulated me with, 'When can we book you again then?' And I knew I'd passed my first test.

The following week a visiting medium at the church singled me out for a message. With tightly closed eyes she pointed directly at me and proclaimed, 'The spirit people would like to work with you to spread the knowledge of a life after death to the people. Many are called but few are chosen.'

I was numbed by her words, but in a strange way moved, too.

'But why me?' I kept asking myself. I didn't fully understand. When you're young you can be right in the midst of important experiences and fail even to register them.

But before I knew it I'd been recommended to nearly all of the churches in South Wales and many took the opportunity to book my services and try me out.

Sundays used to be such boring days but now they were the most interesting days in the month.

Every weekend without fail I travelled out on buses or in other people's cars to churches or halls to take public services; I did many midweek meetings too.

The next few years were packed with unstinting service. I didn't have time to think! I was dashing about everywhere, serving wherever I could: I never refused a booking, and

everywhere I appeared I was asked to return —
and I always honoured my engagements, even if
I wasn't feeling well. An appointment had been
made with my group of spirit friends and I
respected this; I would never let them or the
public down.

Sometimes it was such a rush to reach a
church: after working hard all day I'd barely
have time to dash into the shower then change
before whizzing out. Yet they were happy days,
full of laughter and learning, and hard work and
challenge. But I didn't mind the difficulties too
much because I so enjoyed delivering my
mediumship and trying to help people by doing
the best I could. At last I felt needed and
capable of giving service to the community —
and I was happy.

I served diligently without thought of reward;
there was no charge made for my services and I
even paid my own out-of-pocket expenses for
travelling. If I was lucky enough to be driven by
anyone to a church then they too would often
refuse their petrol money, or put it back into the
church building funds.

And all the time I was growing and learning,
and developing as a person and as a medium.

By doing the work I slowly realised that 'dying'
doesn't change those who pass through it. They
still cared. When Mrs Phyllis Fowler's spirit
father contacted her at a spontaneous séance I
gave, he relayed the surprising news that she
would 'soon go into hospital for tests'. Although
this was Christmas-time and she felt quite well,

he predicted that the date would be between 10th – 14th of January. She received her call from the hospital on 12th January — right in the middle of the two! And of course, her father promised to accompany her in spirit.

Then I received the name of Leo Atkins from a man on the other side. He said he'd been 'a clergyman who'd helped down-and-outs. "Does she remember serving food to the vagrants in St Paul's Church crypt?"' he asked. Mrs Fowler did: it was charity work she'd willingly undertaken.

The Reverend Atkins then mentioned his wife's illness, she was still on earth. Mrs Fowler confirmed these facts and was delighted when he revealed, 'I've met my son and I'm with him in heaven.'

'Oh, I'm *so* glad,' she said. 'His young son was found dead, you see, quite suddenly. Poor Mr Atkins was distraught because he'd loved the boy so much.'

Suddenly a street vagrant appeared before me, so clearly that I was able to describe his features, his ragged old mackintosh and weathered shoes. He tipped a battered hat in salute then held out his hand: there was a coin it. 'Thank her for this,' he said. I did, and she recalled she'd never once passed him without giving something from her purse. Even after death, he hadn't forgotten her kindness.

What a remarkable lesson for us all.

Then her beloved husband 'Idris' made contact. 'March the 31st,' he said confidently — this turned out to be the date of their approaching wedding anniversary.

He sent all of his love 'for nursing me through paralysis for seven and a half years before I died'. She wiped a tear from her eyes.

With him he'd also brought her 'Auntie Gladys', correctly stating she'd died in childbirth: I saw her clairvoyantly, lying in the coffin with both arms entwined around her baby; her long black hair fell down to below her waist.

Mrs Fowler thanked me for her spirit contacts.

'Thank your family,' I said. 'They still love you greatly.'

As my work progressed I lost count of the times I helped psychic organisations out of difficulty. Sometimes of an afternoon I'd be relaxing and a spirit voice would ask, 'Will you take a meeting tonight?' The place was then named. I'd dress up and as I walked through the church door a frantic secretary would beg me to conduct the meeting because 'the booked medium hasn't turned up'. They could never understand why I wasn't flustered by the prospect.

At one such meeting a ninety-three-year-old woman was contacted by her deceased father.

'He says you're not going over yet — there's plenty of work left for you to do on earth!'

'Oh but I'm *ready!*' she gasped in surprise. But I had to report that Dad didn't want her over there just yet.

He identified himself by showing me that the top of his little finger on his left hand was missing. 'A pig bit it off,' she said.

He brought more reassuring evidence when he said he'd 'followed her to St Anne's Hospital where she thought she would die, but she survived the surgery'. He reported that her mother, her grandfather John and he would meet her when her time came to cross into the spirit world. Then he added joyfully, 'We'll have a wonderful shindig — and Auntie Annie'll play the piano.' Dad said they'd lived at 'the Parade' and that a 'Mrs Irene Davis' — their nosy old next-door neighbour — had returned along with 'Mr Harris, the butcher'.

She accepted them all gratefully.

One of the funniest messages I remember giving was when I wanted to contact someone who knew a place called 'Pembridge Way': I'd seen the street sign from the spirit world. An elderly woman claimed this link and her father communicated. I started the message by saying, 'Your Dad says someone is deaf but is too *vain* to wear a hearing aid.'

'Pardon?' she said, 'I didn't quite catch that.'

The whole place erupted into laughter; people were holding each other. I would never have embarrassed her like that but I must admit it was very funny. Unfortunately, she was the only one who didn't appreciate the evidence or the joke.

I recall another amusing contact from a gummy old lady in the spirit world who returned to admonish her bewildered husband. She was furious because he'd buried her without her false teeth. She was vain in life, and death obviously hadn't changed her.

'I arrived without them!' she kept shouting. 'Tell him I'll clip him around the ear when he gets over here!'

Of course, she gave this lovingly and her husband smiled, recollecting that this was exactly the kind of person she was. She now had all her own teeth back in her spirit body, she said, and had appeared without them simply to be recognised.

There were touching communications too. Mrs Sylvia Jones, another recipient, was startled to receive her husband's double-barrelled name from the spirit world. 'Dillwyn-John' communicated and called her 'Tiny'.

'That's my nickname,' she explained. He brought with him 'Jenny, her mother' and also 'Aunt Ethel with her two adored Scottie dogs.'

The Aunt relayed, 'I used to take them everywhere with me,' which Mrs Jones confirmed. 'They were like her children,' she said.

Some emotional moments followed when Dillwyn-John addressed both his wife and his daughter who was seated next to her.

'I miss you both,' he said. And to his daughter he said, 'Please take care of your mother, she's one in a million.'

Everyone was quite tearful.

Moments like these emphasised to me the sacred beauty of spirit communication and why it should always be undertaken with the greatest of dignity and respect for the feelings of all parties involved.

In these early days of learning and experimentation I watched scores of mediums working and, quite frankly, was extremely disappointed with many of them: some weren't even polite to the public; in my opinion there's no excuse for this.

But good manners are not only exhibited by the people of our world however. I well remember a tall blond Second World War airman appearing behind an old gentleman seated in a crowd. This young spirit flyer walked over to me, gave his name then shyly pulled at my trouser-leg and asked, 'Please would you give that man a message from me? I'd be very grateful.'

Mind you, not all my communicators were so friendly. A Mrs Donald's stepfather returned in a furious temper. He identified himself then shouted that he was frantically mad at some of his family who'd disobeyed his last wishes.

'They couldn't wait for me to pop off!' he screeched. 'Then they dived in and helped themselves to my stuff!' Mrs Donald accepted his link because he'd clearly told me, 'There was £400 that went to three people and it should have gone to *four*.' Little wonder he was annoyed — someone had been robbed of their inheritance.

He also mentioned another £200 and kept asking, 'What have they done with it? Where has it gone?'

Mrs Donald enlightened crowd.

'The family sold his treasured car for that meagre sum and there's been great annoyance because no one knows who's taken the profits.'

Mention of somewhere called 'the Cwm' and 'the organ-grinder and the blacksmith who lived next-door' brought more recognition.

To finish off his message her stepfather appeared to me clairvoyantly. He wheeled himself to my side in a wheelchair; his right foot was raised and heavily bandaged.

'That was the beginning of the end for me,' he said.

His stepdaughter confirmed he'd had gangrene in his foot, which had then spread its poison throughout his body.

Another memorable but embarrassing incident involving a witty communicator springs to mind: it occurred when I was giving private appointments in a magnificent English Tudor mansion. It was such an amusing episode, I chuckle whenever I think of it, even today.

There I sat on a blue silk couch, gazing around me at all the grandeur and opulence and thinking: I bet this carpet's worth more than the entire contents of our house, when in sailed an elderly rich widow sporting a one-piece bosom that swayed from side to side as she strode across the room.

I immediately sensed she'd lost her husband. But how grim she looked: her thin mouth was firmly set at 'twenty-past-eight'.

Despite her stately elegance I didn't need to be

psychic to see she was a very dour person. Graciously, she lowered her bulk into a Tudor armchair, diamonds glinting in the shafts of sunlight piercing through the tall bay windows.

'Good morning,' I smiled.

Silence was the icy reply, and her mouth never flinched.

I was just about to launch into the messages when a wizened spirit man suddenly appeared on the antique sofa between us. He sat there nonchalantly reading a newspaper, not one bit concerned by my sitter's presence. I instantly knew this was her husband.

He peeped over his paper and said pathetically, 'She totally dominated me. Dying's the best thing that ever happened to me, my lad! I wouldn't go back to the old battleaxe for all the tea in China.'

Well, you could have knocked me down with a feather!

'Listen,' he said, pointing his finger first at me and then at her, 'she's come in here today for you to tell her how wonderful she was, nursing me night and day. She wants a big pat on the back, my boy. But let me tell you this — *I'm glad I'm dead*!'

How on earth could I relay that?

A flustered silence filled the room.

Her ladyship peered at me through gold-rimmed spectacles, desperately awaiting some wonderful news from her husband; but would she want to hear it?

I plucked up courage and delivered what I still

think of today as a masterful piece of tact.

'You've lost your husband, my dear,' I relayed. Her eyes lit up. 'He's here with us this afternoon, sitting on that sofa.'

She glowered across at the nothingness.

'And,' I continued, 'he wants me to tell you he's *very happy* where he is!'

Her stern face beamed; and the fixed mouth that came in set at 'twenty-past-eight' now rose to 'ten-to-two'!

I sent her husband a sly thought, 'If you want to insult her, sir,' I said, 'you'll have to wait until she joins you and you can do it yourself.'

'No fear of that, lad,' he quickly replied. 'I'll be at the other end of eternity when *she* comes over!' And he chuckled away to himself, then vanished.

When linking with the other side some mediums find full names difficult to obtain, but these featured in my work from the earliest days. Of course, I'm not always sensitive enough to receive them consistently, even today, but on most occasions I'm fortunate to register them.

While speaking to a Mrs Harris I relayed that 'George' was present. She said she'd known two people of that name; so I sent out a request, 'Which one do we have?' And back came the answer of 'Saunders'.

'*Oh!*' she exclaimed with a twinkle in her eye, 'that's the George I particularly liked when my maiden name was Saunders!'

I thought he was quite clever to have given it like that.

Communicators can present some surprising evidence too.

One youngster would definitely *not* accept her grandmother when I brought a message from her. 'Come on,' I said to the spirit grandma, 'You'll have to give me something else. Be more specific.'

Well, she was! She showed me her voluminous whalebone corset and said, 'Tell her I used to hang it up behind the bedroom door and roll up fivers and stuff them down the whalebones.'

'That's her!' exclaimed the girl. 'If you'd brought my grannie back any other way I wouldn't have accepted her.'

Some recipients look quite confused when they're getting their messages. One lady seemed awfully perturbed after I'd taken great pains to meticulously describe a spirit gentleman to her. In desperation I finally asked, 'Well, does that *sound* like anyone you know?'

'Oh, yes,' she said; 'it sounds like my grandad, but it can't be — he's been dead for *years*.'

As if that made any difference!

Other recipients cry with joy, such as the lady who received the ordinary name of 'Bert' from the spirit world. 'He's telling me to let you know he's all in one piece now,' I said — her tears were instantaneous.

'Bert was my son,' she explained. 'He died while underneath a jacked-up car: another car hit his and he was decapitated.' She'd waited years for news of him; little wonder she cried so copiously when this comforting message came through.

'Thank you so much. You'll never know what that means to me,' she said.

I soon learned that the spirit people could build up a mental impression in a medium's mind, which could appear so real that he might think he could reach out and touch it.

While relaying information to a tearful lady from her beloved spirit father I noticed she had a gold tooth right in the front of her mouth. I thought to myself: You don't see many of those these days.

At the end of the meeting she came forward to thank me for her link. She smiled but something was missing.

'Where's your gold tooth gone?' I asked.

'I've never had one,' she said looking confused. Then she suddenly cried out with delight and frantically opened her handbag and took out something wrapped in faded tissue paper.

'My father's gold tooth!' she proudly announced. 'He was giving you the message when you saw it!'

I think my inspirers created this thought-form and superimposed it over the pictures in my mind.

Aren't they clever?

I remember another tooth-related link when a Mrs Cole was so thrilled to hear from her husband in the spirit world that she nearly left her seat; but all I'd said was, 'Your tooth-filling's worked loose.'

'Oh! I've been *three* hours at the hospital today.

No one else knew anything about it! *How could you possibly have known*?!'

'But I didn't know,' I said. 'Your husband told me.'

To further impress me with the extent of their power the spirit people lost no time in making their presence felt, physically — and they took every opportunity to do so. I shall never forget when they gave two friends of mine a real fright.

We were travelling back from a meeting and I suggested calling at my house for a cup of tea.

Dad never encouraged visitors but I knew he was out — so we piled into the living-room. The lads quickly made themselves at home. One lay on the settee, kicked off his shoes, put his feet up and languished with his hands behind his head; and I and the other took an armchair each.

We'd chatted for a few minutes about mediumship when I began to feel uneasy: I wondered what Dad's reaction would be if he were to come home and find us by the blazing fire, supping *his* tea out of *his* cups: he was such a possessive man. Before those thoughts fully registered, a sudden psychic wind manifested through the room. It rapidly shook the closed door in its frame, sounding like thunder crashes: loud and alarming. The wind rushed through the centre of the door, towards me at amazing velocity, then shot straight out through the open window over my right shoulder.

My jaw hit my chest and I caught sight of two blurs whizzing past me and zooming out the door and into the car. Gingerly, I collected a pair of vacant shoes and left the room saying 'Sorry' to the air as I went.

I discovered afterwards that my father returned home much earlier than usual, not long after our undignified exit.

Although it was a startling experience it made perfect sense of those biblical quotes about the 'Wind of Heaven' — and it certainly had the desired effect!

By now, certain people were positive there was something decidedly 'odd' about me. Some, I'm sure, felt I was well on the way to madness: but nothing could have been further from the truth. Unlike many people who remain in ignorance of spiritual and psychic revelations, I was being introduced to the deeper implications of life and living, instead of just skirting over the surface of existence as millions seem happy to do.

Some friends 'walked by on the other side' and others veered away into stores to avoid speaking with me.

My old neighbour, Florrie, had a cousin called Nancy who was a lay-preacher and very prim and proper indeed. She was seventy years old and well respected in her orthodox church, but when she heard of my involvement with mediumship she immediately branded me 'a devil's disciple' and ignored me at a bus stop, looking as though she'd smelt something awful when she walked past me. Yet she'd never seen a medium working or ever made an investigation into the paranormal.

I soon learned that the other side didn't share

this narrow-minded bigotry; at least, the spiritual souls who worked with me did not. My inspirers were not one bit concerned with labels or religions or lip-service codes of conduct. Like me, they were concerned only with people, not with religious fervour. Souls, not labels; and before I helped someone I followed their example. I never asked what religious faiths people held. These are not the most important facets of our lives.

We are all travellers along the One Way, all struggling to find knowledge and seeking happiness and spiritual understanding. Seekers after truth are curious to know about their loved ones — whether they've survived: they want to know if they'll see them again; they want communication with their dear people in spirit.

Millions of people are no longer satisfied by Faith alone — they want Knowledge.

We're all Children of the Great Spirit and that's what I was being taught in those formative years. The spirit people often said, 'We are all small sparks of the Great Spirit's Life Force. This divine spark, which we each possess, motivates us and gives us conscious awareness: it links us to the Creative Mind for ever. We can never be separated from our Creator — the link remains eternally unbroken.'

Therefore we are all Sons and Daughters of the Living God; and if that is so then we're all Brothers and Sisters.

The spirit people taught me to strive always to keep an open mind — and never to close it; they advised me to welcome new horizons of thought, new ideas and beliefs.

And always they instructed me to question everything I was told, no matter who said it. Even their own teachings were to be questioned, reasoned out then accepted or rejected by my intelligence. Never once did they condone a blind faith in anything.

Never once did they dominate or patronise me, or anyone they may have spoken to through my instrumentality; and I came to believe these were some of the hallmarks of evolved souls.

I was often reminded: 'If you believe in anything one hundred per cent, this is dangerous: it is unhealthy because your mind is then closed to any new possibilities.'

That sounded like good common sense to me.

I was also told, 'Seek and you will find. Knock and the door will be opened to you.'

This is as true today as it ever was. And to this they added, 'Turn away and you may miss unique opportunities for greater happiness, knowledge and enlightenment. The choice is yours.'

Although each returning communicator brought a different personal message, the important content was broadly the same. They were often met by those who'd loved and known them in their earth lives.

Only a few of them slept on arrival in Spirit, and all of them found themselves alive and still very real people, complete with all the attributes of mind and character they'd developed here on earth.

Time after time they returned to categorically state that over there they could see now that the important things which matter are:

> *how we live our lives;*
> *how we think;*
> *how we behave.*

Personal religious beliefs carry little weight in the Beyond. But never once did my inspirers decry anyone's religion, instead they said, 'If it makes you a better person then it is right for you. If it teaches you to love, then it is a good set of instructions.'

When my own teachings had spread further afield I was invited to a Christian discussion group. I agreed to speak about the case for survival, and looked forward to finding out what made other people tick.

I arrived at a neat semi-detached house and was ushered in by three charming ladies from the priest's group. Everyone was kind and we were getting along fine, when suddenly my arm was grabbed and I found myself being led away into a study by a middle-aged priest.

He sat me down and warned me that, 'We don't want any messages in here tonight, it's only a discussion.' I assured him I'd perfectly understood this when the invitation had been offered. We rejoined the others.

After an evening of stimulating debate and many questions, the ladies' faces beamed when I revealed that *everyone* survived, regardless of their beliefs or station in life; that even animals had souls and they survived too.

But the priest instantly closed the session — minus his perspiring curate who'd quietly crept away (it had all been too much for him) — and told the listeners that if they attempted to investigate mediumship or visited a psychic or medium in the future, they would no longer be welcome at his church.

But when he left to get my coat the ladies jumped out of their seats and bombarded me with a million questions: and they wanted the dates of my next meetings!

Our minds are such wonderful instruments, I'm often surprised when people don't use them to think matters out for themselves, instead of accepting another's opinions. After all, what's true for one man need not be true for another.

A while before this happened, I'd heard of a spiritual healing group that met every Wednesday afternoon, so I decided to join it to see if I could be of any help.

Feeling light-headed I'd close my eyes and deliver trance healing to the patients. When the spirit world exercised its powers, my hands felt either great warmth flowing through them or icy coldness.

These were physical reactions to different energy rays brought through by the spirit doctors who'd attached themselves to me to work at healing the sick.

Sometimes I'd register no physical reaction

whatsoever, but the power was still working.

One afternoon when a Mrs McDermot attended for healing, the other side drew very close to me. I stood behind her chair and was impressed to concentrate my efforts around her head, particularly around her left ear.

'I don't know what they're doing just here,' I said, 'and I can't feel any power passing through me but they're most certainly doing *something*.'

Mrs McDermot said nothing; but unknown to me she was completely deaf in that ear.

At the next session I was taking off my coat when she dashed through the doors and cornered me with her wonderful news. On the morning after the healing treatment she'd woken up and heard the ticking of the bedside clock — a sound she hadn't heard for years.

Breathless with excitement she rushed to her specialist, who examined her and was utterly dumbfounded. He exclaimed, 'But I can't believe it! The bones of your inner ear, which were out of alignment, have clicked back into their proper places. That's impossible — but somehow it's happened and you can hear. *It's a miracle!*'

As you can imagine, I continued my healing work after this.

The spirit doctors led me to a Mr Earnest Davies. I visited him at home because he was wheelchair-bound and suffering from Multiple Sclerosis. For twenty years the disease had held him in its merciless grip. Occasionally he would feel as though the world was turning upside-down and his arms would shoot out as if he were falling over, and his head would be thrown back violently. After just one visit, these unpleasant symptoms ceased and did not recur.

Each week, more and more patients attended the Wednesday healing sessions and as my mediumship unfolded I became increasingly sensitive, to the point where I could register some of their thoughts and feelings.

One afternoon a thin middle-aged man attended and we exchanged pleasantries; then I recognised him: a few days earlier I'd given him a spirit message from his wife, at my public demonstration.

Too weak to sit comfortably, he was placed horizontally on a flat couch and the healing group gathered around him, forming a psychic battery of power. If I live to be a hundred I shall never forget the look in that man's eyes as he gazed up into my face. He knew the fear of death and longed for the success of this treatment. I smiled gently back at him.

'Try your best to relax,' I said. 'Please close your eyes.' As he did this, he knew I'd read the secret of his heart: this man had cancer, in an advanced state. Unbearably, I also knew his time had come and that this healing treatment would only ease his pain and make his passing more dignified and peaceful. But those haunting eyes, so full of pleading for a longer life, will always remain emblazoned in my memory as a reminder of the great faith, hope and trust that people place in spiritual healers when all orthodox medicine has failed.

He passed into spirit a short while afterwards.

This kind of soul-to-soul or psychic awareness was strengthening within me and sometimes I was called upon to use it. One glorious sunny day a woman rushed in from the street and was directed to me. The poor soul looked as though the weight of the world was on her shoulders. She was more than fretful. 'Can you please help me?' she begged, as she pulled from a bag a small boy's tee-shirt. 'My grandson's only six and he isn't at all well: we're out of our minds with worry. I brought this for you to hold, to see if you can help him.'

Further questioning revealed that the boy was waking every night and screaming out for help. He'd told his grandmother that people were chasing him in his dreams and sometimes they appeared in his bedroom when his eyes were open. The child was desperately afraid and distraught, she said, and so were his parents because no explanations could pacify him.

I clutched the tee-shirt and immediately felt the boy's fear. We established that his name was 'David'.

'Don't worry about him any more,' I told his anxious grandma. 'I'll ask my spirit friends to help him tonight. When you go to bed you can help him too. Send out your own thoughts to your mother and father in the spirit world and ask them to meet David at the point of sleep each night and take him into the sleep-life without any further distress.'

The woman looked at me agog. I suppose she

wondered how I knew her parents had passed over. My spirit friends said her grandson had been wandering around in the astral planes of thought — those worlds on the other side that are nearest to our earth — without any proper supervision.

'Yes, he's such an active mischief-maker,' she confessed; 'it would be just like him to run off on his own.'

'If you do as I suggest,' I added, 'David will not be troubled again.'

She was profusely grateful and we parted company on the understanding that she would return only if the psychic prescription failed and the young lad remained unsettled.

Weeks passed by and her absence proved all was well.

People seem to think that mediums have the monopoly on the spirit world, when communication is open to everyone. Sending out requests to our loved ones often produces success, and no intermediaries, priests or religious authorities are needed to accomplish this.

We are all parts of the Living God within us, and God is listening.

The spirit doctors who worked with me were also successful when they intervened to aid an injured black Labrador dog called Prince. His owners thought he'd been hit by a car but they weren't certain. When I looked at him — and before I'd even touched him — I saw clairvoyantly some words written in golden light, about three inches deep, hovering above his body: they said 'fractured spine'.

'He may have injured his back,' I said to his friendly owners. 'He may have fractured the spine.' I advised he should be examined immediately by a vet. This was done and the diagnosis was a fractured spine, just as the spirit people had said.

Sadly, Prince was put to sleep because he was also suffering from severe internal injuries that were causing him great pain. But this story has a happy ending because his devoted owners 'saw' him again shortly after his transition. He was lying in his favourite spot by the kitchen door looking fine and healthy, with his glossy black coat shining in the sunlight and his pink tongue lolling out of his mouth.

Healing works effectively on animals as well as on people: spiritual healing energies are ever-present cosmic powers that will work their beneficent will whenever they're channelled correctly.

By now I was becoming quite well known as a healer, speaker and platform demonstrator in South Wales, and White Owl delivered a trance address and thought-provoking philosophical teachings at each of my meetings. This was then followed by a display of clairvoyance.

News about my work was spreading fast. London heard of it and *Psychic News* printed reports of my mediumship.

In this way, the evidence and help that had been given to others reached a wide readership of over 100,000 people in seventy countries.

Psychic News

Stephen O'Brien gave evidence to Mrs Irene Lewis.

Stephen said her grandfather, Thomas, was present. He remembered working night shifts to feed the family. This was correct.

In what became a family reunion, Stephen stated that Mrs Lewis' great-grandfather, William-John, her mother, Mary-Ellen, sister, Lily, and three brothers, John, Bryn and Harry, were all present.

Bryn sent love to Lorraine. This is his granddaughter.

The medium relayed details of family history, which Mrs Lewis confirmed as being correct. He said Mrs Lewis' brother, John, was involved with Orthodox clergy. He was a Baptist Missionary.

Stephen added that Mary-Ellen had four sisters with her in the spirit world. He described Mary-Ellen's abdominal troubles caused by difficult childbirth.

The 74 year-old widow was startled when Mary-Ellen recalled a traumatic incident from her childhood.

When Mrs Lewis was nine she ran home breathless and frightened after being chased across the fields by a man. Even after 65 years the reminder of the event still disturbed her.

A neighbour, Mrs Simmons, passed on her thanks to Mrs Lewis for running errands for her when she could not leave the house many years before.

Finally, Mrs Lewis' husband, Bill, was named by the medium as being present.

He correctly related that the communicator had suffered from a blockage of the bowel and had passed with cancer of the stomach.

Through the medium, Mr Lewis told of his sense of shame in being a burden during his long illness. He was in no pain now.

After the spontaneous sitting Stephen left to demonstrate at a Spiritualist church but not before Mrs Lewis had presented him with a small token of thanks: a tin of baked beans.

'I'm not a Spiritualist,' said Mrs Lewis, 'but it made me think. I found the experience very touching.

'I now feel my loved ones are closer to me. My sense of loneliness has been wiped away.

'Stephen is a very good person,' she said, 'whom I think lives what he believes.

'It is marvellous that God is using him as a medium to show us there is a life after death.'

9

Séances

People from all walks of life and from all over the world have sought my help, many coming as a last desperate hope, their lives shattered by tragedy, or their pathways seeming so dark they feel desperately in need of light to show the way forward.

Some of these people were so moved by their communications that they recorded them, and afterwards many freely undertook the development of their own psychic powers as a direct result of being touched by the spirit world.

That's how spiritual knowledge and light spread throughout the world: people share their experiences with others.

When their consultations are over, only the recipients can truly judge what the messages have meant to them. So it's fitting to include a random selection of their accounts here, where they can relate in their own words the effects they experienced.

I hope you find them interesting.

The first report concerns friendship and its undying nature.

Mr Adrian Davie, College Lecturer:

My friend died in an accident and his death devastated me. I felt it should never have happened because he was killed as a pedestrian when a car mounted the hard shoulder of the road and instantly ended his life.

This was the first time death had touched me and I felt lost, hurt and depressed at the time.

Mr Stephen O'Brien gave my wife and me spontaneous clairvoyance. He said he could see 'a pair of leather motorbike gauntlets plus a red crash helmet suspended in the air' over my shoulder.

This identified to me my friend, Alan, whom I worked with for six years. Alan had given me these two items as a gift about a year prior to his death.

The medium brought him forward as being 'twenty-one years old' — the correct age at his death.

Further evidence was given when Mr O'Brien said that Alan was showing him 'a skull and crossbones motif, painted somewhere'. I couldn't recall this but my wife reminded me that three days before this message I'd taken her to Sunderland Museum where there was a photographic exhibition, which included a photograph of my working place. And this same motif was painted on a cabin door in a photograph.

Alan used to work in that place.

This made me realise that he still visited me at work as Mr O'Brien had relayed. To confirm this further Alan gave Mr O'Brien the name of 'Brian'. Brian is the person who has taken my friend's place as my workmate.

Next came a meaningful piece of information. The medium said, 'He keeps saying "Broken back". This was the nickname Alan had for me at work. When I was doing heavy work he used to say: 'You'll break your back doing that.' More remarkable still: I saw Alan's death certificate and a broken back as well as other injuries was listed on it.

I was elated to receive this evidence.

This was the first time my friend had made contact with me in the six years since his death.

When this message came from him it was as though I had found his friendship again, as though he had never died. He had proved his identity to me without a shadow of a doubt. It could not have been any other person but him, and there is no way Mr O'Brien could have known any of these details Alan gave.

Alan's message to me was 'I only died', as though death was nothing at all.

It has showed me that the 'dead' are not in a distant world but are close by, their lives intertwining with ours without us realising it.

If there was more evidence like this, the sorrow of grieving people would be swept aside.

Another account clearly shows us that the spirit people can travel all over our world faster than the speed of light *and* know what's happening long before news of it reaches us physically. Most times, this fact surprises sitters.

Mrs Marion Jones, Shop Manageress:

Back in the mid 1980s I received an extraordinary message from the invisible world of the spirit from Mr O'Brien — quite out of the blue — and this evidence surprised me.

Stephen suddenly described to me a peasant grandmother-figure whom he said he could clairvoyantly see: she was sitting on a rickety chair in bright sunlight, outside a wooden shack. This was a psychic vision that she was projecting into his mind.

He told me that he was watching her while she was cleaning corn-cobs into a basket; and she was obviously living in poverty.

Then he said the old lady was nodding and smiling from ear to ear, and that she seemed very grateful. He said she was thanking me 'for helping her grandson', and that she was also speaking the unusual word of 'Cruz'.

He was puzzled by this word and wondered if it had a South American connection, or if it was a place in that country.

But it was not that at all:

Something he could not possibly have known was that the word 'Cruz' is the surname of a ten-year-old Mexican boy whose education and medical health I am sponsoring through a Christian Charity, which is working in a poor part of that country.

The boy is called Serafin Aragon Cruz.

I was stunned to receive this news because the Cruz family, whom I had never seen but only corresponded with, lived thousands of miles away from me — right around the other side of the world — and yet this young lad's grandmother in the spiritual world not only knew of my association with her grandson, but had also taken the trouble to give me her approval and thanks.

The spirit people can 'follow' our progress through life and in many cases they're walking beside us, quite unregistered by our five physical senses.

This next account proves that a woman who was making her way to her usual Methodist church was most certainly not alone.

**Mr Will Ford,
a Spiritualist Church President:**

Mr O'Brien's clairvoyance contained the highest level of evidence I'd heard for some years.

He told my daughter that she was linked with the medical profession. She is a tutor in St Mary's Teaching Hospital, London.

He also said that a doctor friend of hers had just received some good news. That week, her doctor friend had been accepted as a consultant.

Mentioning that she was concerned over a lady's health was also correct, as she was deeply concerned over the health of her mother.

The medium then gave details of a lady in spirit who had given him this information. Without question, this was my mother.

The medium then spoke to my sister, 'What are you doing here? You're in the wrong church! You were on your way to your own church, you changed your mind, you walked past your own church and came here instead.'

This was quite true. When my sister had left home she had no intention of coming to our church whatsoever.

The medium told her that her husband had died some years ago and that she hadn't yet got over the shock.

This is true. My sister is under medical care for delayed shock.

He then gave a lot of information, which could only have been from her husband in the spirit world.

The spirit people often 'tune-in' to our thoughts, and once they've developed this ability there are no secrets.

They live in a world where thought is King and even though we on earth can hide the truth by closing our mouths or speaking untruths — the mind cannot lie.

Mrs Round's youngest daughter kept a secret from her, but her grandfather in the spirit world 'read' it and predicted an event that subsequently occurred.

Mrs D. Round, Nursing Officer
(Hospital Matron):

One of the most surprising pieces of information Mr O'Brien relayed was from my deceased father concerning the youngest of my three daughters, whom he said would be the first to marry and that this would happen in the very near future.

This statement seemed ridiculous, as my daughter was so young. I laughed at the thought.

But my father laughed last, for he was correct in all he had said; my youngest *was* the first to be married.

This brought me a realisation that my father was aware of what was in the minds of the youngsters involved, although, at the time, they believed it to be their secret.

Some spirit messages can seem quite banal and uninteresting when they're delivered — but the medium and the public can have no true understanding of how much meaning a simple message contains for its recipient, or the way in which it will affect or change his or her life.

Many people have found their communications most encouraging or comforting, and from them they've gained new strength and hope.

Mrs Sandra Meakin, Housewife:

I went to see you at Doncaster. You called out

for a Sandra and said there was a family around me that was breaking my heart. This I accepted.

You brought me 'a rag-and-bone cart and a gypsy man called Sam'. This too, I accepted.

You then gave me 'Alice-Mary'. This was my grandmother's name and you said she and Sam were taking care of me.

Then you said there was a gentleman with me 'who had passed quickly with a heart attack, he was around thirty-nine to forty years old'.

He gave me red roses from a wedding bouquet and you gave me September and felt that he was a husband.

The names 'Wilf and Violet' were also relayed. These people were my husband and mother-in-law and the 11th September was his birthday.

This proof has been second to none and I thank you from the bottom of my heart, for you not only gave me the strength to go on but you also gave me a ladder of life to climb, and I am still climbing it.

Thank you.

I will remember this for the rest of my life.

I seldom get to see people when they first arrive for their consultations; there is usually a chaperone ushering them in, making them tea afterwards and generally placing them at ease. This next record, then, is of particular interest to me.

Mr J. Rees Jones, Oxfam Worker:

I've acted as receptionist for some of Mr O'Brien's private consultations and I've witnessed many different reactions from folk. Often they get something quite unexpected — like the gentleman who emerged rather flushed after a good telling-off from his father, who was unhappy about his son's lifestyle, showing us that even after death we still remain uniquely human, keeping all our character traits.

Or the lady who emerged so astonished that she was almost speechless after receiving such accurate evidence. All she could repeat was: 'I don't believe it. How could he know?'

There have been many tearful and emotional reunions too. Mothers have found their children after agonising years of searching. Partners have been brought together again convinced by pet-names that no one else could have known. And some people, leaving unconvinced, have been directed by their contacts to research certain facts that they had no knowledge of at the time. Then they came back to tell me they'd found them to be correct!

When you've seen a mother weep with relief, finally knowing that her 'lost' child is safe and alive then you truly realise the full importance of mediums and their work.

The media often fail to understand that many who have received personal messages from Beyond, from the people they dearly love, don't want this made public knowledge — in just the same way that most family matters are private and confidential.

Private consultations are exactly that — *private*.

Many accounts in my possession are so touchingly personal that I couldn't allow them to be printed; and I know the sitters would agree with my withholding certain details. The following shortened record of events is such a case.

Mrs Elizabeth Williams' only daughter was brutally murdered by raiders on the shop where she worked. Mrs Williams' letter to me contains compliments about my work and personality, and her gratitude, which I feel are too embarrassing to print. But with her permission I've released some of her comments, which show just how much comfort a spirit communication can bring to people whose lives have been shattered by tragedy.

I recall that in her sitting Mrs Williams' daughter made a specific request to her mother. 'Please don't go to the Inquest,' she begged.

'I'm sorry,' returned Mrs Williams, 'but tell her that I'll *have* to go. I couldn't sit at home while it's in progress.' And much later Mrs Williams did attend it.

It was only then that the horrific details of her daughter's death were publicly released, making clear the reason why she'd wanted to save her mother further pain.

The young woman had been bludgeoned to

death and assaulted; the murderer then doused her body with petrol but fled without setting it alight.

**Mrs Elizabeth Williams,
Voluntary Adult Education Worker:**

I was holidaying in Italy when my only daughter was brutally murdered during a robbery.

We were, as a family, stunned and almost completely broken.

When I felt I was ready I had a sitting with Stephen O'Brien.

And here I must make it quite clear that he knew nothing of my life before the events mentioned.

He did, however, bring my father, my husband and my daughter through to me with details that he could not possibly have known.

This was a great comfort to us all, and during the following months, it was a tower of strength to me. And I can never thank Mr O'Brien enough.

But here's the interesting sequel to this story, which shows that our loved ones' concern for us still burns bright in their hearts and minds.

At the time of writing I received a spirit message through a northern medium who mentioned to me the name of 'Emrys Williams'. Emrys said, 'Thank you for helping my family'.

This man is Mrs Elizabeth Williams' husband

in the spirit world, and he obviously knew her account was to be included in this volume because he mentioned 'the writings' during his link.

I immediately contacted Mrs Williams to inform her of his communication and she commented with a warm smile, 'That's so typical of Emrys — he wouldn't want to be left out!'

10

Spirit Children

Spirit children have often visited me and it's always a great joy to see them. They bring psychic feelings of light and energy, a quick vibration of youthful enthusiasm. Their eyes are bright and open wide, and yet behind them there seems to be an inner knowing that very few earth children possess.

But they sometimes choose the oddest times to call. One evening, I'd just whipped into the bath to freshen up when I heard a woman's voice speak to me from mid-air.

'Stephen, I'm bringing some children to see you.'

'But I'm having a bath!' I said in disbelief, grabbing the nearest sponge.

The voice continued, 'They need education. They haven't lived on earth: they were stillborn babies and miscarriages who have now reached childhood on our side. This could be one of their lessons, if you're willing.'

'OK,' I said, modestly gathering the suds

together.

The voice went on to ask if I'd tell them what sort of daily activities we get up to on earth. I agreed because I'd always thought of myself as a teacher and I love children, which is why they were brought to me — mediums shed more psychic light around them and it's easier for spirit visitors to view our atmosphere from their world if a sensitive is present.

There wasn't a great deal of water in the bath but it didn't stop these beautiful children of all nationalities trying to splash it around. They were giggling at 'the pink man sitting in the bath'. They whispered confidentially amongst each other as children do and they asked me so many questions.

One second they were all visible and the next moment my clairvoyant vision faded — but although my psychic sight tuned in and out of their presence, they were still there, chattering away and having a marvellous time.

It must have been like a trip to the zoo for them!

'What does water feel like?' they asked. 'Does it hurt you?' 'What's that fluffy stuff you're getting on your skin?' I explained all about soap. In fact, after receiving a telepathic request from their teacher I went into explanations about why we on earth needed to wash our skins.

Their eyes almost popped out of their heads when I ended up with, 'And I have a bath every day.' I don't think they could believe it.

One black girl said, 'Our water doesn't make

us wet. It rolls off our skins.' This isn't difficult to accept if the molecular structure of their water behaves in a similar fashion to, say, mercury.

So there I was, one hour to go before a public meeting, sitting in a few inches of bathwater and holding a conversation with 'dead' children. Yet how natural and commonplace it all seemed.

When they left at the end of our class, I heard the children laughing and their teacher said to me, 'A picture is worth a thousand words!'

Another amusing appearance of a spirit child occurred when I was baby-sitting for my brother's children. He was working on nightshift and my sister-in-law had to sleep at the hospital with my nephew Jonathan, who was due to undergo an eye operation. I was asked to look after my niece Claire, and they gave me Jonathan's bed in his little room.

Even though the house was comfortable and I was snug and warm under the duvet, try as I might, I couldn't go to sleep. All the hairs on my legs were standing on end.

There were so many electric presences nearby. I became aware that these were spirit children who were gathering around the bed, no doubt to gawp at the great hulk sleeping there, when they'd expected to see my five-year-old nephew.

Suddenly I felt the hairs on my right leg being tweaked. When I opened my eyes I saw a young lad of about seven, with blond curls and a wicked smile, standing at the foot of the bed. He just couldn't understand who I was or what I was doing there and he became a little indignant.

'Well, where *is* he then?' he demanded, frowning hard.

I immediately knew I shouldn't frighten him with news of Jonathan's eye operation, so I whispered out, 'He's on holiday for a few days. He'll be back on Monday.'

Of course, it never dawned on me at the time that the spirit people don't follow our calendar and dates. However, this little chap turned his head and called out over this shoulder to an invisible person, 'Oh, he's gone *away!*'

As I held back a smile a spirit nurse appeared behind him. 'Come along, Daniel,' she scolded, 'I told you he wasn't here, didn't I?' She clasped his hand tightly and led him out through the bedroom wall.

The psychic atmosphere in the room calmed down after that and I slept soundly. But I couldn't help grinning when I thought of young Daniel coming to collect Jonathan for his nightly visit to the spirit world and discovering me there instead! And if you think about it, it's perfectly natural he should pull the hairs on my leg; after all, Jonathan didn't have any.

But not all spirit children have returned with happy, radiant faces. At one meeting a singing trio were just rendering their final song before I was to give my clairvoyance, when a sad-looking boy appeared to my vision just at the side of my chair. 'I'm Tommy,' he said. I greeted him mentally and asked why he'd come.

He coughed up some black matter, which I thought was probably blood, and said, 'I'm three. I had TB.'

I told the crowd about him and he was accepted by one of the singers in the group when a link with 'Streatham Green' was mentioned. Tommy said he wanted 'John to know I love him and miss him very much.' The singer said this was his younger brother.

Everyone smiled with him when he comically said, 'Mum's washed my teddy bear and she's pegged him on the line!' He didn't seem too happy about that.

This information was to be checked, and if it proved correct how marvellous to know that a little lad like Tommy was aware of his teddy bear's bath.

He then asked the singer to 'Please get Mum to come to a meedjum, 'cos I want to talk to her'.

I can't describe the emotions I feel when this kind of poignant link is made and new hope is put into a grieving person's life.

My work has taught me that stillborn babies and children who aren't carried for their full term of pregnancy all survive death and grow up on the other side. Over there they're loved and cared for by people who dedicate their lives to rearing them, just as good parents and guardians do over here.

I once received a disturbing message about such a child and didn't quite know how to relay it. Seated opposite me at an Open Circle meeting was a young woman, wearing cut-off jeans. Her hair was adorned with coloured rags and beads: it was a deep sandy colour but badly in need of grooming. She had intellectual blue eyes, and compassion shone in them.

When I tuned in to the spirit world, however, I lost sight of her because my attention was drawn to a ball of golden light appearing on her lap: it was shot through with electric blue sparks that looked like a thousand glittering stars. In the centre of this pulsating and protective orb there was a human foetus, all curled up and perfectly formed, just as it would be in its mother's womb. This vision faded into the young woman's body, at the level of her womb.

In that instant a young girl of about four years old appeared kneeling in front of this woman. The child's head was resting on her hands, which were placed across the lady's knees.

The girl looked across at me and displayed the same piercing eyes as the woman, and identical sandy-coloured hair.

'She's my Mummy,' she said.

A spirit helper informed me the girl had been aborted four years previously and asked me if I'd tell the recipient she had a daughter in the spirit world, and that one day they'd be reunited.

But how could I give out such personal details in public?

I couldn't.

I had to find a clever way of avoiding embarrassment and yet get the message home.

Tactfully I said to the woman, 'I think you know a lady who lost a child before it was born.'

'Yes' she replied quietly, her eyes searching the floor.

'Well,' I continued, 'the girl is now four years old. Please would you tell her mother she's alive in the spirit world and that one day they'll be together again? This would make the little girl very happy.'

The surprised woman thanked me.

Having delivered this information with sensitivity, I'd done my job and wrapped up the message so that one else could understand it except the recipient.

I remember another case involving a spirit girl, but this time the child's intentions were not so honourable: it began when I was called in to solve a mysterious puzzle. The parents of little Stephen, a five-year-old, were being woken up in the night by the sound of singing coming from his bedroom; they knew it wasn't his voice that they could hear, so they called me in to investigate.

His mother and I climbed the rickety stairs of the old house and I was led into the youngster's room. The moment I moved within the doorway I felt uneasy; and there, near the sash-cord window that overlooked a steep drop onto a roof, beyond which there was a garden, I could see a spirit girl standing. Her hair was straggly; she was poorly dressed in a faded pink dress that needed washing. But nevertheless there she was, singing away to me to her heart's content.

I couldn't make out her childish song but I watched as she stretched out her hand and crooked her little finger and beckoned me to the window. I obeyed, and in that instant a flash of lightning struck my mind — and a pitiful tale unfolded before me. I turned to Stephen's mother.

'This room was once a kitchen,' I stated.

'Yes; years ago it was,' she said. 'The estate agent told us that when we bought the house recently.'

'Well, I've seen a small girl just there.' I gave a description and mentioned her singing then added, 'She was at the open kitchen window, she climbed onto the ledge and slipped. She fell to her death onto the roof and into the garden below.'

There was stunned pause.

The mother looked rather worried.

'Your son likes to climb out onto ledges, doesn't he,' I stated.

'Yes, he does,' she said in a small voice. But I told her to stop fretting because my spirit people would now take this girl to a place of safety and make sure there'd be no recurrence of these events.

But that didn't satisfy Stephen's mother because she didn't like the thought of any spirit visitors being in her home. Then my inspirers delivered another surprising message.

'You needn't worry,' I said. 'You'll soon be moving from here anyway.'

'But we've only just *bought* it!' she protested.

She'd intended this to be their treasured family home, and even if the place was haunted she had no intention of moving out.

'But your spirit people will arrange it for you,' I said confidently.

And of course, they did move shortly afterwards, as predicted.

I don't know what became of the girl in the pink dress but the young lad has now grown up; and from that day onwards he was no longer lured out onto ledges by his mischievous spirit visitor.

Probably the saddest case I encountered of a spirit child returning was that of a seven-year-old girl who'd been kidnapped, sexually assaulted, then violently murdered.

The newspapers were emblazoned with her photograph and the details of her death — she'd been returning home from school across woodland when her life was so cruelly taken — and a major police-hunt was underway to seek the killer.

To protect her parents, I shall call the girl Sarah.

I was so upset when I read the sordid story that I wept in despair and found myself uttering, 'Dear God, someone please comfort this child, wherever she is. Please help her, anyone who can hear me.'

Thoughts of her desperate mother flooded my mind and increased the sense of horror I shared with this distant family whom I'd never met.

I didn't realise my sympathetic thoughts had

psychically linked me with their cry for help, and that through this link the spirit world would take action.

Thoughts are living things and, as proof of this, the following day when I was meditating in silence I sensed a strange presence in the room; someone I didn't know was drawing near. I heard a child's voice pitifully crying: it was Sarah, the murdered girl. My spirit guide had brought her to my side.

'Tell my Mummy I'm alive,' she sobbed. 'She's crying and she can't see me. Please tell my Mummy I'm *alive!*'

Poor Sarah was distraught. White Owl explained to me that she'd visited her family on earth but none of them had registered her presence.

Instinctively I knew what to do and no time should be wasted: I would write to Sarah's family of her survival; but first I answered her tears. 'I'll do everything I can,' I said. 'Don't worry, Sarah; I'll get in touch with your Mummy and then she'll know you're alive and well.'

I instructed her to follow White Owl, who I knew would escort her to her relatives in the Beyond. She seemed to calm down at this; her presence faded from my mind and I was firmly back in my sitting-room.

I grabbed the nearest pen and sent a card to Sarah's people — the newspaper had printed their address, or at least a part of it. Comforting myself that my mail would reach its destination on a wing and a prayer, I posted it off immediately.

Days passed and I heard nothing from the child's family. Had they received my card? Had it been mislaid? What if Sarah contacted me again; what should I tell her?

Perhaps her mother had read my letter, which informed her that Sarah was 'still alive in another world and grieves because you are crying so bitterly over your loss. But please be happy in the knowledge that Sarah lives on and is close to you', and thought it had come from someone unbalanced.

A fortnight later, a reply arrived: it was a thank-you card expressing gratitude for the message and assuring me that Sarah's mother now believed her daughter was often with her because she had at last sensed her spiritual presence. The relief expressed in those words was clear to see and I thanked my spirit friends.

A more evidential message involving the sudden death of a child was given to young Carla's mother when she came to see me. She was desperate for help.

Carla was ten when she died: she'd complained of a headache to her Mum and was advised to lie down and rest. But when her mother called her for tea, there was no reply. A strange foreboding swept through her mind — frantically she clambered up the stairs and... Carla had passed away.

The coroner's verdict was a massive brain haemorrhage.

I could imagine how this mother felt: one moment her daughter had been skipping out in the park and within an hour she'd gone from her life for ever.

Utterly distraught, she visited her local clergyman. But he offered no comfort; in fact, he upset her even more by declaring that because Carla hadn't been confirmed into his Christian faith she would now be 'burning in the fires of hell'.

This of course is absolute nonsense, which springs from narrow-minded religious bigotry and an abject ignorance of spiritual truths.

Carla's mother was at her wit's end when she sought my help and I readily agreed to a consultation.

Somewhere in a book, not unknown to that insensitive clergyman, it is written, 'And a little child shall lead them' — and that's what happened in this case.

I'd only just started the communications when Carla suddenly appeared to my clairvoyant vision, seated on the settee beside her mother. She had an arm around her shoulders and she carried her 'special rag-doll', which, when I described it in detail, proved Carla's survival — it had been placed inside her coffin, and only her mother knew this.

'I'm all right,' she told her mum. 'My head was hurting me and when I went to lie down I heard a sound like an explosion and then grandad met me.'

She named him correctly then relayed more

Stephen O'Brien, aged 8: 'I was slipping in and out of consciousness. I thought I was going to die and recited the Lord's Prayer over in my mind as they rushed me through the hospital doors.'

Stephen, his mother, Beatrice, and brother John: 'She was everything to us, someone very special; and I loved her with all my heart.'

'At 16, I wanted to enjoy living. I wanted to run free and feel the Great Pulse of Life in my veins.'

No. 10 Rock Street, Waun Wen, Swansea,
South Wales in the 1960s.
Clouds of Light surround Stephen O'Brien (right),
standing outside the room where he was born.
(left and middle: his brother John and a friend.)

'The Nine Arches' and the weir where Stephen played
as a lad. 'On boiling-hot spring days we swam like
fish in the water.'

*'I am your Guardian Spirit. My name is White Owl.
Many on earth have lost their way and stumble
through the Darkness of Ignorance; together we can
bring them the Light of Knowledge.
But I cannot do this alone – I need your help.'*

*The Hands of a Healer: Stephen transmits spiritual
healing energies to a migraine sufferer.*

Antony Hooper, 17, killed by the midnight train, proved his survival to his mother via Stephen's mediumship.

Falklands war hero, Ian Dale, 19, killed when HMS Sir Galahad exploded, proved his continued existence through Stephen's remarkable gifts.

Each year, thousands of people gather to witness Stephen O'Brien's acclaimed spiritual work.

A thought-provoking question-and-answer session.

'I am a voice crying out a Message of Hope from a World of Light. I've been called by the Spirit to serve, and I know, therefore, that my pathway will not be easy. But I pray God will give me the strength to complete what I was born to do.'

comforting evidence.

When her mother left she was a totally transformed being. The stooped, grieving woman who'd entered an hour earlier was now radiantly happy again. She had found her child: she was alive, not dead, and living in a land not far removed from here but nearer than hands and feet.

Once more — not through crusty outdated beliefs, but through exercising the living gifts of the spirit — a broken life had been mended.

We are immortal beings and if our minds are open to revelation our hearts can be made whole again by spiritual truth, which is exactly what happened to another bereaved family.

Nothing could be more poignant than the loss of human life in the 1980s conflict over the Falkland Islands, those distant rocks so far from Britain's shores. Talk of patriotism and defending the Realm probably means little to the parents of the men who were killed in those battles. However, hope is not yet gone.

Young Ian Dale was a Welsh Guardsman in a newly formed Mortar Platoon. He was down below the decks of *HMS Sir Galahad* when an Argentinean bomb from a plane shot down a hatch and ignited the ammunition pile he and his platoon were guarding.

He and several of his colleagues died instantly.

But this nineteen-year-old lad and one of his friends communicated at one of my meetings.

'You know this boy's mother,' I said to a lady seated at the back of the hall. With that, a woman at the front called out, '*Here I am!*'

The young Guardsman then spoke to his 'Mam and Dad' and assured them he was well on the other side.

His best friend also communicated his survival; then Ian told his mother about 'a special tie' that he'd given to someone.

'No,' she said holding up an object clasped tightly in her hands. 'He means this button off his cap' — and she waved it in the air.

But her son was not satisfied: he was mentioning a tie, not a button

What should I do?

Again he said to me, 'No! I gave away a special tie, Mum.'

So I simply checked back with the boy, then repeated his message.

And we had to leave it at that.

But it's strange how things work out because about six months later a lady brought me some refreshments after another of my public appearances.

'You don't remember me, do you?' she said. I confessed she was right, then she identified herself as Mrs Shirley Dale, Ian's mother, and expressed her profuse thanks.

'I researched the evidence you gave me about that tie,' she said, 'and you were right. I telephoned my other son — Ian's younger brother Phillip, who's also in an army camp — and he said Ian had given him his "number two special tie" on the day he'd packed to go to the Falkland Islands.

'I was amazed because we knew nothing about it.'

Following this, she joined her local Spiritualist Church and now she makes the tea and helps out in whatever way she can, to repay the great debt of help she and her grieving family received from the movement's mediums. 'I owe my sanity to Spiritualism,' she said.

Another young man called Robert Thomas performed a similar service for his parents. Robert was sixteen and he'd been riding his motorbike along a straight road when a police car, moving rather fast, came into collision with him. He died instantly.

His family was devastated: the Thomases couldn't believe it had happened, and for a long time afterwards they tried to prove that the blame for the accident lay with the police and not with their son; but all to no avail.

They began a spiritual search to contact Robert, and about three years after his death they were strangers in a large crowd at one of my meetings when their son made a surprising contact.

Robert's mother takes up the story in her own words:

I attended a demonstration of mediumship by Mr Stephen O'Brien and received a message from my son, who had been deceased for three years.

The message contained irrefutable evidence that it was from Robert, and it was accurate.

It mentioned how his body was mutilated, his ambitions about getting a bigger bike and also that his sister still cries for him.

Robert even spoke of 'a secret girlfriend'. We only found out about her three weeks *before* the message: she wrote to find out how he was getting along now.

A lot more evidence was given too: details about his leather jacket with the studs on the back, and he told the medium to 'give Dad a kiss from me'.

My son was killed in a collision with a police car while riding his 30-mph limited-speed bike on a straight piece of road. What the police said had enabled the blame to be thrown onto my dead son, who couldn't speak for himself.

We have always had strong suspicions that this was not the case. This opinion was held by our solicitor also, but due to how the statements by witnesses were obtained, we couldn't prove it.

The point Robert wanted to get across to us most strongly was to say, 'Please, *please* tell my Mum *it wasn't my fault.*'

I cannot express the sense of relief this evoked in us. It was a message we had waited three years for.

You can imagine my feelings.

I must say that I feel great respect and admiration for Mr Stephen O'Brien and the work that he does, and I am unable to convey the peace of mind that he brings to those who are grieving, with such messages as this from the spirit world.

Psychic News, London, and three local papers carried reports about the evidence, after being contacted by this family who wanted to share their joy. As a result of this, the church for which the meeting had been held saw an increase in attendance. So, from the happiness of two people the good news spread outwards and touched others.

There's nothing more touching than when the young die, and nothing more poignant than when they return. Over the years, many children have done so through my mediumship and I feel privileged to have helped them reach their families. There was young Phillip, who locked himself in a discarded refrigerator and was found days later; Trudy and her two brothers who burned to death in a house blaze which left their mother and father desolate and alone, and pitifully wondering 'Why?' John, who drank from a bottle of household bleach, thinking is was lemonade — they rushed him to the hospital but it was too late... and scores of others, all returning with the same message, 'I'm alive, don't cry for me.'

But one young communicator made a big impact upon me: Antony Hooper. His was a tragic passing and a startling spirit return, and I've recorded these in detail for this book.

Antony was seventeen when he was killed by the midnight sleeper-train on its way to London. A British Transport Police spokesman told the court that foul play had been ruled out and that

Antony's leather jacket, gold watch and a £5 note had been discovered alongside the railway track.

Consultant Pathologist Dr Owen Williams confirmed that Antony's death was due to multiple injuries sustained by contact with a moving train.

The Coroner, Mr Francis Wilson, admitted that his death could have been suicide but instead an open verdict was recorded.

His entire family was deeply shocked and couldn't come to terms with their loss: his mother had said goodbye to him at four o'clock and never saw him alive again. For her, each day had no meaning now. On buses, watching other people smiling and laughing, she just couldn't understand why life was continuing so normally.

She didn't recognise it but she was suffering from acute shock.

Having received no comfort from the local Christian community, as a last desperate hope she decided to seek out a medium. If her son was alive 'somewhere' she wanted to know about it. She wanted to hear from him again, to find out how he was and who was taking care of him — if he still existed after death.

Taking courage in both hands, she attended several Spiritualist churches for seven months, always keeping her identity a secret and never speaking to anyone about her quest so that any word from him would be all the more evidential — if it came.

But sadly, no contact was made. However...
Psychic News takes up the story:

A mother spent seven months visiting Spiritualist churches in search of contact with her teenage son who passed tragically. She finally received her reward, a communication through Stephen O'Brien.

'I was so overjoyed. I just couldn't take it all in,' she told *Psychic News*. 'At last I had found my son.'

Mrs Maureen Hooper had seen many mediums demonstrating.

'Although I believed that mediums were able to make contact with people who had passed over, upon searching I have found this is not the case in many instances,' she said. 'Even on a purely psychic level, dozens of mediums have failed to recognise my grief and the fact that I have lost a son.'

As Mrs Hooper's search progressed she prayed for a message from her son, Antony. Yet each time she was given a message, there was no mention of him.

'Nevertheless I kept going,' she told *Psychic News*, 'living in the hope that he would reach me and prove his survival.

'My hopes were shattered and disillusionment set in. I wondered many times where I, and other grieving parents like me, could go to be given comfort via sure proof of survival.

'All I was mostly given were "nuns", "sisters of mercy", "bouquets of roses" and "colourful rainbows". Where was my son among this?

'Was this the highest standard mediums could attain? Or was I expecting too much?'

Mrs Hooper had almost given up hope when she found an advertisement in her local newspaper for a demonstration of mediumship. Deciding to attend, she was surprised at the high quality of detailed evidence, which included full names, place names and accurate dates.

'At last I received a great deal of hope. I continued my search by following the mediumship of Stephen O'Brien and at his third meeting Mr O'Brien brought my son back to me with amazingly evidential details.

'I was given his name, his father's name, and the circumstances leading up to his tragic passing. This medium even told me who was looking after him in the spirit world, Mary Jane, a great aunt.

'At the time of the communication Mr O'Brien even seemed to take on my son's personality; there was a great deal of comforting evidence relayed.

'Isn't it a shame that the majority of mediums do not concentrate on bringing back our loved ones and proving their survival without doubt? While I appreciate that some try to do this, why can't they all?'

When I first saw Mrs Hooper seated in a crowd I instantly registered her grief. As she left, I rushed to clasp her hand and said, 'I don't know who you've lost but if you hold on a while longer, I'm told they're trying to get through to you.'

Her big eyes widened and she could barely say 'thank you' as she left.

A few weeks later, Antony's link arrived; and it contained many details not published above, small evidential remarks that conveyed both his personality and his style of speech.

On the day he'd died, Antony Hooper had been drinking and had stolen a car and taken a joy ride with three other boys. The car crashed and was a write-off. Antony made his way across fields to reach his father's Auto Garage and those were his last moments on earth — the railway tracks stood in his path.

When communicating, he mentioned these events and also talked of personal family matters, even commenting on the 'new central heating' his mother had recently installed adding, 'It's about time too!' Mrs Hooper said this was a typical remark, especially as the heating had been planned for years but had never materialised while he was on earth.

Mrs Hooper rang everyone in the family with the news of her son's first words from beyond death.

When she told Antony's father, he replaced the receiver and within ten minutes he'd left work and was sitting in the front room, eagerly listening to the story.

Antony's elder brother Gary held on to his mother and cried, sobbing with relief. And Phillip, his younger brother, listened intently, numbed by the news.

After these initial contacts, Mrs Hooper was so

overwhelmed that we got talking and eventually I became friends with her and her family, and this meant that we hadn't heard the last from Antony Hooper. He'd found his medium and was determined to make use of him.

Through me, he told his family he was studying what he called 'a contact course' in the Beyond, 'to learn how to transmit messages correctly'. He proved a good student too, for we heard from him again.

One evening when I was speaking with the family, I heard Antony's distinctive voice calling to me. Taking up paper and pen, I wrote down his statements exactly as he said them. They were an intelligent and carefully worked out set of facts, some of which had to be checked in a bid to rule out telepathy by his medium.

He was successful.

No medium can read details from a sitter's mind if the information isn't there. Antony knew this approach would be more convincing to his Mum. With Mrs Hooper's kind permission, here is what Antony transmitted, word for word:

ANTONY	*RESEARCH*
My jeans were fought over by my two brothers after I passed; but it didn't matter to me who had them.	Correct: checked out. Gary and Phillip had fought over his black canvas jeans—this was the first time Mrs Hooper had heard about this.

ANTONY	RESEARCH
My pair of yellow briefs: there was a small hole in them and they were thrown out.	Correct: he tore them in an embarrassing accident.
I wanted a racing pigeon but didn't manage to get one.	Checked. Accurate. His best friend kept racing pigeons and he would have liked one.
My thick belt, with the large buckle and studs on it. I don't know where that went. Did they burn it with me? I want to know.	His brother Gary had secretly kept it as a memento.
Who's been thinking of my birth certificate? I've received the thoughts but don't know who it is.	Phillip, the youngest, had been searching for it that morning, unknown to Mrs Hooper.
There is one single daisy growing by my stone on the cemetery floor.	*Expedition*!

This final remark bundled us into a car with some torches and we were off to the cemetery: it was two o'clock in the morning on a bitterly cold night with no moon. We crept through the church gates into the chilly graveyard and the night air took our breath away.

Our shoes clicked along a pathway, where we located Antony's stone, and there, right beside it, was *one solitary daisy*. There were no others — just this one, exactly where he'd said it was.

We were dumbfounded.

No other flowers were out at that time, yet this single daisy had freshly opened, maybe on that day.

What is more amazing, Mrs Hooper later asked every family member if they'd visited the cemetery recently. None of them had: the last call had been *three months previously*. Therefore, no one belonging to Antony had any knowledge of that flower.

Furthermore, that was the first time I'd ever been to that churchyard; if you asked me to go back there now, I wouldn't know the way.

We were greatly impressed by Antony's ingenuity. Not only had he proved his existence but he'd also foxed the psychic researchers who declare that mediums simply read facts from people's minds.

He'd beaten them all, and very cleverly — with one daisy.

Weeks later, when visiting this family again, I described a spontaneous clairvoyant vision I saw near Mrs Hooper — it was 'a red jumper with a broken seam' floating next to her shoulder and she immediately recognised it as her son's.

Grabbing paper and pen, I quickly scribbled

down this letter from Antony to his mother:

I'm very happy where I am, and I'm in touch with all the family by thought.

I've withdrawn my presence because now I've almost mastered the ability to register thoughts, as my previous list of evidential statements proves.

I'm living in a sort of small flat. It's great! I don't have to clean up after me at all!

I wasn't in the church tonight and I'm very aware of what you were supposed to have received from me. I'm sorry, Mum, but I didn't transmit a thing.

This remark refers to a message that Mrs Hooper was given by a local 'medium' earlier on that night. Antony goes on:

I do know how difficult it's been for you on times since I went.

As I remember my last few hours, I know it was a stupid thing to do. In drink, no one's in their right senses really.

I'm not present in the room. My thought waves reach down often as they do now. I want you to know I'm safe.

Information can always come down to you about which you know nothing.

Did my daisy surprise you? Hope so.

I've been with Nanny Hooper recently. We've shared some lovely times together.

I haven't got any solid evidence to transmit tonight, more of a friendly, kind note to let you know how I am.

My leg doesn't hurt any more — this new body's great! And I've grown a few inches and my hair has darkened a bit.

Mrs Hooper recalled that he'd broken his leg eighteen months before he'd died and that he'd lightened his hair when he was here. Antony finishes:

Love to Dad. I love you all, Antony...
— will be in touch again but will pick my mediums carefully. No dopey ones!

And true to his word, Antony Hooper, the young lad who was killed by the midnight train, has returned dozens of times to his family. He's even rapped walls and furniture in his mother's home in answer to questions. Time and again he's returned to prove his survival.

Other mediums have often brought him to me. They named him and added, 'He says you are his friend.' And so I am. But I never knew him on earth; he is a messenger.

I can do no better than close this chapter with some encouraging words from Mrs Maureen Hooper to all those who have lost a child.

I think her remarks will bring you hope and comfort:

To all mothers who have lost children I would say: Your child is not dead but still alive. Don't believe they're at rest, because they're not.

Don't believe that they have gone for ever, because they have not.

And I know through good mediumship, with patience and determination to keep on searching, you will find them again.

Rain Pools

Rain Pools,
Rain Pools,
Watering the ground;
Splish splash
Rain Pools,
Water all around.

Snowflakes,
Whiteflakes,
Floating on the air;
Pirouetting Earthward,
Watch the children stare.

Grey hail,
Dark hail,
Bouncing off the pane;
'Look, Mum!'
'Yes, John,
It's only frozen rain.'

'Sleep, John.
Rest now;
It's been a tiring day.'
'Right, Mum.
'Night Mum.'
And soon he's on his way.

As Jonathan sleeps,
His mother weeps,
Unable to understand
Why the one she loves more than life itself
Must soon slip from her hand.

'See the X-rays,'
The doctor said.
'There isn't any doubt.
Your little boy is dying,
And time is running out.'

Rain Pools,
Rain Pools,
Johnny's favourite sound;
Splish splash
Rain Pools,
Watering the ground.

Summer came
As Winter left,
And little boys grew tall;
All, that is, bar Jonathan French,
Who, too weak to move,
Too frail to breathe,
Daily lost his strength.

John's fragile frame grew smaller
As each day came and went.
His body became thin,
His face drew in
Till all his fight was spent.

'Mum, the sun is shining!
Take me to the window, please?
Just ignore what the doctor says,
I want to see the sun again,
I want to feel the breeze.
I want to watch the raindrops
Splashing on the ground,
Making little Rain Pools —
That's my favourite sound.'

So Johnny's Mum
Lifts up her son
And carries him to the light;
And her tears fall, so quietly,
Hidden from his sight.
(Such a kind boy,
such a good boy;
It doesn't make sense at all.
He's done no wrong,
He's far too young,
Too innocent and small.)

(Just eight years old
and he won't see nine,
Or ever know a wife;
He wants to watch the raindrops fall:
Please God, spare his life.)

(Let my son be well again,
give *me* what ails him so.
It's fit that I should end my time:
Spare John and let *me* go.)

But God, it seems, was busy;
For He didn't heed her cry.
And from Beyond He called John's name
And little Jonathan died...

Rain Pools,
Rain Pools,
Watering the ground;
Splish splash
Rain Pools,
Johnny's favourite sound.

And there in a dusty graveyard,
Kneeling all forlorn,
Is an aching grief-stricken mother,
Her wrecked life shattered and torn.
'John, I've come to see you again,
It's so hard to forget your pain.
But it's better that you're at peace, my son,
Than to have suffered and remained.'

'Daddy loves you, darling,
And Susie's tears still fall;
And all your friends still think of you, John,
But I miss you most of all.'

And she places her eight red roses tall,
One per year of his life
(Which blossomed and now is run),
And her constant tears incessantly fall,
Making little Rain Pools
On the grave of her special son.

Rain Pools,
Rain Pools,
Watering the ground;
Splish splash,
Rain Pools;
    John still hears the sound...

11

Animals Survive Too

It was pitch-black night and the car sped along the motorway, lit by successive pools of orange lamplight. Suddenly a black cat shot out of the shadows and pelted across the dark road, keeping close to the ground and increasing its speed as it flew past the front of the car — but we were moving too fast. There was a scream from underneath the passenger wheel and the vehicle jolted as it ran over the animal.

We screeched to a stop about a hundred yards up the road — I flung open the door and in a panic ran back along the tarmac, dodging traffic as I went. The dark patch of shuddering animal came nearer until I was right beside it: the poor cat was bleeding from a cracked skull. Its eyes were wide open and staring, its mouth was pulled right back in terror. As I watched the last throes of life ebbing away I felt so helpless. But it wasn't my driver's fault; before he knew what had happened the cat was under the wheel.

Suddenly the creature arched its back,

shuddered, then freed its soul as the lifeless body contracted. The cat's spirit dashed across the road into nearby bushes and freedom.

That was the first time I'd ever been involved in the killing of an animal and it was an horrendous experience.

We stood there, my driver and I, both deeply shocked and full of regret.

Although it was 2.30 a.m. we took a shovel and dug a grave for the body in the roadside grassland, scratching and scrabbling at the hard earth to give the cat a decent burial.

'Do you want to say a few words?' I asked my driver, then I left him alone while I tidied up the roadway. When I glanced back he was crying with remorse.

I reported the incident to the police but the duty officer just wasn't interested. 'It's only a reportable offence if it's a dog,' he said boorishly, which annoyed me.

'We're not one bit interested in your traffic rules,' I said, 'we're concerned about the feelings of the cat's owners, should they contact you.'

I've always loved animals and since childhood I've been aware of a spiritual kinship with them. When I was a boy we kept two chickens that laid fresh eggs every day. It was such a thrill to collect them straight from the coop. But after a few years the grown-ups decided they were to be killed and prepared for the table. Horrified and incensed, I pleaded for their lives. 'What harm have they ever done? Why should they be destroyed and eaten?'

But shout as I might, no one listened and a friend's husband was called in to do the killing.

Mr Morgan was a course and unfeeling man who relished the prospect of his task. But I don't think he'd bargained for my opposition. When he arrived I stood against the back door and barred his exit to the garden.

'Come on, son, clear out of the way,' he snarled.

'No!' I exclaimed, bracing myself against the door jambs. 'I won't let you near them! They've never hurt anyone and I won't let you do it!'

But he brushed me aside like a feather and strode into the sunshine, a sharp knife glinting in his hand. I pulled madly at the scullery door but he'd locked it.

I clambered awkwardly onto a stool and craned my neck to see through the window. It was a bright spring day: sparrows were singing in the garden but our chickens were minutes away from their deaths.

Pummelling the glass, I screamed out again and again to save their lives, but with a smirk and a few cruel twists of his hands, he wrung their necks before my horrified gaze.

I ran upstairs, threw myself onto the bed and sobbed and cried for hours.

The bodies were later plucked, cleaned and made ready for the table but I wouldn't touch them.

I point-blankly refused.

The whole episode made me feel physically sick.

On that day, I realised there were unkind

people who just didn't care about our fellow creatures, the animals.

Many owners are distressed when their beloved pets die and are eager to know if their friends survive death. I can happily report that they do. I've lost count of the times spirit animals have returned through my mediumship to their beloved masters and mistresses. In most cases they bring a tremendous feeling of warmth and gratitude for the concern and love shown to them when on earth.

When animals have shared a close bond with us they've been helped into a greater awareness of their individuality, which in turn assures not only their survival but also their spirit return. Even creatures other than domestic pets live on into eternity.

At a meeting in Yorkshire, England, an elderly spirit miner contacted his niece in the audience with some good news. 'Uncle Ernie' asked her, 'How's it going, lass?'

'Tell him I'm fine,' she called out.

'Good,' he replied to me. 'Eh, you'll never guess who I've got over here wi' me, lass? Remember old Nellie and Jessie?'

'Oh, yes!' exclaimed his niece. 'They were the two pit-ponies he took care of down the mines.'

'That's them,' he returned. 'And can you remember, lass: they were down't pit for so long that when they retired t'surface, they were both blind as bats?'

'Yes, I do remember,' she said. 'He loved those ponies as though they were his own children.'

At this Uncle Ernie beamed and called out joyously to me, 'Well lass, I still love 'em I do! And what do you think? *They can both see now.*'

When I looked around the hall nearly everyone's eyes had misted up.

But horses were not the only deceased creatures to pay me a visit while working. During one question-and-answer session the audience began to look at me rather strangely because they couldn't understand why I kept grinning and scrutinising the air above their heads. They didn't know I could see a bright blue-and-green spirit budgerigar dive-bombing the crowd then flying high up into the rafters again! It was such a comical sight and so real a vision that for a moment I thought he'd got in through an open window.

When I told everyone what was happening, he flew from the top of the hall and landed right on my shoulder. I could feel his little claws digging into my skin (my etheric skin, of course). Then a spirit woman appeared, took him onto her finger and relayed a successful message to her relative, saying, 'I've got Edgar with me.'

'Oh, I'm *so* glad. He only died a few days ago and I've been worried about him.'

But there was nothing to fear because 'Edgar' was still very much alive, chirruping away and swearing as he did on earth!

Another happy return of a much-loved pet was that of my beautiful chinchilla rabbit, Smokey, whom I'd kept when I was fourteen. She was a slate grey cuddly ball of fun and fur, and she was so affectionate. Every time I entered the shed where she lived she'd come hopping over to greet me and sniff at my pockets to see if I'd brought her fresh food. But sadly, after an illness, Smokey died.

Tearfully, I buried her body in the garden.

I missed her terribly.

When I cleaned out the shed I found hundreds of teeth-marks in the wood where she used to sharpen her ever-growing incisors. But a few days later, while I sat in the lounge reading, I felt something pulling at my shoe. When I looked down there was nothing there: all I could see was the sole of my shoe being physically tugged and I could feel it being gnawed. In that instant I knew Smokey had returned. She'd never been allowed in the house but her love for me, and her desire to be near me, had brought her to my side.

How marvellous to know that our lesser brethren survive. Or are they lesser? When I look at their gentle behaviour and loyal trust then measure this against man's nature, I sometimes wonder who is the more evolved.

There have been many occasions when unusual creatures have made spiritual contact. Can you imagine my astonishment when a fully-grown Indian elephant appeared in the aisle at one of my meetings? I took a deep breath and ventured a description.

'I'm not getting a name,' I said, which tickled the audience; 'but I do see a distinctively-dressed Indian boy who's looking after him.' I described in detail the young lad's clothes.

'Here!' called out a man near the front. He revealed that he'd been a gamekeeper in India and recognised the spirit lad, and also the elephant.

Thank goodness for that, I thought, feeling quite relieved, because just behind the elephant I could see a giraffe coming into view! Oh well, if he's taken the one he's bound to accept the other, I thought — so I offered out the giraffe, to which he replied:

'Yes. I can take *two* actually.'

Everyone fell about laughing and boggled their minds, wondering how I was going to sort it all out.

I simply said, 'Well I don't know which one we've got here because they all look alike to me. But it's the one that was close to the elephant.'

'Ah, yes!' he exclaimed. 'I perfectly understand' — much to the amusement of the crowd.

In contrast to this link, there followed an emotional message when a blind man accepted his golden Labrador guide-dog from the spirit world. Even though death had separated him from 'Sandy', his first companion sat quietly at his feet. The man wept like a child when I named his faithful friend. 'He's there because he loves you,' I said; 'and because you love him.'

Sandy's loyal presence shows us that the bonds of love can never be broken — not even by death.

People have often asked me if their pets are

psychic and the answer is *yes*. Animals' minds are uncluttered and free of stifling prejudice and social etiquette. Even the most humble of pets can see or sense the spirit people, an ability which most humans seem to have neglected.

I used to visit a large pet shop in an open market and in one of the tanks lived a black-and-white Moray Eel. Whenever I approached the stall, his innate psychic senses immediately recognised me: he'd swim to the front of the tank to greet me before he could actually see me. We'd struck up a kind of unusual friendship, I guess.

'Hello,' I'd whisper. 'Still here then? Never mind, someone will come along and give you a good home. You'll see.' And whatever people may think, that Moray Eel 'knew' what I was saying because he seemed to settle down after that.

One rainy day I called on my friend to find that he'd gone. I really hope he got a kind owner.

I feel so sorry for caged creatures and tanked fish. It must be a far from ideal life for them, all cooped up in those confined spaces. We wouldn't like it. We put people in small places like that as a punishment. But what have the animals done?

Animals know instinctively when they're safe or in danger, and Woody was no exception. He was a wild pigeon who used to perch on my bedroom windowsill. He did this every night for several years: he'd rest peacefully on one leg with his head tucked underneath his wing. Timid creatures normally need a long association with us before they gain our trust but Woody sensed psychically that he was quite safe with me; no matter how many lights were flicked off and on or how many doors were banged in the early hours, Woody never flinched.

A part of his mind reached out and touched mine: his spirit knew beyond doubt that no harm would come to him at my house.

This kind of soul power is resident in every living thing. Animals are extremely sensitive beings: they can register human emotions because their psychic abilities operate freely; they, like us, are spirits working through physical bodies.

My faithful cat and childhood companion, Tibby, was such an animal; but she went out one night and never returned. Eventually we got word that a school caretaker discovered she'd been killed at the roadside by a hit-and-run driver; it was a sad goodbye to a lovely friend.

She was a remarkable cat. She used to chaperone my mother down to the shops, sit at the kerb until the traffic was clear, and walk her safely over the crossing. Only then would she go off and play.

There's no doubt about it, I'm a cat man!

In later years (long after I'd left home and was living alone in a flat in northern England — more about this later) while taking a fundraising meeting in aid of an animal sanctuary, I was moved when I read a banner the organisers had hung above the platform. On it was written: 'If you show kindness to these my lesser brethren, you have shown kindness unto me'.

I wholeheartedly agree.

The meeting went well and it was followed by a delicious home-baked vegetarian feast, to show any carnivores present there's an alternative way of titillating the palate without cruelty to animals.

From that same northern animal sanctuary I became the proud owner of Sooty, a grey-and-white female cat with black tiger stripes on her coat. She walked like the cowboy film star John Wayne, was into everything, and was bossy and very independent.

We grew to love one another greatly and she wouldn't let anyone tickle her stomach except me.

Sooty always loved company, which is why, when she was an energetic kitten, she kept bounding on and off my bed at night when all I wanted was a bit of peace to go to sleep. In the end I couldn't settle until I'd placed her basket outside on the landing and firmly shut the bedroom door. But her spirit was not a bit deterred.

In the middle of the night I was rudely awoken by the pressure of her feet pounding over the bed. I could actually feel her full body-weight pressing down on me through the duvet; and it was only after I'd 'thrown' her off with my legs that I realised she wasn't physically in the room at all. Her body was *sound asleep* outside on the landing — her spirit had walked right through the locked door and bothered me again!

This fiasco was repeated night after night until one evening, as well as Sooty's spirit feet bouncing on the sheets, I also registered a tight 'ball of fear' crouched in the bed, close to my left knee. There were *two* spirit animals present. Before I had time to be perplexed the sensations faded away.

But everything became clear when some friends of mine rang to plead, 'Will you take another cat from the animal sanctuary?'

I agreed, and a few days later Bess arrived on my doorstep. She turned out to be the 'frightened ball of fear' I'd felt huddled next to my leg. My invisible inspirers had brought her to be introduced.

When I finally prised Bess out of her cardboard box, she dived into my arms, buried her head in my jumper, and stayed there for three hours without moving.

I gently sang to her, smoothed her dark coat and massaged her tight neck muscles to try to reduce her tension and fear. Only after forty-five minutes did she suddenly purr like a train! After that she spent three days in her own basket, too petrified to move: she just sat there resting her head on outstretched paws and watching Sooty with wide eyes as she sauntered past.

Would they get along? I wondered, because the

sanctuary told me she'd never known life in a house before.

If anyone approached she buried her head in her comfort blanket.

Whenever she took a few brave steps out of her box Sooty thought she was live target practice and pounced on top of her, wrestled her to the floor and triumphantly pinned her down by the neck.

Another victory for John Wayne!

The sanctuary had advised me to return Bess if she couldn't cope, and after a while I could see their point. I began to despair, thinking she'd never feel at home with me.

Then I heard a clear voice inside my head saying, 'Please love the cat.' On the strength of this, I kept her — and was so glad that I did. She turned out to be a real lady; not at all like Sooty. Bess developed a quiet, gentle personality, in contrast to Sooty's wicked mischief.

They soon got along fine and went everywhere together: they became inseparable, two great pals. They'd clean each other's coats until they shone, then they'd twirl around each other, cuddling up on cold nights to keep out the draughts. They were a smashing team.

But I didn't realise what that spirit voice really meant when it had begged me to keep Bess. As time went on, her behaviour began to change. One day I scolded her for not using her litter box — this was her second accident — but then I noticed something was wrong.

She'd always wobbled a little when she walked; friends had nicknamed her 'Wobbler'. But now she positively reeled from side to side, bumped into furniture and ended up staggering against a wall for support. I then realised she hadn't used her litter tray because it was down on the lower landings and poor Bess couldn't manage to descend the stairs without pain.

I rushed her to the People's Dispensary for Sick Animals where they diagnosed a possible brain tumour and meningitis, an inflammation of the brain membranes.

After this, her health deteriorated quickly. Antibiotic treatment brought only temporary relief. She was falling in and out of blindness, was incontinent and had no sense of balance.

For three months I nursed her: I made a special waterproof bed and lined it with old newspapers, but poor Bess was failing fast.

I tried to teach her to walk again, to overcome the paralysis in her hind limbs, but she cried out in pain so I stopped. She fell extremely ill; she was terribly frustrated and couldn't bear the indignities she suffered.

One Sunday night I knelt by her basket and closed my eyes and prayed. I asked that if she was to be taken across into the spirit world, the next day at the PDSA, that my grandfather, Grancha Price, would be there to care for her. I instinctively felt this would be her last night on earth, and as I finished the prayer I sensed my spirit friends moving away. They'd received the message.

At the vet's they advised that because of her great distress and personality change — she should be put to sleep.

I was stunned and silent.

What should I do?

My mind was numbed by the responsibility. Such a decision should never be made lightly.

But poor Bess was suffering...

Against my better judgement, after wrestling with my conscience, I nervously read the paper.

A lump came into my throat when I signed it with a shaky hand.

'I want to be with her,' I said in a whisper. They gently cut some fur from her front paw and prepared the injection.

'Will she feel any pain?' I asked.

'No. It's an overdose of barbiturates. It'll be instantaneous.'

'She mustn't feel any pain,' I said quietly, resting my hand on her head.

'Don't worry, she won't.'

My heart was thudding against my ribs.

From somewhere a nurse appeared and helped to smooth Bess, who gave a little trembling stretch.

'Lie still, sweetheart,' she said. 'There's a good girl.'

I bent down and kissed Bess again.

'Shh,' I whispered gently. 'Goodbye, my Bess... safe journey...'

And then the injection was given.

Her eyes opened fully.

Her heart stopped beating.

Bess was gone.

Tears streamed down my face as I kissed her again and smoothed her fine dark coat. I was too upset to stay any longer and left quickly, clutching my empty box and pushing my way through a waiting-room full of people's sympathetic sighs.

I was shaking with tears.

I was shocked. I had betrayed my friend.

I'd taken Bess to the doctor in good faith and she'd trusted me to help her and then I'd signed a form for them to take away her life.

I couldn't speak.

How could I have done such a cruel thing?

I couldn't catch the bus home. I walked all the way, uncontrollably sobbing.

When I got in, I collapsed onto a chair and broke my heart.

How could I have made that decision? How could I live with myself after that? I felt so terribly guilty; I would never forgive myself.

And I still don't.

Even though people said it was the right thing to do, the heavy burden of guilt lingers with me to this day. I killed my friend, just as surely as if I'd given her the injection myself.

Sooty and I missed Bess terribly that bitter northern winter. The place seemed so empty and life just wasn't the same without her gentle presence. Sooty would sit on the landing and sigh, staring across at the box Bess had slept in. Then she'd look at me as if to say, 'When is she coming back?'

I sat at the piano and composed a piece of music in tribute to our friend and called it 'Gentle Bess'.

Then, one night, while Sooty and I sat quietly in the music room I heard Bess cry out from beyond the door on the landing. Sooty sat bolt upright.

She'd heard it too. Then there was scratching at the wood.

I dashed across and opened the door. I couldn't see Bess but sensed her walking in, swaggering along. Sooty ran over and greeted her, sniffing the air and playing with her invisible friend. Sooty's happy face was a picture.

I felt so relieved to welcome Bess back into our home and to ask for her forgiveness.

A little while later, when sitting in meditation my psychic vision opened up and I saw Bess again, in the spirit world. She was stretched out in a patch of sunlight under some flowering bushes. She always did love warmth. Behind her the house door opened and out stepped Grancha Price. He was much younger than when he'd died and he went over to Bess and stroked her fine coat with loving hands. Then he raised his head and smiled at me.

And I couldn't help marvelling at the power of thought and the power of love. How mighty they both are.

My prayer had been answered.

Bess had arrived safely on the other side, no longer in any pain and completely free of disease. Furthermore she was under the loving care of my grandfather, just as I'd asked.

The Voiceless Ones

Voiceless Ones,
The Voiceless Ones;
Who will hear the cry of
The Voiceless Ones?

Fighting fish;
Wrenched by your mouth
From the deep —
Killed —
And served up in a dish.

Gentle Sheep;
Stolen from your mother
And pushed along an aisle of death,
Too afraid to weep.

Featherless Chicken;
Standing on wires,
Laying eggs for man,
Who'll cook your bones
And pick them.

Turkeys, Ducks and Geese;
Will killings ever cease?
Still slaughtered in your millions
To praise a Prince of Peace.

Voiceless Ones
The Voiceless Ones,
Who will hear the cry of
The Voiceless Ones?

Frightened Fox;
Chased for sporting blood,
Or caught in a gin-trap
That cracks your limbs and locks.

Majestic Giant Whale;
Killed by a spear
Through your brain,
Then turned into cosmetics
For profitable sale.

Monkeys; Dogs; Birds and Cats;
Seals and Calves; Mice and Rats;
Imprisoned by Science:
Electrically jolted,
Shaved and moulted;
Fastened to contraptions,
Strapped and bolted.
Cannot move,
Cannot rest;
Unspeakable cruelty
In the name of progress.

Skins for fashion,
Furs for clothes,
Meats for the belly
Bludgeoned by blows.
When will it cease?

When man sees that all these creatures
Are friends not foes.

No need for meat;
There's much to eat:
Fruit, nuts, plants and others —
And lest we forget:
Man is also an animal,
And animals are our brothers.

And it's foolish to think
This has nothing to do with you,
For you contribute too,
Whenever you buy meat,
Fur coats, cosmetics,
Or leather shoes.

Thoughtless man —
Put away your guns,
And pity the cry of
The Voiceless Ones.

12

Psychic Powers

The telephone rang.

'Would you come and see us, Mr O'Brien? Our radio station's haunted.'

Well, it was one of the strangest requests I'd received. How could I resist it?

I was interviewed 'live' at about 11.30 at night and I was to conduct the séance at around midnight. I'd told the presenters that time was irrelevant, but it didn't seem to matter to them.

After my talk the switchboards jammed with callers as usual, but I didn't know that then because I was moving along a dimly-lit claustrophobic corridor with a reporter creeping behind me, armed with a cassette recorder.

'I won't tell you where they say it is,' she whispered.

'No need,' I replied. 'It's right here.' And the air was cold all about that spot.

I didn't answer any more probing questions because I could see a ghostly form gliding into the energy fields around me. She was a kindly looking soul, wearing an old-fashioned long grey nurse's uniform, or what looked like one. She carried a wooden bucket of clean water, rolls of bandages and a wad of dry rags.

The reporter peered into the dimness and glanced at her watch as midnight approached, but she couldn't see the vision that transfixed my gaze.

This nurse of long ago bent down close to the ground, which was below the current level of the corridor floor. Just as she neared the tiles, a soldier came into view: he was dying, taking his last breath; and I sensed him calling out for aid.

She wiped his brow with a damp cloth and tended to his wounds. So great were the emotions of gratitude emanating from him and the feelings of pity radiating from her that my eyes shone with compassion for these two forms who were no longer of our world.

This pair of apparitions from centuries ago were not real spirit people making a visitation — they were merely energy pictures caught up in the atmosphere.

Then I was interviewed.

'She comes along this corridor,' I said, 'and is seen just here where this chilly spot is in the psychic atmosphere.'

'That's perfectly correct,' confirmed my baffled companion. 'This is exactly where the sightings have occurred.'

'I think if you'll check,' I continued, 'this was the site of a particularly bloody battle centuries ago. In fact, I feel many conflicts have occurred here on this ground. Your "Lady in Grey" was a nurse of sorts who tended to the wounded and dying. She was allowed to walk amongst the injured without harm. When she approached a soldier just here' — and I indicated the exact spot — 'the powerful emotions they both released, blended and "pictured" them in the atmosphere, in the psychic energy fields. So your ghost is not a living, communicating entity, she's a picture from the past.'

The reporter was visibly impressed and replied, 'I can now reveal that historical records show this place was a battleground in centuries past; several battles were fought here actually. That's amazing, Stephen.'

I don't know if they saw their 'Lady in Grey' again but she couldn't harm them. How could she? She was only a psychic snapshot.

This kind of soul sensitivity was quietly building up within me and it heralded a new area of my work.

Mediums can use their own soul powers or psychic energies to register vibrations of sight, sense and sound which don't necessarily reach them from the spirit world. I wasn't contacting the other side when I saw the 'Lady in Grey', I was purely exercising my own sensitivity.

Instead of directing my awareness towards the spirit realms Beyond, I channelled it a little nearer to home, so to speak. This kind of psychic sensitivity can provide some startling information if correctly used, and many people are aware of it operating in their lives.

I use these soul powers when I read the human aura. The aura is made up of a set of electro-magnetic and spiritual fields of swirling psychic energy, and these vibrations encompass all things living and inanimate.

Much research has been undertaken in recent years which proves that sensitives have not only seen the aura but have also accurately described it.

In fact, there are several auras radiating around people and objects, but they mostly blend to form what looks like a sort of translucent soap bubble of rainbow colours — ever changing, ever moving and vibrant.

The aura can hold within its spiritual and magnetic fields all kinds of interesting information, as I soon discovered.

A lecturer approached me to use my sensitivity in an unusual but constructive way. He had dozens of students in his care but one of them, he felt, was responsible for the anonymous letters he'd been receiving: they were of a disturbing sexual nature and indicated that their sender was in need of professional, medical help. But which student had penned them? Could I help? I said I'd try.

When I was present before a class of forty students, none of whom knew why I was there, I extended my auric energy fields by an act of will and embraced the class within my power.

I then used my clairvoyant ability to carefully scan each person, quietly and privately.

I soon made a discovery.

In the fields of light around a female student I found some telling information: hovering within her mind I saw the selfsame details that were contained in the disturbing letters.

I privately named the student to the lecturer and my findings were later proved correct, which led to the youngster receiving the professional help she needed.

Sensitives can read the life story of objects by becoming attuned to the vibrational fields that surround them. Of course, they sometimes interpret these visions and impressions incorrectly, but a reasonable success rate can be achieved.

Once, on a sightseeing trip to a museum, another medium and I decided to 'tune in' to the mummified remains of an Egyptian priest called Tem-Hor: this kind of exercise is known as *psychometry*.

We placed our hands on the glass cabinet through which the mummy's swathed body could be seen and moved our minds towards the lifeless form.

We closed our eyes and, to the background sound of clicking footsteps echoing through the far rooms of the museum, we concentrated on the man in the coffin, and visions started appearing in my mind.

Even though the last earthly impressions of this Priest of Isis had been placed into his body's vibrational fields about 220 BC, more than 2,000 years ago, we received a scant picture of his life.

Between us, we saw this man moving through rich hanging draperies in a magnificent palace, where he was consulted by royalty. The colours of the visions were glowing; the palace was beautifully ornate and decorated with gold and precious gemstones.

Then I saw Tem-Hor sitting at some kind of desk; he was writing on clay and parchment, probably papyrus. As I watched, an awful sensation overcame me: cold metal was thrust into my back with a deadening thud.

I felt he'd been murdered.

My colleague saw the funeral procession and got the feeling he wasn't considered an important man and that the proceedings were undertaken out of quick necessity rather than out of love.

The impressions faded and we stood once more in the cold museum, being eyed rather suspiciously by a warden.

How strange to think we each leave our spiritual 'fingerprints' on everything we touch.

I did another interesting psychometric reading when I was handed a peculiarly shaped stone. I clasped it tightly and immediately began to register sensations. The link was so strong, so very real, that as I relayed my impressions I spoke as if I were the voice of the rock.

'I'm in a wall or part of a castle,' I said. 'I can smell gunpowder smoke and hear the cries of dying men. Just down the grassy bank there are swans on the moat; they're fleeing from the noise in terror. There's thunder in the dark skies above me.

'Now the rain comes... I can feel it bouncing off my surface, cooling me after the hot sun.'

The scenes shifted when I tuned in to another part of the rock's past.

'The clash of metal is all around me and those cries of pain are here again. There are men dying and lying dead on the grass under a leaden sky; some of them are calling out in agony and giving up the spirit. I can hear canons firing and a spear has just glanced off my surface. Oh God, someone's being killed up against my vision... blood is splattering all over my sight.'

My mind quickly dismissed these gruesome impressions and found another area to view.

'That scene passes now, thank God, and I can see a small flickering campfire. It is night. The air is cold but stilled. The battle's over I think: it finished days ago, and these men I see have been clearing the ground of the dead and taking any treasures they wanted.

'They're gently singing songs and drinking ale. I think they're pleased with their day's work. One of them, a big chap, is sneering and tossing gold coins in the air. He's taken these from one of the dead...'

I 'tuned out' and came back into the present-day room.

The researcher then explained that the piece of rock had been prised from the walls of an ancient castle which had seen many battles, taken from the wall at about a man's height, overlooking a dry grassy slope that would have once been a moat.

Isn't it amazing that so-called 'dead' objects can photograph and capture for all time the sights and sounds they've experienced? This makes it easy to accept the beliefs of the Native American Indians, particularly those of my Guardian Spirit, White Owl. Many times he's said, 'You think you have so much knowledge, but indeed today's civilisation has lost many of the great truths known to man in the past. We knew, the people of my race, that what seems lifeless to the slow heavy senses of the flesh is not without life at all: it has its own consciousness, its own specialised form of spirit awareness.

'To you the dead rocks and stones are immovable and of no great consequence to mankind; yet they exist through time much longer than man's puny physical frame. The rocks have their own lives to lead. They move over the centuries. They breathe the great breath of the Spirit.

'How foolish is man to assume that he is the epitome of all growth. One day he will retrace his steps back to the ancient wisdom that he has so conveniently forgotten.'

White Owl has often told us that he himself was a medium when on earth and that he could psychically 'read' the plants and stones. When people or objects were lost, the Native Americans — those sufficiently gifted and trained — could 'ask' the countryside if it had seen the missing articles or people. My guide's stories of the past are always so fascinating.

The word *psychometry* comes from the Greek. Literally translated it splits into two sections: *Psyche* (broadly meaning Soul) and *Metron* (meaning to Measure). *Psychometry*, then, is the means whereby we can 'measure the soul of things'.

But to prove that this works we need feedback, facts that can be verified beyond reasonable doubt, and I've helped to provide these on a number of occasions. A good example of this was when I was suddenly called out onto a platform by Gordon Higginson, the Principal of a College of Psychic Studies, who unexpectedly conducted a psychic experiment. He blindfolded me then placed some jewellery into my hand and said, 'Stephen will now psychometrise this ring.'

I began rattling off facts and details about its owner, having made a connection with her through the psychic vibrations around the article: the ring had become a kind of 'key', if you like, opening a doorway through which I could contact her.

The recipient was not allowed to speak to me, only Mr Higginson's voice was heard.

I discovered later that the ring belonged to a Mrs Judd. She was a rather jolly lady of considerable proportions, and that's why the whole audience chuckled when I confidently announced, 'Whoever owns this can tap-dance!'

The mental picture of Mrs Judd's well-endowed figure tripping the light fantastic had titillated them.

But back came Mr Higginson's voice, 'Yes — when she was younger.'

I went on, 'This person is worried about some documentation she's specially gathered together to present a case of some kind. I feel she has the papers with her and intends to make her case known.'

All this was accepted; afterwards Mrs Judd revealed to the students that in her possession on that very afternoon she had twenty-six signed affidavits concerning a legal matter which she intended to bring to the attention of her solicitors.

The audience gasped at my final statement when I confidently declared that, 'Whoever the owner is, she — because it is a woman — has a strong link to Portsmouth.'

'I live there!' she called out.

Over the years, several people have asked me to use my psychic powers to help them: one was an eminent healer.

'Stephen,' she asked rather worriedly, 'will you take a look at one of my patients for me, and see what you can see with him?'

I agreed, and tuned in to the man sitting across the room; he was receiving healing from two smart ladies but I was concerned about the emotions he was radiating. Despite the fact he was outwardly serene, some other feeling lurked in the background.

Afterwards I relayed my impressions to the healing group leader.

'As well as being deeply in grief —'

' — Yes, he's recently lost his wife.'

' — I'm afraid he's thoroughly enjoying the closeness and touch of your female healers.'

'That's exactly what I'd suspected,' she replied with a bob of her head.

We agreed it would be a good idea if a male healer were to treat him in a bid to stem these emotions, which would only have caused distress if they'd continued.

The following week he was healed by a man, and the week after that he didn't return. Of course, the healing group continued to send him help through the spirit world, but I don't think they saw him again at their sessions.

Many people have come to me in distress, seeking aid, and although they speak their thoughts freely they don't always tell the truth — or else they withhold information they feel might embarrass them.

Such a case was the woman who claimed she was being pestered by a 'dead' man who wouldn't leave her alone and constantly questioned her about sex. But something was not as it seemed.

While she was busy speaking, private investigations into her auric fields revealed she had a history of mental illness. The spirit people confirmed my observations. 'She is still mentally unbalanced,' they said. 'Be careful with your words; be as tactful as possible.'

I questioned her about whether she'd sought medical help. At first she categorically denied she'd ever been ill, but then she reluctantly admitted it. We helped her as much as we could.

At the time of writing it's against British law to diagnose illnesses unless you are a qualified doctor; so, whenever I've been asked to demonstrate this ability, I've always done so to closed groups of emotionally stable people who understood psychometry and weren't vulnerable to the power of suggestion.

In one lecture I 'read' the auric fields of a female student, concentrating particularly on the physical aura, which radiates about an inch or so in depth all around the body: in it are contained our health problems.

'I see three difficulties here,' I said. 'There are shadows over your left ankle, over the right kidney and also at the top of your neck.'

The astonished lady replied, 'I broke my left ankle last year; I'm under supervision for kidney problems, and last week I was diagnosed as having osteo-arthritis in my neck.'

Many people have experienced similar psychic feelings — for example, those inexplicable sensations of entering a room full of smiling, happy people, and yet you 'know' that a raging argument has just taken place there. That's your auric energy registering the true atmosphere in the room.

Our perceptions can be *wrong* of course, and we must never deceive ourselves into thinking we're right all the time, because we aren't: it takes years of careful development to perfect these psychic skills.

But I was spot-on when Kenny, an officious under-manager where I once worked, smiled and said, 'Stephen, the top Management want you to do some overtime at the weekend. How about it?'

I had never liked this man.

I looked him in the eye and replied, 'But that's a lie. The Management want you to do it; and you want to coax me into taking your place.'

The poor man was dumbstruck: I'd read his secret and he never bothered me much after that.

Sometimes these soul powers can produce strange sensations. On occasions I'd get the peculiar feeling that someone was calling out to me, as though people in *this* world, and not in the next, were wishing to hear from me.

One week I kept receiving telepathic calls from a Mrs Scott who lived in England, miles away from me. I hadn't seen her for ages but I just kept thinking I should telephone; so, at the end of a nagging week I dialled her number.

'Oh hello, Stephen. How lovely to hear your voice. It's a wonder your ears aren't dropping off, I've been talking about you all week!' She went on to reveal it was the anniversary of her husband's passing and that she'd been feeling dispirited.

Her thoughts had reached out and made a psychic link with my mind.

Speaking of the telephone, I got rather good at knowing who was on the other end when it rang, which was an extremely useful skill, particularly when it was a difficult person on days when I wasn't up to scratch.

I wasn't always right, of course, but some of my friends doubted my ability. 'Pick it up then,' I challenged, 'and see if I'm right.' And nearly always, I was.

Possessing visionary powers has its price to pay, and I was sometimes called upon to make investigations that others would have run away from, a hundred miles in the opposite direction. One such event occurred on Scottish soil, in Glasgow.

I was taken to a small terraced house situated in a rough council estate. 'There's definitely something *awful* in this place,' confided my trembling hostess to me and the small group of men and women who'd gathered for the unusual event. 'Please take a good look about, Stephen.'

'Certainly.'

Armed with youthful pluck and the knowledge that my spirit friends supported me in all my psychic efforts, I wandered through the humble rooms. There was positively nothing malevolent or even spooky on the ground floor, but as I climbed the staircase the emanations of a powerful dark force reached out and touched my soul. Unfortunately I whispered to myself, 'By the pricking of my thumbs something evil this way comes,' not realising that half of the group had heard what I'd said and then fled down the stairs and run out into the street!

As I approached the upper rooms I sensed nothing untoward in two of them, but when I neared the third door I knew I'd struck gold. I was just about to say to my hostess, who was clamped nervously onto my arm, 'It's in here' — but her strained expression told me not to bother; I was right.

Furtively, I opened the bedroom door and felt the most sickly sensation of hatred I'd ever experienced. I took a courageous step into the room but bumped into a solid wall of psychic power and was visibly thrown back a few feet.

'Oh God,' she said, 'that happens to me too.'

Undaunted I marched across to the door and just as I was about to thrust myself forward — it suddenly slammed shut in my face.

'I don't think we're welcome here,' I murmured feebly.

So down the stairs we trouped and she made a cup of tea while we chatted about 'him up there'.

I was convinced that someone from the other side had taken up residence in her bedroom and a few quick words with White Owl confirmed this.

'I'll remove him,' he said. 'He's too strong for your world to do this. He's nearer to us than he is to you. Leave it with me and I'll deal with it properly.'

And so we did as he asked; and shortly afterwards we heard some scuffling from that bedroom — and after that, silence reigned. The 'heavy brigade' had gone in and taken 'him up there' away.

Another unworldly visitor made himself known to me in a similar way, but he was not a malicious entity, however, and he lived in an eighteenth-century farmhouse in a place called Glyncorrwg in Wales. The house was beautiful, steeped in character: the original oak beams still spanned the ceilings and walls. History oozed from every stone in the building, which had been lived in and loved for centuries.

While taking tea with the owner, all at once I heard the sound of heavy footsteps dragging along in the room above the ceiling. I kept quiet about it, but then it came again.

I looked up.

'What's the matter with you?' asked my hostess.

'Oh, nothing... There's a man walking above us,' I said glibly, 'and he's got really *huge* feet. He keeps dragging them along, scraping the floorboards. I can hear him. Can't you?'

She couldn't.

The sound disappeared into a bedroom and then away into thin air: there was no room where I could still hear his footsteps, just a sort of old attic area.

'Whoever he is,' I said, 'he used to live in that attic' — and I pointed upwards.

'Pull the other one!' she said. 'Who'd live in that scruffy place? You can barely swing a cat in there and it hasn't been used for years.' But I was adamant, so she checked it out.

Enquiries revealed that decades ago there had been a mentally sub-normal man living at the farm. The locals were afraid of him but he was a gentle and harmless soul; and although he was now 'dead' he obviously still lived in his attic room.

One of our informants also recalled, 'He was a strange, heavy man. He was hugely built: that's why the children were fearful of him, I think. But the oddest thing about him was his feet. They were *enormous* and he could barely drag them about behind him.'

In my years of searching and developing psychic and mediumistic skills I've learned much about the power of thought. I've also experienced, or rather encountered, thought-forms on many occasions.

In Ancient Egypt the Priests of Isis meditated within a dead Pharaoh's tomb and created by the power of their minds 'guardians' or 'thought-forms' to ward off any intruders or grave-robbers after the burial. They placed these thought-forms at the sealed entrance to the tomb, which probably gave rise to the 'Curse of the Pharaohs'.

But is there any truth in these accounts?

I think there is.

Once, when I entered a friend's home I was surprised to see clairvoyantly the figure of a faceless hooded monk, wearing a black robe: he was standing quietly against the wall by the threshold. The form was motionless. I passed it warily and said nothing about it until suppertime.

When I described the monk to my hosts, one of them sniggered. He'd read about these psychic guardians placed in the Valley of the Kings and had created his own to test my clairvoyance, and to see if the theory worked.

These thought-forms, or to give them their more popular name, ghosts, cannot communicate with us in the way that a living, vibrant spirit person can. Ghosts have no conscious personalities of their own. Sadly, many mediums have not yet mastered the art of distinguishing between thought-forms and spirit communicators and have fallen into the trap of confusing the two.

This happened to me in my earlier years.

I recall demonstrating once at a Remembrance Day service; as the audience fell silent and the lights were slowly dimmed in respect for the War dead, I clearly saw two servicemen — both had been killed in the Second World War — standing behind a woman. Well, actually they weren't behind her, but sort of *hovering* at the back of her. I could see only their faces and shoulders, and they didn't speak to me.

When I described these men she replied, 'Oh yes, I've been thinking about them all week.'

I realise now that these weren't spirit people but merely thought-forms, memories she'd unknowingly pictured in her auric energy-fields.

In more recent years I had another unusual soul experience around the date when the world was deeply shocked and angered by the Chernobyl Nuclear Reactor disaster in Russia, where huge amounts of radioactive material was burnt and released upon an unsuspecting world. Britons were told that the radiation cloud wouldn't reach the United Kingdom. But while out walking one day I really did feel most unwell. In fact, I cut my journey short and called on a friend to ask if I could rest for a while.

'I feel strange,' I remember saying. 'All my body's tingling and seems to be "alive", as if I'd been under a sun-lamp for too long.' And I lay down gratefully on a bed for half an hour.

That evening on the six o'clock news the BBC announced that the toxic cloud from Chernobyl was directly over our region and that background radiation levels were now ten times greater than normal.

There is no doubt in my mind that the price one pays for mediumship is sensitivity.

Critics of mediums are fond of accusing them of reading their sitters' minds. In fact they claim that the evidence given by the spirit world doesn't come from the Beyond at all. I find this a rather presumptuous statement to make because if only *one* case for survival is proved, then the mediums' claims carry weight.

Aware of these allegations, I began to seek for proof that would satisfy my sharp intellect. I reasoned that because there was no one more critical than I, if I could be convinced that telepathy was being ruled out, many others would be too. The spirit world obviously caught these thoughts, for upon investigation of the messages they relayed through me I discovered that sometimes certain facts were not acceptable at the time: they had to be researched.

If proved correct, the theory of telepathy on the part of the medium had to be discounted. Mediums can't read details from a mind that doesn't possess them.

To prove my point I have in my possession a signed affidavit, one of many, which contains spirit-supplied evidence that was outside of the recipient's knowledge.

Here is the statement signed by Mrs Valerie Johnstone, and it speaks for itself:

Stephen O'Brien told me he was talking to my 'two uncles in spirit, both brothers,' and he named them as 'Uncle John and Uncle George'.

I strongly disagreed, telling him that I only had one uncle there, namely Uncle John. But Mr O'Brien stuck to his guns.

'There are two uncles,' he said. 'Ask and you'll find I'm right.'

So I did ask my mother, and to my astonishment the facts proved correct. My Uncle George had died before I was born and I had no knowledge of him whatsoever.

This message impressed me because it contained evidence which could not possibly have been read from my mind.

How can information that is not present in my memory be gleaned from it?

The only fitting explanation was that my two deceased uncles were speaking to the medium.

13

Poltergeist

After my kind teacher, Mrs Palmer, had suffered a sudden heart attack and passed quietly into the spirit world that she had dearly loved and so conscientiously served, her sisters gifted to me one of her belongings: a pure crystal ball.

I'd never held one before, but when I gazed into it as an experiment, to my great surprise I could see moving pictures. I saw a high-speed train shooting along the tracks, then a Guardsman outside Buckingham Palace — and before I knew it I was fulfilling a prediction she'd made two years previously. She'd seen me entering London's Spiritualist Association of Great Britain — in those days the largest of its kind in the world — at 33 Belgrave Square.

The SAGB had nurtured within its walls, and had connected to it, many famous British mediums: people like Estelle Roberts, Helen Duncan, Coral Polge, Doris Stokes, Doris Collins, Eileen Garrett, Helen Hughes, Gordon

Higginson and Mary Duffy, to name but a few. And now I'd joined their ranks. Working at the Square was challenging because its audiences were cosmopolitan. Many people from overseas travelled to London just to consult the mediums there.

I was in my twenties and this was my first ever appearance in Britain's capital. The work was stressful and difficult because I had to pronounce the foreign words I received from communicators; some people have peculiar names.

But I worked there for only one hectic week packed with private appointments, group sittings and public demonstrations, and it was bedlam. I'd dash out of a meeting, shoot upstairs in the lift and into another room to take sittings. After the first day I knew this kind of pressure wasn't for me, so I decided there and then that I would give a guest demonstration only, whenever I could get to London in my holidays. But the experience was invaluable.

Back home, working in a department store was driving me mad: the hours were long and the pay was pitifully poor. Then I had an idea: part-time store work, part-time mediumship; that seemed quite sensible to me. I decided to give it a try, reasoning that by cutting down on store work I could devote more time to my spiritual work and serving the public.

So I wrote to all the places I served, explaining the position. About thirty-five letters went out around South Wales, and silence followed.

The days dragged by and no word came.

Why didn't they reply?

Was something wrong?

Was £2 a meeting too much to ask for my service expenses? Surely not. But did their committees think it was?

Then I received some of the cruellest shocks of my life.

Nearly every church slammed its doors in my face.

I couldn't believe it.

Had they forgotten the years of unstinting service and dedication I'd given to the spirit world and to the public? Those years during which I'd refused to accept any fees and paid my own travelling expenses, even when out of work? Was this really happening? I couldn't believe they were rejecting me with such bitter statements.

I was terribly hurt.

They had used the medium but they didn't care about the man.

It was like a nightmare and their selfishness haunted me for months.

Why had they done this? Surely they weren't jealous of my success?

Rejected and disillusioned, I renounced all my responsibilities and cancelled further engagements: I got right off the Spiritualist roundabout and took a complete rest. I stopped and took stock of my life and its meaning.

I kept my part-time job going, its meagre wages barely allowing me to survive the wilderness months that followed, months filled with heartache and indecision. I had plenty of time on my hands but I couldn't erase the deep wounds those letters had inflicted upon my spirit. I wandered round the city shops, lost in thought.

What could I do now?

I was an outcast in my own nation.

I'd been charged by a world beyond time and space with a message of love and hope, but my own people had rejected its transmission through me.

In those days, I knew what it was to be a prophet without honour in his own country.

Dejected and alone, I went up onto a mountain to pray. In the silence, I sat on the summit in the midnight mist and gazed at the distant city lights, twinkling under a black sky thick with stars. I took in each lamp-lit house beneath me as far as the eye could see. There were lonely people there; sad and grieving people; people who needed new hope or purpose in their lives; seekers who needed to hear the voice of the spirit. I could bring them that voice. But my enthusiasm was broken, and I yearned to be accepted by my own nation.

What had happened to my dreams, my desire to touch the souls of people in need? They seemed to be slipping away, along with the purpose of my days.

As I stared at the cold stars, a teardrop hit my hand.

Listening to the distant buzz of the city I

realised that I was learning another of life's hard lessons.

Spirituality is rare.

Slowly and painfully, the months tumbled over one another. Winter turned to spring and it took a long time before I felt I wanted to enter a Spiritualist church again. But when I did, a young medium immediately singled me out for a message.

'The sheep have deserted their shepherd,' he said, 'but one day they'll realise that the shepherd was right all along.'

But that was small consolation, for the church people held their narrow-minded ground and refused to open their doors.

Quite by accident (?) I learned that groups of churches had been in telephone contact and unkindly advised each other not to favour me with bookings.

Were they such inadequate people that they seized this opportunity to exercise their self-proclaimed authority over a vulnerable young man?

I thought so.

All communities with strong belief systems live with the ever-present danger of closing in upon themselves: then, in blinkered isolation, their members become Kings and Queens of their own small worlds.

In my quiet times, White Owl drew near and told me over and again, 'You leave as a boy — you will return as a man, with power and understanding.' He seemed to think they would be in touch. Was he right?

I didn't know.

But they say that when God shuts a door, somewhere he opens a window; and in my case He did just that.

I first met psychotherapist the Reverend John Jewsbury, BA, and his wife Valerie, a schoolteacher, at one of my public meetings. They invited me to help out at their Thursday clinics in the Unitarian Church (a free-thinking body of seekers), where I was called upon to counsel certain patients suffering from mental and emotional problems.

The three of us worked well as a team, and it was such a joy to be amongst truly kind people again.

I attended each week for the next two years and sometimes gave patients a private consultation, if the need was there. I tried my best to help manic depressives, schizophrenics, and people suffering from obsessional neurosis.

Remembering a patient called Sue evokes pathos even now. She was completely out of touch with reality: she had bizarre dreams in which her dead mother encouraged her to commit murder. There was very little that psychotherapy could accomplish here, for poor Sue was psychotic.

The spirit people instructed me, 'She'll have to come to a realisation that what she believes is not founded upon fact but upon fantasy. Once this realisation takes place we can get into close proximity to her mind and help her to rebuild reason.'

But sadly, even though spiritual healing did calm her down and bring her more peace of mind than she'd ever known, she remained ill.

One day Mrs Jewsbury got an emergency call for help. 'Stephen, will you come with me to see a Mr Kaye? He says he's possessed by an evil influence and needs urgent help.' I readily agreed and Val and I set off immediately for a poor area of the town near the docks.

We arrived at Mr Kaye's dilapidated house and passed through the weed-bound garden. When I knocked on the door, a heavy-jowled woman tweaked apart the lace curtains and frowned hard. She was obviously fearful — she stepped back instantly. Then a wizened man opened the door, a thumb's width wide.

'Are you the people?' he asked in a low voice.

'Yes.'

We were ushered quickly inside a musty, damp-smelling living-room.

Mr Kaye was small, painfully thin and absolutely positive he was possessed by an evil spirit, and nothing we said could shake that conviction. 'It stops me enjoying myself,' he grumbled, and gave precise details of how 'the demon', as he called it, robbed him of sexual pleasure with his wife.

She sat on a stool by the fire, all hunched over and heavy-hearted. She was large in body and small in expression, and whenever her name was mentioned she tilted her head forward and her long greasy hair removed us from her sight.

I felt so sorry for them.

The evil 'demon' turned out to be nothing more than a portion of her husband's own personality, which he'd suppressed for years. As a lad, his mother had never allowed him to be discourteous, to use foul language or even to think bad thoughts. In short, she dominated him and tried to make him as 'pure' as possible in mind and deed. As a result of this, early in his life he'd reasoned that his bad thoughts couldn't possibly belong to him. They must have originated in someone else — but there *was* no one else, so he created someone: 'the demon'.

Mr Kaye was a classic case of a split personality; a schizophrenic, and he refused to listen.

'But Mr O'Brien can see into the spirit world,' encouraged Mrs Jewsbury, who then turned to me. 'Have you noticed anyone with Mr Kaye?'

'No,' I said. 'I've searched around you and there's no one evil there.'

We took great pains to educate him but his mind was closed: as far as he was concerned he was 'possessed'.

But the sad truth was that Mr Kaye was *obsessed* by the idea of what his mother considered purity to be.

Some parents have a lot to answer for.

Before we left we tried to prevent him from visiting a 'renowned' exorcist. 'God forbid he should be ridiculed by that completely unnecessary experience,' I confided in Val.

However, when we returned the following

week, as arranged, they'd packed up and moved house, and were nowhere to be seen.

Back in the Jewsbury's private psychic development circle, which I led, the spirit people asked me to sit for physical mediumship, which would afford them a closer contact with our world.

I agreed.

After a few sittings held in a blacked-out room lit only by a dim ruby lamp, I soon fell into a trance state. Sometimes I was totally unaware of my surroundings and at others I was semi-conscious of what occurred. The teachings were usually of a highly educational nature. They had to be: three of the sitters had University degrees and the fourth was an undergraduate. But there was still room for fun.

When a young lad called Bobby spoke, he rapped so hard on the antique bookcase glass that it sounded just like a stone pelted at a window and we all jumped out of our skins. We fully expected to find the glass smashed but there wasn't a mark on it.

During another séance, after which I was to stay the night in their home, we heard three deafening thuds high on the ceiling right above me. Bobby again. But I didn't give it another thought until I retired, with nothing on as usual. Imagine my surprise when I laid down on spiky pieces of gravel!

Bobby's ceiling raps had been exactly underneath my bed. What a cheeky lad! 'You'll have me punctured,' I admonished. 'If you must bring gifts, Bobby, bring money!' And he laughed.

But the most remarkable phenomenon we obtained was Transfiguration. Each week, with the ruby lamp shining on my face, the other side took control and withdrew ectoplasm from us then gathered it around my head. They slowly condensed this power into a mist, into which the communicators moved and made their features visible.

The circle reported many successes. But one night I decided to call it a day after an unnerving experience. The misty-skin had formed and I felt my head tilting right back in my chair until my face was pointing at the ceiling. My eyes were tightly shut. In a semi-conscious daze I heard a man speaking through me to the sitters: This is silly, I thought, I'm talking to the ceiling and the sitters are replying.

But after the circle I was stunned when they said *my eyes had been wide open and my head had remained directly facing them when the man had spoken.* 'But that's impossible,' I frowned. 'My face was pointed upwards and my eyes were closed.'

'No, your eyes were open,' they countered, 'and what's more they were light blue, not brown.'

I was shocked.

If my eyes had been open, surely I'd have seen the ruby lamp and my friends looking at me?

But I hadn't.

The only explanation was that my spirit-head must have exteriorised then tilted backwards and faced the ceiling, while my physical head stayed facing front. I'd been conscious in my spirit-head and not in its physical counterpart.

After this, I decided to keep firmly in control of myself, so these sittings were suspended.

But that didn't mean my work for the other side had stopped. Far from it: in fact, it steadily increased and I was called upon to deal with a constant stream of new experiences. One that sticks in my mind concerned our neighbour, Willy, who lived next-door with his two sisters.

One day our front door crashed open and one of Willy's frightened sisters stood gasping for air in our hallway. 'Please come quickly!' she gushed emotionally. 'It's Willy, he's collapsed blue-faced on the stairs! He's fighting for breath — please help us!'

My father and I dashed next-door and lifted Willy up the stairs and onto his bed. I raised his feet above the level of his waist to aid blood flow but I could see what the others couldn't. Willy's spirit had passed. What we witnessed emotionally was only the last throes of the body's nervous systems fighting valiantly to keep alive. But Willy had died.

They sent for a priest immediately but he was too late. Nevertheless he performed the last rites to ease the anguish of Willy's sisters. Everyone thought that was the end of Willy's adventures on earth; but we were quite mistaken.

The following night I was sitting quietly by the fireside reading a book, when my hackles rose: a strange presence had entered the room. Then I gasped in surprise. It was Willy. His body hadn't been committed yet but here he was gliding through our living-room wall, which joined us to next-door.

Angrily he shouted at me, 'Why can't they hear me in there? They're ignoring me! What's the game?'

So I had to tell a 'dead' man that he had 'died'.

I explained it all very calmly to him then advised him to call for help to be taken to meet some of his family over there. But he shrugged off my suggestion, and still rather annoyed he ran off through the wall, presumably to shout at his sisters again.

A few days later, one bright morning I saw Willy's brother sitting on a bench near town — and as I passed I had to rub my eyes to see if I was dreaming: there was Willy too, sitting right beside him. He obviously had no intention of moving on to better things. He was keeping to his normal routines and no one over there could interfere with that, of course. So off they both went to the pub — one in the spirit and the other in the flesh. I didn't hear from Willy again, but I'm sure he reached his spirit relatives safely after his short spell on earth.

As time slipped on, Dad and I passed through our darkest patch yet. We'd never got along but now our relationship was so bad that I'd moved upstairs to get out of his way. I now stayed in my bedroom. We lived in the same house but didn't share the same space.

He'd taken a swipe at me on a few occasions; and even though I was paying him £16 a week from my meagre £21 wage packet (and I was buying my own food on top) one night he stormed up the stairs in temper, switched off the radiator and removed my one-bar electric fire. 'You're burning my money!' he shouted.

He then banned me from taking a daily shower and from using the washing machine twice a week, for the same reason.

Like his mother he was mean. The 'sins' of the parents can certainly be passed on to their children, and down to the coming generations.

Since my mother's death he'd tolerated my interest in psychic matters, though he'd never approved of it, and had said so, frequently and loudly. But I stood my ground.

'This is *my* life, Dad, not yours — and I intend to live it *my* way, not yours!'

This aggravated the situation even more.

I'd tried everything in my power to get a peaceful life but it was no use: it was a pure personality clash, impossible to resolve. Silently I vowed that before I'd tolerate any more harassment I'd move out and sit on an orange-box in the street — if that was the only way to be let alone.

Someone, somewhere, must have been listening to me, for that's almost exactly what happened.

I'd already received a letter from the Council Housing Department informing me I was now at the top of their list after a two-year wait, which was just as well because while walking home a different way one evening I spotted a furniture van outside some maisonettes. I now realise I was inspired to see that place; I'd never walked past it in my life before. I immediately applied for the tenancy and within two days it was granted.

I told my father I'd be moving on the day before I left, and I think he believed I'd be back in a week, but I knew differently.

I threw my possessions into thirteen black plastic bags (mostly books and clothes) and some friends helped me to walk to my new flat, a quarter of a mile away in the Brynmelyn district.

So there I was, installed in the first home of my own, albeit a shabby rented one. I sat on the floor gazing at the bare walls and carpetless tiles. Everything would have to be scrubbed and disinfected. There was such a lot of dirt everywhere — the previous tenants obviously weren't as particular as I was. So I spent my last few pounds on cleaning materials and then I was penniless.

I was sitting there, wondering why it had all come to this, when it struck me that my silent wish had all but come true.

I had absolutely nothing.

No money, no chairs or furniture, no table, not even a stove. I didn't even possess an orange-box to sit on. I had an empty, echoing flat, my single bed, and that was about it.

But despite this, I felt happy because at least I could come and go as I pleased without constant harassment. At long last I had a place of my own and the peace of mind I'd prayed for so avidly.

But then strange things started to happen around me and I began to realise that I wasn't alone. My flat had another occupant and he wasn't of this world.

I'd moved in with a poltergeist.

On my first night I decided to sleep on the floor and lit a few night-light candles for company. But as it turned out, I didn't need them because the air buzzed and hummed with psychic activity, making it impossible for me to close my eyes. People were peering at me and sneering; but worse was to come.

Lights were flicked off and on, and wire coat hangers were thrown across the landing upstairs; and from a spare bedroom there came a man's loud coughing and the sound of his footsteps walking the floor above. The next night, this troubled spirit physically ripped a tapestry from the wall and tried to pull the bedclothes off me.

The following day, I asked a friend to sleep over until I'd tried to 'clear' the house. Little did I know it would take three weeks to accomplish this; it would be a long, difficult haul.

Just when I thought I'd frightened off the intruder, I discovered some of my important papers scattered all over the living-room floor, and I clearly heard a man's voice saying, 'We'll get him tonight.' Then I caught sight of the culprit. There he stood as large as life, screeching out that I should leave his property at once.

He said his name was Tom and that he was the rightful tenant. I showed selfish Tom the rent book but that didn't do much good.

'*Get out of my house*!' he screamed until he was blue in the face. '*Get out or I'll do something I'll regret*!' And with that he snarled and disappeared into the storeroom, where I heard him talk with two other spirit people.

Once again I'd failed to realise that my psychic powers had provided the spirit people with an energy-boost, vibrant strength that enabled them to create havoc around me. And of course, my annoyance must have projected negative energy into the atmosphere for Tom's use.

But I was determined he wasn't going to win. This was *my* home now, not his; and he would have to see sense and leave.

White Owl proved most helpful, not in removing Tom and the others — I had to do that — but in the advice he gave me.

'Ask about the property,' he inspired, and 'This man had a police record when on earth.'

These were the two clues that helped me to clear my home.

Enquiries revealed that my flat bad been a troubled spot. There was once an active prostitute living there and then a family who kept a horse in the lounge, followed by people who were in and out of prison all their lives. Little wonder the psychic atmosphere was disturbed!

When I thought about my guide's words, I guessed that selfish Tom's involvement with the police would be the chink in his armour, so I determined to make full use of it — I had to; I'd tried everything else and still he wouldn't budge.

So when next he manifested I threatened him with calling the police and gave him twenty-four hours to move out or else. I found it difficult to make it sound convincing — but it worked. Tom and his companions left my home and were helped to find their rightful place in the spirit world. Gradually, my little maisonette transformed itself from a psychic nightmare into a relative haven of peace.

But these first days on my own were extremely difficult.

I was now out of work and had no money. My stomach began to rumble and I lost weight. My clothes started to fray and there was nothing new to replace them. Life was gloomy and my days were full of uncertainty and a deep insecurity about making my own way in the world.

On top of all this, back came that chillingly haunting sensation of 'not belonging on earth'.

Living almost as a recluse, I was swamped by a devastating sense of loneliness. This wasn't a personal, physical loneliness. I'd long-since discovered that the most important relationship I'd ever have is the one that I have with myself — no matter where I go or what I do, I cannot ever get away from myself and therefore this relationship comes first, and all others are secondary. No: this loneliness was the blackest shroud of universal aloneness I had ever experienced.

I felt as though my mind was expanding, stretching outwards to the very darkest Edge of Time, and with this expansion came the fullest knowledge that I did not belong on earth.

I felt lost and far away from my true home: the Realms of Spirit.

In these sombre hours I was told by my other world companions, 'We cannot promise you true happiness in your world, only in ours.' And I fully understood them.

Stranded on some tiny speck of cosmic rock and dust, washed by pale blue seas, I was only visiting this planet.

These reflections were interrupted by the growling of my empty stomach and the cold bare floors and walls of my shabby flat. How would I manage to survive from day to day?

When I turned out my pockets, they were empty; and I didn't know where the next meal was coming from.

14

Prediction

All through Christmastime the snow never stopped falling. In my bare living-room I sat at the window and admired the crystal rooftops. All the nearby slums had vanished and in their place was a glistening white blanket of silence.

Every night my tipsy old neighbour, Muriel, went to the pub across the road and she was determined the snowdrifts wouldn't stop her from whetting her ancient whistle. Two boozy men came over and shovelled a pathway to the block of flats then slipped and slid her ample form over the ice so that she could down her usual nightcap.

Afterwards, they carried her home swaying and singing at the top of her slurred voice, '*I did it My-y Way-y!*'

As usual I went to the cupboard and, like Mother Hubbard's, it was bare. I had no money, no food, and on top of this, no decent footwear to brave the elements.

It was one of the worst winters Britain had

seen in decades. Thick snow covered cars and obliterated houses and gardens. Transport came to a standstill. Farmlands and villages were cut off from civilisation and phone lines fell in the drifts. And I was crunching through the snow wearing my only pair of shoes, which leaked through splits in either foot. I wrapped two plastic bags around my feet to try to prevent the ice from seeping through, but this failed.

I contacted the Social Security Department (known locally as the SS) for some new footwear but they refused.

How hard and bitter red tape can seem when you're genuinely in need. So I suffered in silence... until the day I exploded at their staff. In the midst of my shouting, a feisty girl at the back of the queue yelled out, 'Don't bother, love! If you dropped dead in front of them, they'd ask for your death certificate to prove it!' And an elderly woman said, 'God help him, he's a genuine case, too.' Everyone clucked in agreement.

Well, you're on your own again, Stephen, I thought — and I was. So I trudged home to my ice-cold flat again. I kept saying to people, 'It's never been so bad, I don't have tuppence to call my own.'

Then one morning I awoke drowsily from a deep sleep and rubbed my eyes. Was I dreaming? There on my bedside table were two old pennies, both out of circulation. They were gifts from the spirit world: one was an English King George V, dated 1920, and the other was an Irish penny dated 1937. I was thrilled with them and kept flipping them over to delight my friends, until a spirit voice said, 'We took them from an old grave.' I immediately let them drop.

'You might have told me sooner,' I complained. 'I'd have washed them first!'

How much more helpful it would have been if my spirit friends had brought me £200; but of course, this was another valuable spiritual lesson:

I knew what it was to be destitute.

Reluctantly, I realised that because work was so scarce I'd have to try to return to the theatre, which was something I didn't want to do; I'd left the world of make-believe far behind me to enter the real world of spiritual values. But what else could I do?

I had to support myself, and I didn't intend to starve.

So I wrote away and was fortunate enough to be accepted by an agency that got its clients television walk-on parts; only we weren't referred to as walk-ons, we were Supporting Artistes, if you please.

It was tough going, too: whenever there was work I'd be up at 4 a.m. then off in someone's car to the Cardiff studios for a costume call at 6 a.m. I did only three assignments, I think; and on one of these we were filmed on a freezing cold mountaintop and we had to pretend it was a warm summer's day. But it was the depths of winter with hail lashing down on us. Even though the countryside had been lit by huge orange arc lights to create a warm sunset effect, we Supporting Artistes were perishing cold and dozens of us huddled together in the long grass. Shivering and ill-at-ease I remember thinking to myself: I must be mad. But I wasn't: I was just flat broke.

Filming work was very sparse and assignments were so irregular that I waited months between those few calls. So, never one to vegetate, in my spare time I helped out at a local playgroup.

About fifteen toddlers attended at the YMCA and they were full of beans. It was easy to see why their mothers left them with someone else for four hours. They'd scoot around in pedal-cars, bumping into my shins and screeching with delight; and when storytime arrived I'd be swamped by children clambering up over my back and shoulders.

But this was charity work, without payment.

It was then that White Owl said to me, 'How can you help those who stand in great need, if you have never experienced harsh conditions yourself?'

Of course, he was right: I had to attain the spiritual quality of Acceptance and the Grace to go with it.

I turned to the creative arts to fill my hours and recorded some of my thoughts in poetry: it was a soul-stirring exercise that helped me to understand my life and most of all myself. Even though I was down to my last twenty pence I managed to retain my sanity and inner peace.

But then I had to borrow money, for news came that my grandfather was dying.

I immediately travelled to see Grancha Price. Entering his silent bedroom, I was shocked to find him just a shadow of the man he once was. Nana was desperately upset and we both felt great sympathy for him: his cheeks had hollowed out and his eyes had sunk well back into their sockets. He had cancer; and I couldn't help remembering my mother and her passing.

When I took his hand the old man opened his tired eyes.

'Hello, Stephen,' he said, and a smile lit up his face: he'd recognised me.

Weakly he muttered, 'I've seen them, Stephen. All my family's waiting for me across the river...'

'I know,' I replied softly. 'Why are you fighting this, Grancha? Why don't you just lie back and relax?'

His lips half-flickered; he knew what I meant.

Just then, the wall behind him faded away and in its place there came a sphere of luminous golden light. Within this stood a beautiful young woman in a silver robe, her arms were outstretched and her long dark hair cascaded over her shoulders: she was the loveliest sight. She radiated such purity. Smiling at me, she spoke:

'I'm waiting for him, Stephen. Two days.' And with that the light faded and the wall was back in its place.

But who was she?

Not wanting to disturb Grancha further, I didn't mention her but placed his hands inside the warm covers. Then I reached over and kissed his forehead. 'Goodnight; God bless you,' I said, just as I had done to my mother.

Exactly two days later, Grancha died.

Weeks after this I heard a spirit woman say to me, 'I am Myra. I met your grandfather.' Enquiries proved revealing. Myra was his daughter, an aunt of mine whom I'd never known because she'd been stillborn about forty years previously.

How comforting to know that she met him; and I like to think she was also there when his lovely wife, my Nana, joined them both a short while afterwards.

By now, Wales had woken up to the fact that I was still alive and mediating. Glowing reports of my meetings started to appear in the psychic press, and suddenly I was overwhelmingly in demand again. The Spiritualists are certainly quite unpredictable folk: even though I'd never thought of myself as one of them (I needed no label), they'd now decided to welcome me again and hail me as a 'personality' virtually overnight: I was once more warmly embraced by my own nation, and no longer outcast.

And as my spirit guide had correctly foretold, I had returned as a man 'with Power and Understanding'.

Coaxed by the spirit world I began travelling further afield with my work (something I'd never wanted to do!) and eventually I became a nationally recognised visionary within the Spiritualist Movement. People started booking small halls for me in which to demonstrate my mediumship. Then I was invited to teach in England at the Arthur Findlay College of Psychic Science in Stansted Hall in Essex — thought of then as the magnificent stately home of Spiritualism. The place reverberated with peace and power and top-class mediums, from whom I learned valuable lessons about psychic science and the presentation of mediumship.

'I could live here in the manner to which I'm unaccustomed!' I wittily quipped. But the work was extremely taxing: I knuckled down to private consultations, lecturing, teaching and demonstrating my mediumship to students from all parts of the world.

On the last night of one week, everyone had had such a good course that they stood up and sang the Welsh national anthem in a moving tribute to my work. As the beautiful melody rose and the words 'Land of My Fathers, how fair is Thy Fame' rang out, my throat clogged with emotion.

They applauded loudly. It seemed I had 'arrived' as a recognised medium.

Back in Wales, my public engagements were increasing and other requests started pouring in too. The first funeral I took was that of a pensioner called 'old May'. I restlessly turned in bed thinking about the service, which was to take place on the following morning. What on earth could I say about her? I'd have to be careful for she was such a crotchety old girl in her last days, probably because of the pain she suffered. Nevertheless, everyone knew she'd always been a difficult person. Then suddenly I heard some aggressive spirit-raps in the dark bedroom. There was a loud thump on the floor and from within the mattress came a dull thud. Startled, I turned around and saw crotchety 'old May' standing directly in front of me. She furrowed her brow then poked me hard in the ribs with her walking stick. Her voice was commanding.

'See that you get it *right*! And do it *properly*!' she ordered.

But she needn't have worried; with the spirit people's inspiration the service flowed beautifully. But I still smile when I think of her visit, even today.

Demand for my services steadily increased and this led to a public meeting being organised by twelve dedicated seekers at a pavilion on the seafront.

I was closely involved with it and suggested that the monies raised be given to two charities, the Friends of the Blind and a local handicapped children's society.

When the news got out and the big day arrived, my telephone rang. On the other end was a television producer requesting an interview. 'What, *live*?' I gasped.

'No, we'll record it for later transmission.'

I turned him down flat.

But he persisted and wouldn't take no for an

answer.

Some media people think I'll be flattered by their interest and will therefore not only bow to their requests, but also be grateful for them.

Wrong.

He wore himself out talking.

I've always held deep reservations about the media: presenters and producers often have hidden agendas; many aim to ridicule or sensationalise. But in the end, just to placate the poor man I agreed to an interview, provided it would be conducted with dignity.

They sent a car and as quick as flash I was chauffeured to their studios, where they whisked me down a warren of corridors and into a make-up room.

On the set we were counted down and silence fell about us as three huge cameras slid silently around like menacing robots...

When I left the TV station its switchboards jammed with callers. Outside, my chauffeur smiled at my bright orange face: I still had the make-up on. I called out, 'Home James! And don't spare the horses!' And we sped down the motorway to try to get me to the public meeting on time.

The next thing I knew we were desperately trying to find a parking space outside the pavilion: the meeting was a sell-out and people were milling about and squabbling over seats we didn't have — but eventually I pushed my way through to the dressing-rooms.

The other two renowned mediums, Gordon

Higginson from England and Mary Duffy from Scotland, were pacing about like caged lions, while I tried to relax quietly. Each medium has his or her own way of tuning-in to the spirit people, I've found. Mary was chain-smoking like a chimney.

Suddenly the door burst open and a white-faced organiser cried out, 'It's like a mad-house out there!' Then she took a huge breath and flung herself bravely back into the fray.

The 700-strong audience sounded like a football crowd before a match and my stomach tightened. Worse still, I couldn't get a link with the spirit world — and I was to go first.

I began to feel anxious. Had the trip to the studios exhausted me? I couldn't go on stage without a message for someone. But not a psychic sight or sound entered my mind. Then we were called to commence and the door opened and a wall of excited voices nearly bowled me over. The atmosphere was filled with electric anticipation — every seat was taken. A more than capacity audience stood around the walls, sat on tables and there were no aisles left. This was to be my first big meeting.

Hundreds of eyes stared at me as I gingerly took my seat. There were people all around me, to the left and right; some of them had touched my jacket and called out greetings as I'd made my way through the crowd. And still I had no contact in my mind.

As I looked about the hall I wondered if I could possibly meet the needs of these folk. What was it they expected of me, of us? So many demands, so many hopes. Could we satisfy at least some of them?

The deafening applause petered out, and still no voices reached me.

The £500 we raised was presented to the charities and the capacity crowd lifted the roof with clapping and cheering. I'd kept my promise to help people in need but now I was in need of help myself.

Where were my voices?

Why couldn't I hear them?

Through the microphones the chairperson said, 'Ladies and gentlemen, representing Wales tonight, will you please welcome: Mr Stephen O'Brien.'

I didn't need to get up — the thunderous applause lifted me from my seat.

I stepped nervously to the microphone... and suddenly a spirit woman said, 'We're Gwen's mother and father.' (Thank God; *at last!*')

After a few nervous comments I delivered the link, which was instantly accepted, and the evidence flowed without fault. After that, my confidence burgeoned and my demonstration rolled along fine. One message followed another: husbands were reunited with their wives, daughters with their mothers, neighbours with their friends. It all went smoothly: the other side had not let me down.

When I resumed my seat the audience clapped and cheered and people whistled out from the back of the hall.

The event was a resounding success.

Later on, I watched a video recording of my television interview that millions had seen; and what an horrendous experience that was!

The following week, with much public acclaim (and with twelve colleagues) I opened the Swansea Psychic Centre in the city, and dedicated it to the service of those in need and to people seeking greater spiritual knowledge. I became the Vice-President of this educational establishment, and for the next few years conducted psychic workshops, took lectures and discussion groups on spiritual subjects, and trained mediums to develop their powers to serve mankind.

The Centre's audiences grew so large that we often had to turn people away — so we moved to bigger premises in the city. Remaining faithful to the decision I'd made when younger, I supported many worthy charities through my Psychic Centre meetings, including Save the Children, Mother Teresa of Calcutta's Mission, an Ethiopian famine appeal, local hospitals needing oxygen tents for ailing babies, and societies for the blind. I also raised money for a school of physically handicapped children. The thirty pupils needed their own hydrotherapy pool. Their head teacher told me, 'If you could only see the children's faces when the water gives them their freedom, you'd realise why we want our own pool. At present I have to choose one handicapped child from thirty every fortnight to travel fifteen miles to the nearest pool. Which one would you choose?'

I couldn't say. They were all beautiful souls but their disabilities were great. Little James, who was lying on the floor because he was unable to support his own weight, looked just seven years old, but in fact he was sixteen.

It was a great privilege to help them.

My days were now full to the brim with organising seminars, teaching, counselling distressed people, and demonstrating my mediumship. I didn't have time for a private life, and personal relationships didn't get a look in. Like a priest I was married to a Cause, and my thoughts were entirely centred on spiritual work. And my presence at the Psychic Centre attracted the interest of practically every well-known medium in Britain, all of whom visited and served the people of South Wales at packed-out meetings. It was not uncommon for dozens of people to be turned away at each event.

Although the organisation was now well-established, and its work, as well as my own, had gained national recognition, somewhere in the back of my mind a strange feeling stirred within me. I became aware that a new stage of my life was about to begin, and I told my colleagues of my unrest.

Then — quite suddenly — I knew I should move away from Wales.

I now see that this inspiration was given to me by the spirit world: I just 'knew' I had to work in pastures new. I'd made some good friends in the north of England during my nationwide travels, and this seemed to be the place that both attracted and called to me: there was spiritual work to do up north.

My invisible friends were quick to confirm this: they also showed their remarkable powers of reading the time-stream by delivering an accurate prediction from it. And this was how it came about:

Following my inspiration I registered my council maisonette on the national exchange lists on 14th August and on that same night two friends declared, 'Let's have a table-tilt.'

Without further ado we sat in dimmed light, our fingers lightly touching a wooden table. The other side immediately sprang into action and the table leapt up and began rocking and swaying to and fro with great vigour. Then it tapped out a message for me, one tap for each letter of the alphabet:

Within ten months
you will move to Newcastle-upon-Tyne,
in England, to continue your work.

The table became still.

There wasn't another movement — the séance was over.

I informed my Psychic Centre colleagues about this prediction and began training more vigorously the up-and-coming mediums to shoulder my responsibilities in preparation for the move.

Time passed, and I heard nothing from the

housing departments.

Just before the ten months was up I said to White Owl, 'You've never been wrong before but you are *this* time.'

But once again the spirit world had the last laugh.

That evening, the telephone rang. I shouldn't have been at home but my lift was late. I answered it and on the other end of the line was a man's voice.

'I'm on long distance,' he said. 'Do you still want to move to England?'

My heart jumped into my throat. Could the prediction be coming true?

The rough voice came again. 'Hello? Do you want to come to Newcastle?'

'But what made you ring me?' I asked.

'I saw your address at my local Housing Offices.' And then came the mind-shattering statement: *'I've only just read about your details.'*

But my guide had predicted this move ten months previously.

How could the spirit world have known?

I looked at the calendar: the date was 13th June — just one day *within* the ten months foretold by my friend.

White Owl was right.

The next few weeks were hectic and exhausting. Bit by bit my home was packed away in cardboard boxes. Because I was still living below subsistence level, I sold some items to rent a three-ton truck; then six friends helped me load my possessions into it.

283

Within two hours there was nothing left of my little home — just bare floors and hollow, empty rooms. Moved by gratitude, I touched its walls and gazed around it for the last time and found myself whispering, 'Thanks, we've served each other well.'

Then I closed the door and hurried quickly down the stairs and out into the rain, biting my lip.

Three drivers sat in the truck cabin, as I hugged my friends and kissed goodbye to the hills and valleys of Wales.

With tears trickling down my face I entered the back of the truck and closed the doors.

It had all happened so quickly.

I couldn't believe it.

And so began the most bizarre journey I've ever made. For the next ten hours I sat in semi-darkness, coughing and spluttering from exhaust fumes, until 400 miles later I arrived in northern England. Then like royalty I was slowly lowered by the hydraulic van lift to a burst of applause from my northern friends, who made me kiss the ground that was to be my new home.

PART THREE

Rays of Spiritual Light

If you walk in the Light
your heart is lit.

If you breathe in the Light
your soul is filled with radiance.

When you live in the Light
you become the Light,
and its rays will shine out
to relieve others of their darkness.

Stephen O'Brien

15

Passing Through the Veil

'I'm afraid to die, Stephen,' whispered my friend
Pat, who was a nurse.

'Don't be,' I said. 'There's another life awaiting
you. There's nothing to fear. It's just a crossing,
an awakening to a New World.'

Her tired body had been ravaged by cancer for
over two years: her hair had fallen out, her skin
had become pale and drawn and yet despite all
this she kept a sparkle in her eyes.

My words seemed to comfort her but she was
truly set at peace only when I described the
presence of her long-dead mother, who arrived
surrounded by rays of golden spiritual light.

'She's holding out her hands to you and saying,
"I'm offering the hand of friendship",' I said.

'Oh, Stephen,' beamed Pat, 'Mother always
used that phrase.'

This knowledge eased her suffering and
calmed her anxious mind.

'She promises to meet you at death's gateway,'
I continued; and she kept her word when Pat

made her transition a short while afterwards.

No matter where I've lived or worked, countless people have wanted to know exactly what will happen to them when they 'die' — not only at the point of their 'death' but also on their arrival in the next world. I do my best to offer them spiritual knowledge and, I hope, some comfort.

You 'die' every night when you go to sleep. Just as soon as your physical body has relaxed, the spirit body within you starts to loosen from it and you leave your sleeping form and can travel into the spirit world. On some evenings you may not travel out. On these occasions your spirit body exteriorises a little way from your physical frame, but remains close to it in a state of semi-sleep. This gives your spirit body the chance to absorb the invisible health-giving cosmic energies all around it, and channel them naturally to your physical self.

One morning when I awoke I couldn't move my left arm: it felt as heavy as lead and was freezing cold and numb. Then I watched clairvoyantly a dark shadow of its exact shape and size floating down and aligning itself with my physical arm in the bed. Circulation increased and my 'dead' arm woke up.

On another occasion, before I could move my body upon waking, I only *thought* about taking a shower and immediately shot out through the bedroom wall, feet first, horizontal in my spirit body, and landed in the bathroom. Taken aback, I gasped, then shot back into the bed. That was the quickest shower I'd ever taken!

I've also seen the spirit-forms of people whom I knew personally: they appeared to me when they were fast asleep, but I knew they hadn't passed over because they didn't radiate a bright psychic light, as permanent spirit visitors do.

I've seen strangers in this form, too: one bright starry night when the sky was black, cold and deep, I was wandering along some clifftops and a 'sleeper' appeared in the air about thirty feet above the whispering waters. He must have wondered what the sea was like and been instantly transported there by his thoughts.

Once we realise we can project out of our physical bodies and still remain conscious, it's only one small step to acknowledge that the seat of consciousness is not the brain, and that we will survive the dissolution of the body.

Thousands of people have reported out-of-the-body experiences in all kinds of circumstances; many have undergone them on operating tables and then returned to describe with remarkable accuracy all that transpired when they were clinically 'dead'.

But exactly what happens to us when we pass over?

Sudden deaths, such as accidents, cause many people to go into a state of concussion. Just as the earthly body is knocked unconscious, likewise the spirit suffers from temporary sleep. But this soon passes and awareness returns in the new world.

When long and protracted illnesses are

suffered, the passing is taken more gently and loved ones in the spirit realms gather to meet travellers as they cross the threshold of death to life.

Every transition is different; but in each case there is no pain involved. Pain belongs to the physical form only and it isn't present in the energy body.

There are people over there who watch for new arrivals, whether they pass over suddenly or gradually. These trained watchers are especially evident in world disasters such as wars or large-scale tragedies.

People in states of coma are already passing in and out of their physical bodies: as the casket sleeps, the spirit is released into worlds beyond earth. When the Nazarene said 'Lazarus, come forth!' he called back a wandering spirit, but the body wasn't dead. If death had occurred then no reanimation could have taken place. When asked about Lazarus the Nazarene is reported to have said, 'He is not dead: he sleepeth.'

The same principle applies to people on life-support systems. If the spirit has vacated permanently then the person has 'died' and the body is kept 'alive' only in a mechanical sense. Switch off the machine and the body dies because the spirit is gone.

The most qualified people to talk about the process of 'dying' are those who have experienced it; they alone can speak with authority. Through my mediumship I've obtained several of these accounts but the following two may interest us most because they come from my mother and my spirit guardian. They dictated their stories to me and I recorded them.

There is no need to fear the Dark Angel called Death, for he isn't a Dark Angel at all: he's the Brightest One.

Here is my mother's passing as seen from her viewpoint:

You were all gathered around the bed. I don't know if you knew that I could see you all, but I could. My old body was wracked with pain and numbed by morphine to combat the agony of the cancer, but my inner body was alive and well.

My physical eyes were half shut but my spirit eyes were wide open. Gradually, as my strength ebbed away, I slowly lost sight of the bedroom: it just faded away like a scene from a film, and superimposed over it was another scene forming. As earth faded out, my New World faded in.

I hadn't gone anywhere. I was still lying in the bed but I was losing sight of you all. I was so worried I'd never see you again but someone inside my mind said, 'Lie still. Be at peace. All is well.'

Your physical forms became heavy and grey to my vision. A mist appeared around you. Then inside this mist, a light began to shine. As earth faded out, your physical bodies turned into a grey mist and I then saw your spirit forms, much lighter and brighter.

The bedroom wasn't duplicated in my new world where I'd arrived. Instead I was in a sort of light-coloured room. I heard you crying and watched you go. I was alone in this room. I couldn't move. I suppose if I'd wanted to, I could have, but the newness of it all made me lie still, as the voice had asked.

Then someone — I thought it was one of you boys — came into the room again. I studied the misty grey form with its light inside it but I couldn't recognise who it was. But someone must have been watching closely because that voice spoke to me again. 'It is Mary, your best friend,' it said. Then my vision cleared and I could just make out her features. I saw the rosary beads she was running through her fingers and by some kind of miracle I heard her thoughts. They were quick and clear and packed with love for me.

And then, I knew I had died... Mary was asking for my soul to rise to God and to be loved and taken care of there and I remember thinking, 'It's finished now. Please God, no more suffering.' And my next thought was, 'Please God, take care of my boys. Look after them for me — and Ron, too. Don' t let them be alone.'

And I thought of the grandchildren and John's wife and all the others I'd loved.

Then I wondered where you were, son; and that voice spoke up again saying, 'Stephen's being comforted. Lie still now, close your eyes and relax, Beatrice. Trust and sleep. Close your eyes and sleep.'

And I closed my eyes to rest for a few minutes, and then I must have lost consciousness, or the person belonging to that voice must have put me to sleep; I'm not sure. Anyway, after that I didn't remember anything until I woke up a while later.

When I opened my eyes I was in a pleasant rest room. It was very spacious, with pale lemon walls and french windows overlooking a garden full of roses and trees. The sun was bright. I think there was an orchard beyond the garden. The colours were beautiful, very bright and pleasant.

The room had three other beds in it but they were empty. But I wasn't alone. A middle-aged nurse came through the french windows from the garden and said, 'Hello, Mrs O'Brien, how are you feeling now?'

'Very well, thank you,' I said. 'All my pain's gone. I feel at peace for the first time in months.'

She took my hand, and when she did I felt a wonderful peaceful feeling as though she'd given me energy. I can't explain exactly what I felt, but I now know it was healing energy. 'All your suffering's over now, Mrs O'Brien,' she said as she smiled at me. 'There'll be no more pain or tears. And just as soon as you like you can get up and walk with me in the garden. The roses are gorgeous. Would you like to come?'

I said I would and pulled back the crisp sheets, expecting to have pain when I swung my legs over the bedside, but there wasn't any.

And when I stood up, with her help, I could stand straight: I wasn't pulled over by my operation scars like I was on earth.

We walked to the window together. But on the way this nurse, whose name was Totty, must have heard my thoughts because she smiled reassuringly and said, 'You're worried about your family but you needn't be, my dear. They're quite safe, and all is well.'

'Have they had the funeral yet?' I asked. 'What time is it? How long have I been here?'

'Now don't fear,' said Totty, 'they haven't had the funeral yet; and there's no time over here, as you'll soon learn. So I can't tell you how long you slept. But I don't think it was very long. Look at the gardens now. Aren't they beautiful?' And she showed me the fresh flowers, and the birds were singing their songs as though the sun had just come up. It was the loveliest view I'd ever seen — just what I'd imagined heaven to be like.

Totty must have heard my thoughts again because I instantly remembered the family, especially Claire and Jonathan, for Totty said, 'They're all well on earth; and just as soon as you're ready we'll go back, shall we?'

'Can you take me back?' I asked eagerly.

'Only on a visit, my dear — and that isn't my work. But shortly someone will come and go with you to see them all on earth. I promise you.'

And that was how my mother entered the next life.

But White Owl, my Native American spirit guide, arrived on the other side in a completely different way; and in his poignant recollection he also reveals how he first learned of his future work as a guardian soul:

The love I held for my woman, Running Deer, was well known in our tribe. She was lithe and beautiful: her eyes outshone the brightest stars and her smile welcomed me each time we met.

Other men consorted with many women but I kept only to her. She meant life itself to me and this caused jealousy among the other men of my day. One, whose name was Tomahawk, wanted Running Deer as his own. We had often fought for her love and each time she expressed it only to me.

One day she and I had been bathing by the river near to the waterfall when, unknown to us, Tomahawk crept up behind me as I stood gazing across the banks at the woodland. As swift as the lightning that travels across the heavens, Tomahawk struck me a fatal blow at the base of my skull with his hunting hatchet. I was told these things after I passed from the earth plane — at the time, I just felt a shuddering crack of numbing sound in my neck. Then blackness overcame me.

Before I lost those last seconds of life, I felt my body falling into the river. I heard Running Deer scream and cry out. But the murderer had taken flight on his horse.

I swam to the bank and clambered up, exhausted by the blow, trying to gain my breath once again. I saw Running Deer wade into the current and drag something from the river's grip. She struggled and panted for air as she pulled the heavy object onto the grass nearby.

I shouted out to her, 'I'm all right! He's gone now!' But she took no notice.

Still struggling, she didn't even see me running towards her. But as I approached, I saw what she was kneeling by, crying and mourning over — it was my blood-stained body.

I sat on the riverbank, dumbfounded by the thought of my own death.

And then a brilliant light flashed over the moving waters and I saw the radiant form of my great-grandfather floating across the river. He didn't walk, but glided in the light. His ancient features that I dimly recalled as a boy were just as I'd always remembered them. He spoke to me.

'Take my hands, little one,' he said. 'The river of life has finished with you now. There's nothing you can do here for this woman. She must mourn her loss; but for you it is gain. A new sun will shine on you now.'

'But you have been long in the spirit world,' I answered him.

'Yes, and you have now joined me. Come, little one... the memory of White Owl is now a subject for fable and storytelling around the fire of the young ones.'

'But I can't leave Running Deer,' I protested. He gripped my arm, holding me firmly at his side. 'I can't go yet,' I said; and he released his grip.

I walked over to her and knelt beside her weeping form. I touched her bronzen skin once more. I kissed her slender neck... but she felt none of these things, and I was distressed. When I called her name, she did not hear my voice. Then I was aware of great-grandfather nearby.

'You cannot do any good here now,' he told me. 'You are a medium who speaks with the spirits of our ancestors. You should know it is not all who possess such a treasured gift.'

And deeply vexed, my tears joining those of my beloved woman, I agreed to follow him.

'Do not fear,' he said; 'I'll bring you to see her soon... just as soon as you understand.'

And together we floated out across the river and into a great engulfing light. The power and brilliance of it swamped my vision, obliterating the scene I'd just left, as I watched Running Deer drag my lifeless form onto my horse, Silver Cloud, and gallop away to give the news to our people.

'Do not be afraid,' said great-grandfather, 'the light will heal you. It will soothe your soul, my son. Just breathe it in.' And I did so; and then it faded away and a new countryside came into view.

I questioned my friend. 'We are at the Hunting-Grounds?'

'They are everywhere,' he smiled. 'But in this small part of the Great Spirit's land you and I shall sit and talk awhile. There is much I have to teach you.'

And we both sat on the dewy moss and he told me many wondrous things. He spoke of my new life, its ways, and the future that he said lay before me. He introduced me to my brother, Lame Wolf, who had passed into spirit before I was born.

'Why does the sun stay high in the mountain sky, grandfather?'

'Because there is no setting of it here, White Owl. Here there is rest for those who seek it but no darkness of the night. Come now, we have spoken enough: I must take you on a journey.'

'Have we to travel very far?'

'No, my son. We are going to the top of the mountain.' And he pointed out the highest peak above us.

'It'll be a good two days walk.'

'No, it will be shorter than the time it takes the lightning to jump the great clouds when the rains come. Give me your hand —' and as I did so, we were standing on the mountain peak.

'But, how…?'

'There is much for you to learn. Behold the valleys and the Great Plains.'

And together we could see way into the distance, right out to the far horizon.

'All this is God's Land?'

'This is just a small part of it. See how the hills slope down into the green valley? Look, just there. There is the place where you were brought into Mother Earth; and here, just to its side, is the river that watered our people and the land of our forefathers. But now, you are here. All this, as far as the eye can see, is over for you, my son.'

And the old man saw my tears falling gently. 'Do not cry for the past — pray for the future. You shall once again go back to the earth.'

My eyes lit up with expectation. Could I dare look forward to being beside Running Deer again? But great-grandfather heard my silent prayer.

'You shall not take up the flesh again. There is a greater task before you. Somewhere in the time yet unborn, you shall stand beside the soul of a man. This man is not of our race or tribe; he will be born far from our peaceful valleys in a time of turmoil and strife, in a land where many people will have forgotten the meaning of loving, giving and caring.'

'How do you know these things, grandfather?'

'It has been revealed to me, White Owl; I see many things with my inward eye which others cannot perceive. Your task is to bring the white man some peace and truth. In time, you will see what I have seen.

'When the Great Spirit reveals these visions of another world to you, you will feel pity for those races yet unborn. They will have lost their way. They will need our simple truths of the spirit to guide them back onto a pathway of peace, a way of caring for one another and Mother Earth.'

'I don't understand,' I said.

And great-grandfather took my hands and with the most beautiful smiling eyes I had ever seen he assured me, 'It is written, White Owl. You shall be a messenger. You will see. I have never lied to you.'

Pausing to gather his thoughts, he stretched out a hand and moved it across the vista before us, and with the utmost conviction reaffirmed:

'In a time yet to come, in a place far from these beauteous mountains, you shall play your part. With a man yet unborn, you shall stand; and together you will bring the Truths of the Great Spirit to all who will cease their wanderings and listen.'

16

Behind the Scenes
at Séances

I've often been asked what it's like to communicate with the spirit people and to reveal how I cope with the problems that arise when messages are being relayed from one level of being to another.

The processes are intricate, to say the least, and it requires a great deal of skill to manage a public demonstration or a private consultation correctly, especially when many communicators are trying to gain my attention at once, which has sometimes happened.

So here's a medium's-eye view of what occurs behind the glare of the spotlights in a public meeting, or privately when I receive communications from people in the next world.

I arrive at city halls or theatres and accustom myself to the surroundings and settle technical arrangements with sound and lighting engineers, then I retire to my dressing-room to change. If letters and greetings cards have arrived I don't open them or have any contact with outside information, such as inscriptions on bouquets or gifts. As much as these kindnesses are appreciated I must keep my mind free from anything that may influence it prior to the demonstration.

Eventually the theatre doors are opened and the public flood inside. From my dressing-room I hear the droning buzz of hundreds of voices and sense the excitement mounting among the people. At this point I remember that many in the hall are desperately hoping for contact with people they've loved and seemingly 'lost'; some may have held on tightly to their tickets for months. To them, their tickets are passports to renewed hope.

The needs of these people cannot help but keep sensitives humble. I know can't possibly reach them all, so inwardly I ask that everyone will find the meeting helpful.

As the seats fill, the noise of talking swells until it sounds like a massive swarm of bees circling the building.

I relax as much as possible: in the silence of my mind I send out thoughts to those who help me, asking that their evidence may be clearly communicated and that they'll bring accurate details which can be readily understood. I ask to be given the full name of the communicator and of the recipient in the hall if possible, so that between us we can establish the correct contact quickly (I know then that the messages will flow through me).

Sometimes I receive part of a message at this point, before I face the public. A man might appear and ask for a connection to his wife who he assures me is in the auditorium; or a child might be heard giving a name and a message for its mother. If this happens I respond immediately with something like, 'Stay close to me and we'll try to get your message through.' Or, 'Stay with me and I'll do my best to help you.'

The clock ticks away and the final minutes before I take the platform rush toward me.

In the early days, my solar plexus used to tighten with anticipation, but not now. Before I gained confidence and learned to trust my communicators implicitly I used to be anxious to the point of worry, but experience has beaten this fear out of my system. Yet slight apprehension remains because communication, even at its best, is always an experiment: so many processes can go wrong, as I'll explain later.

Now I'm ready to start the meeting.

In the shadowy theatre wings I pause and compose myself, aware of the great responsibilities placed upon my shoulders. I will be representing the spirit world and the organisation I'm serving, of course, but I also recognise that by the power of the word I could help to rekindle the happiness of lives shattered by grief. Words can encourage, give comfort and offer startling evidence of survival, if they're chosen carefully and delivered correctly.

The audience falls silent and the meeting commences.

I'm introduced; the curtain rises and I take the platform, stepping to the microphone and acknowledging the welcome.

While I explain to the public what I'm about to do, my consciousness begins to register the nearness of the spirit world. But it's sometimes difficult to 'block out' the psychic atmosphere generated by the crowd seated before me; those seas of expectant faces, each one telling its own story, many praying for specific contact with the Greater World.

I always commence with a talk, which may prove helpful to the hundreds listening. I might relate an uplifting true story of a spirit-return or a comforting experience. I speak because I know that with the magnitude of the gathering and the time allotted me to work I can't possibly touch everyone with a spirit message. When I address a crowd I feel I'm talking to each individual, personally; it's a little something from me to you, if you like: some spiritual knowledge or thought-provoking ideas inspired by the people on the other side.

I'm soon surrounded by rays of spiritual light and energy.

But the public are waiting, so... where is my first contact?

All anxiety vanishes when a communicator gives me information about him- or herself, which may comprise of places, names, dates or other family matters.

My first job is to place the link.

The right connection must be made before the evidence can be relayed because if the message goes to the wrong person the whole object of the evening is defeated.

Placing links can sometimes be difficult: even if I receive the full name of the communicator and the person he wishes to contact, it's not uncommon to deliver this to a wall of abject silence. Audiences often feel nervous and apprehensive, particularly if this is the first time they've experienced a medium's work.

Alternatively, several hands may rise to claim the connection. Some wave because they genuinely believe the information relates to them; but others, driven by grief or greed, may claim a message just to have some kind of help, even if they know it doesn't belong to them.

At this point I become a kind of telephone-operator between two worlds, though vision and sense are also in use as well as sound.

When two or three people try to claim the information I ask the communicator to bring more facts — and this is where we really get to work as a two-worlds team.

The next pieces of evidence usually pinpoint the correct recipient and this, in itself, displays an invisible intelligence at work.

I can't possibly select each recipient individually: in some gatherings all the people cannot even be seen — they're so far away from me and the glare of the spotlights doesn't help. This is why the spirit people contact me directly on the platform, although I do frequently see them standing next to their relatives in the hall.

Once the link is firmly placed, the communicator acknowledges this with more evidence, then the messages flow and usually reach their target.

Most messages are direct and to the point. Sometimes they're simply worded, but on occasions they've been so complicated that only the recipient could unravel them.

The communicators bring whatever they can to be recognised and prove their survival. But they may mention remote family details about which the sitter knows nothing. When this happens, people are asked to research the link to see if it's correct. This often provides the best evidence of survival because the facts relayed were obviously not stored in the recipient's mind, which rules out telepathy by the medium — a charge often levied at sensitives by sceptics.

I've learned that those who do not wish to believe, will never accept — even if the evidence is so startlingly accurate that it takes their breath away.

The fact is this: the messages can only be fully understood by those receiving them and those sending them. What may sound 'trivial' to the witnesses can often convey a wealth of meaning to the receiver. The link might contain 'code words' or intimate references known only to the two people involved.

Who can say?

I recall delivering such a seemingly 'unmeaningful' message to a man once, but it proved to be exceptionally evidential.

I'd given him the name of a spirit woman. 'Yes,' he said.

This was his wife.

'She's giving me a strange vision here. She shows me her right hand with the fingers outstretched but only two of them are painted with red nail varnish. The other three nails are normal. Now she takes this hand away and brings it back: only this time, all five of her fingernails are painted red.' I was completely perplexed. 'Does this mean anything to you, sir?'

'Yes,' he replied quietly, but offered no explanation.

Sceptics might declare these statements to be void of survival evidence, but in making this assumption they would never discover the jewels glittering in the dust.

The man later explained, 'My wife was painting her nails red when she took a heart attack and was rushed to hospital, where she died. I made the usual funeral arrangements; but when I saw her in her coffin I noticed that two of her nails on one hand were varnished but the other three weren't. So I painted the other three fingernails for her. I was alone at the time; no one, not even the undertaker knew what I'd done.'

The spirit people will use any means at their command to prove their presence to those they love.

The witnesses in a public meeting can judge the accuracy of a medium's work only by the quality of the recipient's response.

If a recipient is sullen, quiet, too amazed to speak or unenthusiastic, even the most astonishingly accurate evidence will remain unnoticed. How can anyone know if the medium is right unless the recipient says so?

Unresponsive crowds can ruin a demonstration of mediumship.

However, success is thwarted not only by the audience: I smile when the spirit people get their transmissions mixed up. The other side inhabitants are just as human as we are, and they certainly can and *do* make mistakes.

I recall a spirit aunt contacting her niece and telling her she was 'with child'. The delighted young woman confirmed she'd only just found out.

The aunt then brought before my eyes a pair of blue baby gloves and stated quite clearly her niece would have a healthy boy. Everyone was pleased with the news. But months later, this young woman reproached me, having given birth to a girl.

'What does it mean?' she asked.

'It means your aunt was quite wrong,' I said.

She'd probably felt a 'hunch', as many women do, and then voiced it as a fact.

I think we all learned a lesson from that.

I maintain that the best evidence of survival contains accurate details of present circumstances or important facts about a communicator's past. Predicting the future is not really the job of a medium; though prediction is possible of course, and I've often been used to deliver it, both publicly and privately.

In all my years of platform work I've never had to sit down because I had nothing more to give. In fact, if extra time had been available I'm sure dozens more spirit people would have communicated at each meeting.

From the first time I appeared in public the services flowed, but that's not to say I've never been in difficulty, because I have.

A breakdown in communications is more likely to be the medium's fault. After all, we're trying to 'tune in' to higher frequencies of the mind, and that isn't easy.

Mediums are rather like human radio sets; but whereas radio tuning is more or less fixed, the medium's mind is trying to register constantly fluctuating spirit-wavelengths. This registration is carried out by the mind, under the discipline of the willpower.

Often I catch everything that is given to me by my communicators but sometimes I miss pieces of the message.

Some spirit people play a part in a communications breakdown too. They forget things or get flustered and give the wrong information, just as we would at such an important time. Add to this the poor recipient who's been singled out to acknowledge facts before hundreds of strangers and you can see

311

that nerves can prevent the public from recalling even powerful emotional memories brought by their loved ones.

It's rare for a spirit message to go completely unaccepted, but this of course has happened. There are many valid explanations as to why some links are unclaimed; and often the fault lies with people who are reticent to speak up. They may feel embarrassed about others recognising their voices when they just wanted to sit unnoticed in a crowd to witness the proceedings; a few may have groundless fears that family skeletons will come waltzing out of the cupboard.

No medium can have control over these hindrances, which can, and sometimes do, prevent successful communication taking place.

I try never to allow communicators to humiliate or embarrass recipients. I often tone down, edit or even reject what I receive, because death doesn't instantly change those who experience it, and the public platform isn't the right place for family feuds to be aired.

A good example of an unaccepted message that was subsequently confirmed was the one relayed for 'a Mrs Gaynor'. She wasn't at the meeting when it was delivered but her friend was; but although she recognised it, she didn't claim the link.

Apparently I'd declared, 'There's a message for this lady, who's holding an appointment card for next week at the hospital.' There was no response; so I continued with, 'Someone here understands this but isn't acknowledging it; nevertheless I'll give the link. Harry says he'll go with you to the hospital and the test results will show perfectly clear. There's absolutely nothing to fear: you're healthy.'

Over a year later, Mrs Gaynor introduced herself to me in a charity shop and said, 'Harry is my husband on the other side. I was booked to go to the hospital and was quite fearful, but that message helped me greatly. The tests were clear just as Harry told you.'

Because Mrs Gaynor's friend had relayed this message it fulfilled its purpose and brought hope and reassurance to a bereaved widow. But the success of the meeting wasn't helped at the time by her remaining silent. Indeed, if she *had* spoken up, Harry might have had more to say.

I can only hope that other 'unplaced' links found their targets.

I've learned to trust and depend upon the voice of the spirit.

I've learned to flow *with* the stream of evidence reaching me, and not battle upstream by arguing over minor details that seem important to the recipient but not to the communicator.

When spirit communication takes place we on earth are passive receivers; the communicators are the active transmitters.

Of course, the medium must *combine* these two skills: he must maintain a central core of passive mental attention in order to hear his inspirers, but also take an active role in delivering the evidence.

If a medium doesn't speak his thoughts, the spirit world remains silent.

When I work, I'm engrossed and can lose all sense of my surroundings. Once, while delivering clairvoyance to a crowd, a woman seated no more than eight feet away from me was taken ill with an angina attack and escorted from the hall with quite a fuss made; but I didn't know what had happened.

This demonstrates that when a medium is working properly a shift of awareness is operating.

The contacts flow to me and I'm happy to deliver them for as long as time permits. When the evening draws to a close, about two and a half hours after it starts, the audience is sometimes upset: there have often been sighs of disappointment and people have even called out for more. Once a lady yelled emotionally, 'Please don't finish!' This kind of remark highlights the unique service mediums provide and the great need there is for it.

As I break my connection with the spirit world, its nearness fades and I become attuned once more to my worldly surroundings.

Sometimes, meetings have a question-and-answer session included and these have always proved interesting and sometimes positively absorbing.

As I bid the audience goodnight there is applause; on occasions they've stamped and cheered. But, however embarrassing the noise might be, I'm grateful because I know it's their way of saying 'thank you'.

Communication is never easy.

Mediumship has to be developed over a period of years: it has to be channelled correctly and nurtured carefully like a growing plant or a delicate child. It has to be fed time and patience; and if it's undertaken then it should be done only in a serious and responsible manner.

To dabble with anything is unwise; to master anything is always fruitful.

Each day, to strengthen my links with invisible friends, I sat in silence and spoke with them, mentally.

Being in touch with the Worlds of Light brings happiness: sometimes my mother or other family members greet me. While attuned I may receive wise advice if the conditions for contact are good.

I may be asked to read certain books to build my spiritual knowledge; I obey: once I travelled 300 miles to get them because they were out of print. Sometimes I was asked to write guidance for people who needed help. I was thanked with, 'Post it off. Sorry we can't supply the stamp!' In this way many people's prayers were answered.

My voices gave me plenty of work to do and often reminded me that the task of a spiritual medium is to serve.

Towards the end of a meditation I'd sometimes be told that if I would rest my head on the back of the chair I'd receive spirit healing energies. I never refused. I'd soon relax and feel exceptionally light-headed as the spirit power gathered around me... half an hour later I'd wake up refreshed and reinvigorated.

After one exhausting day's work my body felt like a lead weight and I slumped into a two-seater settee. When I closed my eyes I heard a loud *crack* in my mind and my head quickly dropped to my chest, but before it touched my breastbone my spirit body was lifted out of my physical form by two pairs of hands. How light and wonderful that feeling was; the sense of perfect calmness was marvellous. I still had my spirit eyes shut tightly when I was gently placed at the other end of the settee.

A woman's hands took hold of mine and affectionately smoothed my palms: I realised then that this was Mrs Palmer, repeating the gesture I'd done to her when I'd visited her in hospital and given her spiritual healing not long before she'd passed into the spirit world. By stroking my palms she'd cleverly indicated her surname.

Then somehow I disappeared into oblivion and awoke half an hour later in my physical body, which was back at the other end of the settee.

This occurred at a time when my workload was prolific and stress was high; and it proves the adage that 'Those who serve, are served'.

Other private communications occurred when I lay quietly at night, just before sleep overcame me. I'd crash into bed extremely tired and then feel the room 'shiver' — a feeling rather like a water-ripple in the atmosphere — this meant that someone had suddenly 'arrived'. They'd announce themselves and I'd see coloured spirit lights, of different shapes and sizes, floating about the bedroom.

In the darkness my friends would give a healing treatment; I'd feel their hands smoothing my skin and would receive a little prod in my stomach or side when they'd finished. That would be about all I'd remember until the sun greeted me at dawn and the noisy seagulls cried their screes and gracks as they fought over the titbits I'd put out for them.

One night I received a remarkable private link. I was shaken from deep sleep by hands and was shocked to see a figure watching over me as I lay in the bed. A spirit woman had fully materialised and was standing there — a solid human being. The orange glow of the street lamps filtering through the window lit her spirit robes, which were draped over one shoulder and up around her head, leaving her smiling face clearly visible.

I suppose I should have been grateful for the visit but I wasn't: it was like discovering a burglar in the room. The fact that she stood there in her flesh-and-blood body with loving arms outstretched made no difference, I'm afraid; I was only twenty years old and caught unawares. I dived under the sheets and thought speedily, 'If you love me, please go away!' And, of course, she did.

I invited her to return many times after this, but she never did.

Nearly all spirit messages are prepared in the

other world before they're transmitted. I can recall a fascinating example to illustrate this. When a woman on a psychic training course booked a private consultation with me, her grandfather communicated, gave his name and began speaking to her for about two minutes — then the messages stopped.

'I'm sorry,' I apologised, 'but I don't receive anything more for you. There seems to be a confusion in the spirit world. All I'm hearing is the name "Hutchinson".'

So the appointment was terminated and we agreed to try again the next day to see if our luck had changed.

It had; this time the sitter was pleased with the results and she explained the previous day's failure. The unsuccessful sitting had actually been booked for her father, *Mr Hutchinson*, but at the last minute she'd decided to commandeer it.

The spirit people had obviously been taken by surprise!

Mediumship by its very nature behaves like fluid: it flows and fluctuates in its operation, as indeed we humans do. That's why I always advise people to make a lengthy investigation before making a judgement upon the soul's fate after death.

The conviction that life is eternal comes only gradually as piece after piece of evidence is delivered, maybe over months or years, as if each fragment were a brick in a rising wall. After a while the wall becomes so high, so overpowering in its immensity, that the seeker cannot then say 'I see no wall'.

But what exactly constitutes evidence of survival?

What convinces one man may seem like nonsense to another.

I believe that what sceptics demand from the spirit world wouldn't entirely satisfy them. They ask for full names, telephone numbers, cheque-book account numbers, dates of death and other 'precise' information. To a degree this kind of accuracy is necessary, of course, and all good mediums should strive to develop it. But I firmly believe that it is the seemingly trivial and intimate memories, the everyday phrases and personal characteristics that spirit communicators bring, which often present the most convincing evidence to the average seeker.

The evidence is carefully prepared for the benefit of the recipient and not for the approval of media-men, reporters or even the other witnesses.

There will always be those who are unready to accept the fact of an afterlife; there will always be people who will remain seemingly untouched by a display of spirit power. I say seemingly, for who knows what really goes on inside another human being's mind?

The hardened sceptic who refutes the fact of survival and leaves a séance with nothing but scorn for mediumship may be the person who holds the greatest fear of dying. One day, perhaps even on his deathbed, he may dimly remember the demonstration, and this thought may ease his passing and bring him comfort in his hour of need.

Nothing is ever is wasted.

A shrewd businessman who attended one of my meetings, but didn't receive a personal contact, challenged me afterwards.

'Without doubt you can hold an audience's attention and present your case well, but nothing you said tonight convinced me there is a life after death.'

He'd obviously overlooked the man in front of him who'd received so much detail from his deceased wife that his tears of joy couldn't be contained.

'But I'm not out to convince you of an afterlife,' I replied. 'I'm here to serve the spirit world: to link wife with husband, mother to son and father to daughter, so that shattered lives may be pieced together and people can obtain new hope and peace within themselves to face the future.'

His brow furrowed.

I continued. 'When a medical specialist heals the sick, does he do it to prove that medicine works? Or does he do it to serve and cure the suffering?'

There was no reply.

Sensation-seeking individuals have asked me many times if I've delivered clairvoyance to rich and famous people or others holding high office. Some are convinced I've given consultations to royalty. But when pressed for details my answer is always the same: a private consultation is just exactly that — private.

It doesn't matter to me if kings or paupers come seeking help from the spirit people.

Worldly rank and titles do not impress me.

Whether the seeker is a rich man, poor man, beggar-man or thief, to me they're all souls on the pathway of life, dealing with its rigours and challenges as best they can. Irrespective of the status people may think they hold, they are all individuals seeking Light. We're all motivated by the same basic emotions, and we all hold the same basic concerns.

This world of ours makes much of pomp and ceremony, and it treasures public acclaim as a mark of importance, but in that Greater Life what we call ourselves or how important we think we are will be of little account.

It is what we really are, what we have done with our lives, which matters. These are the only eternal treasures we can possess.

Although mediumship comforts the bereaved, heals the infirm and gives new hope and meaning to countless millions of people, I believe there's a greater purpose behind its function. These comforting aspects are simply a means to an end; they are not the goal itself. Writing through my hand, my spirit guardian sums it up perfectly:

It is our function to touch the soul of man and to make him think, helping him to become aware that he is a mind, evolving through experience.

We desire to make people aware of the infinite possibilities and potential within them, so that they will turn away from the false worship of materialism, which creates bitterness, greed and cruelty.

It is our hope that people will learn the value of peace and love, and project these out into the troubled earth so that the children yet unborn may find a better world in which to learn their experiences when their time for birth is ripe.

If we can lift one soul, help one person towards the light of patience, tolerance and genuine caring for its fellow creatures, including the animal kingdom, then our task has been worth while.

For these reasons, and many more, we return to your dark earth, bringing with us our light of understanding, which will sweep away all creeds and dogmas and false divisions between nations, and replace them with the knowledge that all life is linked and is One under the Guiding Influence of the Great Spirit, the Giver of All.

The God Force is within everything, behind everything and through everything.

When man learns these truths and lives them in his life, with the respect for creation that these truths bring, then peace will be his.

And for me, these words ring true.

All we shall take with us through the gateway called 'death' is ourselves.

There are no pockets in shrouds; no status symbols or earthly aggrandisement on the other side.

We shall simply take with us our minds and characters, our soul-growth and moral attitudes, along with all the facets of our true selves.

Over there, we shall not be the person *we* think we are, nor the person that *the world* thinks we are. We shall be the person we *truly* are.

Seek Thyself

Seek Thyself; search not for any other prize,
But quest to find the *Real You*, rather than devise
A plan that leads your search astray:
  Glittering baubles all break and die
  And worldly pleasures perish away
  (Toys of one life only)
But your spirit stands for always
And you hold the only key.

  Lustrous jewels and paper-wealth
  Are just for a moment loaned,
  But nothing in this world of clay can ever match
  The pricelessness of your timeless soul.

A Life Neverending awaits each one at death,
And through the Gateway all must pass:
  None can escape,
  None can linger at the last breath, but
All must enter the Land where Thought is King;
  An adventure through the looking-glass, wherein
  We will only possess our Total Selves,
  No more, no less;
When we reach Home at last.

So Seek Thyself, 0 Thee of flesh and bone;
And rest not till the task is done:
  For once You are found
  You can never feel lost;
And when at last Great Peace is yours
You cannot count the cost.

                                        Stephen O'Brien

17

Questions and Answers

So many people are seeking spiritual truth that I sometimes incorporate a question-and-answer session into my large public meetings.

Over the years, investigators have posed some deeply searching and meaningful questions regarding life and its purpose, all aspects of the paranormal, mediumship and spiritual healing, God the Life-Force, and other fascinating topics such as out-of-the-body experiences.

Here's a selection of stimulating questions, which I hope you will find meaningful or educational.

Do we all survive death?
Yes. Survival of the consciousness after death is the natural birthright of all.

Do animals and domestic pets survive?
Yes, indeed. Many of our fellow creatures have returned through mediumship and proved this.

Do you have to believe in God or a specific religion in order to survive?
No. We're all a part of the Eternal Life Force or Great Consciousness and it is this which links us to everlasting life. All people, all forms of being have this Spirit within them and therefore all will survive death.

It isn't necessary to believe this or to follow a particular faith. What really matters is *how* we live our lives on earth. When we pass over, we will gravitate to a sphere of existence that we've earned for ourselves by the building of our character and the growth of our spirit.

So there is more than one spirit world?
Yes: there are worlds within worlds, within worlds, within worlds. 'In my Father's House there are many Mansions', many · spheres of existence.

Who selects the sphere we will live in?
The selection is automatic. It's all a question of soul-growth. Every kind deed, every truly compassionate thought or noble act increases the stature of your soul and the intensity of your psychic light; the spirit within you becomes more tolerant, more patient, more loving.

These character developments increase the frequency or rate of vibration of your spirit body and the psychic light it radiates.

When you pass over, your soul 'frequency' or 'wavelength' is naturally attuned to the sphere of spirit life where it belongs. 'Like attracts like', and 'Birds of a feather, flock together'.

So all the evil people have their places and the good have their own spheres?
Broadly speaking, yes — but I'm not happy about that word 'evil'. 'Misguided' is a better term.

Are you telling me we don't change when we die?
We're the same people one second after death as we were one second before it. Death doesn't confer upon us abilities or qualities of mind and character that we haven't earned for ourselves in this life. However, development is open to everyone.

We can change for the better if we wish to: infinite opportunities are afforded us to progress.

Do aborted babies survive?
Yes, and they grow to maturity over there just as they would have done here on earth.

When does life begin?
The two life-forms from the male and female involved in the creating of a child are both already alive. The seed and the egg have movement and consciousness. Therefore I maintain that from the moment of conception, life for that 'new' personality has begun.

But some specialists don't agree with you. They say the child isn't alive, as we know it, until it's

served its full term then taken its first breath.
Even with all our current medical and scientific knowledge we cannot be one hundred per cent certain. That's why I would always give the child the benefit of the doubt.

But should babies be aborted?
I can't answer that. In normal circumstances the mother is responsible for this decision. I believe in personal responsibility.

What do you mean by personal responsibility?
We're personally responsible for what we say, think and do; no one in this world or in the next can take away from us the mistakes we've made. We alone must rectify them, and hopefully learn from the growth-experience of overcoming our challenges.

It doesn't seem fair that very wicked people can get away with the most heinous travesties of human rights. Why doesn't God stop them?
But they don't get away with it.

In committing these acts they degrade their souls and thereby 'lower' their spirit body's frequency-rate.

One day the realisation of what they've done, and of the misery their influence has caused to many people, will become crystal clear to them.

They'll reach a time when they'll feel acute remorse and the need to put 'right' what they've done 'wrong'.

We are our own judges and juries.

There is no celestial panel awaiting you when you pass over. You will confront yourself with the memories of your acts — either 'good' or 'bad' — then pay the price your highly-sensitive spirit conscience dictates.

How are the acts repaid?

Usually by seeking forgiveness from the one we've wronged, then by an inner urge to serve them and others until we feel the records have been put straight and we can once again live with ourselves in peace.

As to why God doesn't stop people committing cruel acts: we have free will, freedom of choice, the right to govern our lives as we see fit. This knowledge, of course, brings with it personal responsibility for our thoughts and actions.

But our free will is limited. For example, we can't drink the oceans dry in one gulp, even if we wanted to.

There are eternal natural laws at work all the time, cosmic restrictions that curtail our freedom. These laws, which you can find in all areas of being — emotional, physical, mental and spiritual — are manifestations of what some people call God. I prefer the terms Life Force, or Great Spirit, Consciousness Itself. Some call this God The Law-Giver.

The power to choose is ours. God gives us this right, but it's up to us how we exercise it. We can create beauty and joy or wreak havoc and destruction.

Why are some people born with such terrible physical and mental handicaps? It doesn't seem fair.

This is such a difficult question: it needs to be viewed from an eternal viewpoint. If we examine these issues from a material standpoint only, our judgements will be wrongly made, based on transient and unsound information.

Behind everything there's a purpose operating. Handicapped people — and we're all handicapped in some way or another — are assumed to have a poor quality of life, yet they may be perfectly happy souls.

If the handicap is particularly severe the sufferer will need to dig deep down into his soul to find the courage to bear the burden. This is never an easy task for anyone, but by meeting this challenge and hopefully mastering it, soul-growth is achieved.

These challenges may be necessary for the individual to gain experience, so that his spirit can express some of its hidden beauty.

We are *all* affected by these forces, every one of us.

Man's soul also has spiritual debts to repay, lessons to learn, which may spring from wrong-doing in previous lives.

Physical and mental problems are usually explained as genetic faults in the early stages of life. But, having said that, I believe we inherit the body we need in order to spiritually progress.

332

Viewed through eternal eyes, this earth life is just an eye-blink in the stream of never-ending time. Earthly suffering is transient: it soon passes away; and there's no handicap in the spirit body, it functions in perfect health.

The immense courage, fortitude, and great optimism shown by many handicapped people are fine examples for us to follow.

God is perfect, so why did he allow Thalidomide babies to be born with no limbs?
There are two sections to that question.

First of all, how do you know God is perfect? God may be slowly evolving, just as we are; and imperfect beings make mistakes.

Secondly, the drug Thalidomide was created by research chemists and released upon an unsuspecting world before adequate testing had been completed. Mothers took this drug in good faith and, sadly, we know the results.

Are you saying that God allowed this scientific disaster to take place?
I'm saying God's Spirit is in all of us and that certain portions of this Spirit — the scientists involved — exercised their free will to develop and dispense the drug, then mothers decided to take it in good faith.

You say the spirit body is healthy. What about people who have lost limbs: will they be replaced on the other side?
In our world, if you lose a limb, only the physical

body suffers. Your spirit limbs are undamaged.

Cases have been reported where people on earth have undergone surgery to remove a leg, for example, and afterwards they've walked normally on the missing limb for a few steps then realised the true situation.

I think the spirit leg supported them.

Will there be a nuclear war?
I sincerely hope not; but it isn't my finger that's on the button.

Is there anything we can do to prevent it?
Yes: create harmony and peace. The more people know about the horrendous effects a nuclear war would have and the untold misery it would bring, the more governments will realise that in a full-scale nuclear war, there can be no victors.

I don't like the idea of living for ever. Who says life is eternal?
The people in the next world.

But it would be so boring!
Maybe. But then, what is time? We judge it by the ceaseless ticking of the clock, the rolling seasons, the rising and setting of the sun.

But in the next stages of life, there seems to be one never-ending day. The sun doesn't set; therefore clock-time is irrelevant.

Our sense of the passing of time is relative to our experience of it.

You can spend five minutes being absolutely bored out of your mind and it seems like for ever to you. Every second drags along.

But on other occasions you can spend a whole day with good friends and it seems to shoot by in what seems like five minutes.

So what is time?

It is an illusion, as we measure it.

It's all a question of individual perception. I've written a number of poems discussing these topics.

A medium told me my relatives in the Beyond would solve my problems. What do you think of that?

Not very much, I'm afraid.

Our problems are our own. They don't belong to the people on the other side of life and therefore the solving of them is our responsibility.

Although our loved ones can give us advice I very much doubt whether many of them have the power to interfere with our world to that extent.

My niece is on a life-support system and has been pronounced 'clinically dead'. Who has the right to make the decision to switch off her life-support machine?

All of us can exercise free will and therefore we all have 'the right' to make decisions.

In this case, however, the medical profession places the responsibility jointly upon itself and the next of kin.

Whoever makes the decision will have to be perfectly sure — at least, as sure as anyone can be — that the right choice has been made.

Does it matter if a child dies without being 'christened'?
No. All those who pass over will inherit eternal life whether they've been linked to any set of religious teachings or not.

If a woman marries twice, as I have done, which husband will she live with in the next life?
The marriage pact is a man-made institution: it is of the earth and all earthly things will pass away. Legal papers carry no importance in the Beyond.

The woman can live with anyone over there; it is her choice entirely, exactly as it is here on earth.

If a couple divorce and one partner still loves the other, will they meet up in the next life?
Again, that's entirely up to the individuals involved. True love will always seek its own.

Do the spirit people know everything?
No: most certainly not. They're only people, just like us. Older minds in the Beyond will probably have more knowledge than younger ones.

Do you think euthanasia, 'mercy killing', is right

or wrong?

Decisions are made according to our levels of understanding. What seems right to one man may seem obviously wrong to another. The acid test is the motive for performing our actions. When all is said and done, we have to live with ourselves and answer both to our consciences and to our victims for the acts that we commit.

Is everyone met when they die?

I would say yes, but not necessarily immediately or by the people they might think would be there to greet them.

But no one is forgotten in the scheme of things. There are watchers whose job it is to know when a soul is about to pass.

In cases of illness, when the family on earth gathers so does the family in spirit.

Why are some houses 'haunted'?

But the spirit people are everywhere! Their worlds interpenetrate ours; therefore every dwelling is haunted so to speak.

In homes where you find individuals who possess psychic sensitivity you'll probably hear of a sighting.

However, ghosts are not the same as spirit people. Very often they're merely energy-pictures held in the psychic fields of activity surrounding the walls and atmosphere of a building.

What is the difference between a ghost and a

spirit person?
A spirit person can communicate with you; a ghost can't.

The spirit person has a personality and is able to express it. But you can talk to a ghost or energy-picture until Kingdom come, but you won't get an answer.

Can the spirit people see the future?
Evolved souls in the afterlife may have acquired this ability, but I don't think many of the ordinary folk we've loved and known would be able to foresee events — not unless they've developed this special kind of perception.

Should we believe all that mediums tell us?
No. Test everyone and everything with your powers of reasoning and intelligence, whether you receive their teachings or truths from this world or from the next.

Test them all; think them out for yourself and dissect every word until you believe you've discovered their validity or otherwise, irrespective of who speaks these 'truths' to you.

People holding a great name do not automatically possess wisdom because of it.

Do you believe scientists should conduct experiments on animals?
No, because the animals are not asked to give their consent.

Do you for one moment think that animals would agree to vivisection, or to having their children stolen from them to be butchered for people to eat, or for their skins to be stripped from their bodies so that people can wear them?

The answer is no.

Man experiments on animals because he foolishly deems himself to be higher in importance than our fellow creatures.

Man would do well to remember that he is also an animal.

I take it you don't eat meat?
That's correct; I'm a vegan/vegetarian and I touch no animal produce.

Is it wrong to commit suicide?
Actions are only deemed to be right or wrong when each person weighs them against his or her own understanding and moral codes.

But there are a few factors to consider in these cases.

Suicide solves no problems.

Committing suicide doesn't extinguish your life, it simply terminates it here and places you in another world. In the majority of cases people who commit suicide do so because they can't cope with their lives on earth. If they can't cope with life here, it's unlikely they'll be able to cope with their lives over there, because they'll take this 'inability to cope' with them into their new environment.

But suicide victims are helped to progress on the other side. There are compassionate qualified specialists in the next world who help people to try to find contentment and a balance in living.

I've heard that if a person commits suicide he will be in a darkness, a gulf, in the next world, where he must stay until his 'appointed time of death' should have occurred on earth. Then he'll pass into the spirit world. What are your thoughts on this?

I don't accept it. Some suicide victims have returned through my mediumship before their own funerals.

When life terminates here, it continues over there. That is a universal law.

However, I wouldn't advise anyone to take his own life because the purpose of life is growth. Growth cannot come only in the sunlight, it probably occurs better in the shade.

All life is comparison. We must know tears and joy, happiness and sadness, pain and peace within.

Taking your life doesn't solve your problems because after the act you're still alive.

It's better to learn to cope with life here on earth; seek professional help if you must, but learn to grow spiritually through your struggles and hardships.

Some people say it takes immense courage to commit suicide, but I think it takes even greater courage to remain on earth and face your life as it is.

Are our lives planned out?

If they are — and this has long been a debatable point — then we are the planners. It must be that way because we each have personal responsibility.

Do you think our lives are mapped out?
Yes I do.

Do you think the death penalty should be given to people who commit murder?
If you take a life, you send a vengeful soul into another world and give someone else your problem instead of solving it yourself.

Capital punishment doesn't treat the root cause of crime, which would be to help the criminal to redress his character.

Do we have bodies in the other world?
Of course we do! Your earthly form exists only because it's built around the blueprint or energy-pattern of your spirit body. Take your spirit away, as in death, and your flesh decays because it loses its animating force.

When you discard the physical you'll register through a finer vehicle of expression, the spirit body, which is the counterpart of your present form. In its own world it is solid and real; it can be touched and sensed, and it occupies space and dimension.

Can you tell me what happens at death?
The physical body ceases to function and the spirit body, which is now the vehicle through

which the individual expresses himself, moves away from the earthly casket. Separation occurs; and once this has taken place the physical body has played its part and will begin to break down into the elements from which it came.

The individual will become aware of a different environment, another phase of life.

Is death painful?
No, disease of the body is painful but death is painless; it is simply the release of the spirit from the earth. I often think of it as a happy release, for in many cases it is.

Do you think people who charge money for their mediumship services are taking advantage of the bereaved and the vulnerable?
No one forces people to pay mediums.

But does a minister get paid for taking a funeral service? Does the undertaker commit the remains of a loved one free of charge? Do doctors receive payment?

Are prayers answered?
Yes they *are* answered, but not always in the way anticipated or as immediately as expected.

Prayer is a stream of spontaneous living thought; it's born of desire, and someone, somewhere, will hear those thoughts.

Just like a pebble dropped into a still pool of water, thoughts are born and radiate outwards.

However, some requests are so futile or so

materialistic that I doubt they would bring a response from advanced Beings in the Beyond.

In the main, requests that would accelerate soul-growth, or perform good service towards yourself or others, tend to bring the most fruitful and visible results.

The Universal Laws stipulate that by the very act of praying and opening up the heart to seek help from a Higher Source, the petitioner makes himself available to the great influx of inspiration waiting to be poured into the minds of all those who seek its help.

Prayer can be seen as a personal exercise of one's own spirit, through which it seeks refreshment, guidance or aid from those who are in attunement with it in eternity.

By opening the soul to stimulate our thoughts and energies, we strengthen our contact with the higher part of ourselves, our higher minds; and in this way we can be healed and renewed.

How should we act towards others in order to advance spiritually?

This subject is vast and I couldn't possibly give a short definitive answer; but for your consideration I would suggest these basic guidelines as a starting-point:

- ◆ Try to be patient with yourself and others.
- ◆ Try to really *understand* yourself and others.
- ◆ Through self-examination, attain peacefulness within and then radiate it.
- ◆ As far as possible in your life, adopt the

principle of harmlessness towards all living things.

+ Be truly kind and genuinely loving towards all Creation.
+ Exercise moderation in all things.
+ Think positively and act likewise.
+ Keep cheerful and try to be optimistic.
+ Exercise tolerance towards yourself and others.
+ Take full responsibility for your thoughts and actions.
+ Recognise that all things are passing, that nothing remains in a constant state. Life is about movement and change.
+ Change what you can; and gracefully accept whatever you can't change.
+ But above all: love and respect one another, and serve each other with a willing heart.

Why do you continue with your mediumship, Stephen?
Because there are souls in the next life who are desperate to dry the eyes of those who are grieving for them on earth.

I carry on because the Spirit has called me to serve and educate, to stimulate thought and proclaim that to love is better than to hate; and that peace should be written in every heart and mind.

I believe that might is not always right, and that materialism is a mental disease which leads to greed and selfishness, poverty and the breakdown of human dignity.

I hope that by using my voice to cry out a message of hope and reassurance I can suggest an alternative road — the same ancient path that one man spoke of many years ago.

Like him, I too point to the sign at the crossroads which says: *Love One Another*.

Windrush

Dead leaves billowing in the air,
  Blowing, fluttering, not by Chance;
  Windrush green trees all a-gently swaying,
Bright leaves clapping out an Ageless dance.

Mankind breezing down through Time,
  Twistering forward through Earthlife's Game;
  Windrush children seeking and searching,
Learning vital lessons with unimportant names:

Growing minds
  Not one of them the same,

Trying to figure out
  Why they came...

Stephen O'Brien

18

'O, Great White Spirit...'

*(White Owl delivers an Invocation,
prior to rendering public service.)*

O, Great White Spirit,
Thou who art Omnipresent and Omnipotent,
the Power which marks even the smallest
sparrow's fall,
I raise up my mind in simple humility,
as would a little child,
and through the act of prayer
I seek Thy Blessing upon this, Thy work,
from the deepest
and innermost Realms of Light.

I ask that Thy Messengers
may come forward to guide and inspire
all these efforts,
which are undertaken so that man may know
more of Thee and Thy wondrous Laws of Life.

It was Thee who fashioned the Universe
in all its beauty and vastness —

and it was Thee who brought into Being
the Mind of Man,
and linked him for ever
unto Thy Great Creative Consciousness.
And for these Unending Gifts of Life,
we are eternally grateful.

And it is the Prayer of these,
Thy Peace-Loving Servants in the Spirit,
that this vital task of spreading
Knowledge of Thy Eternal Truths
may continue
and thereby reach all Souls
in need of Food for their Spirits.

This we ask of Thee.

And for all Thy Blessings,
both hidden and seen,
we send Thee our grateful thanks.

19

Touching Souls

The train windows closed in on me and the passing countryside blurred into an unrecognisable streak. My head swam and buzzed and I felt uncontrollably sick. In a daze I rose unsteadily from my seat and staggered along the aisles into the cloakroom, where I was so violently ill I felt I wanted to die.

How I got back to my seat I'll never know: there were flashing lights in my vision and I was mentally whirling into delirium. I didn't know what time it was; I didn't know where the train was. All I knew was that I needed urgent medical attention. For six hours I'd suffered agonising pains and my endurance was now spent; I dimly recall pulling a passing Guard's coat and asking for help.

The next thing I remember was being carried off the train onto a freezing cold platform and strapped into an invalid's chair then wheeled into a Buffet Bar on the station. I was hundreds of miles from home and over thirty miles from my destination and the last thing I needed was the piercing stares of nearby travellers, who all stopped sipping their teas to gawp at me as I sobbed in my wheelchair.

What an humiliating experience.

As I wiped my eyes I just kept thinking: Why couldn't they put me in a private office?

After twenty minutes of public scrutiny and a series of loud and embarrassing questions from two ambulancemen I was whisked across the city to hospital.

Too weak to stand, I was carried into a curtained-off room, put into a loose gown and left on a bed in a corridor.

My body was ice-cold: the sickness and nausea had been so bad that a Sister injected me in the thigh to ease the pain and then left me alone. But I kept calling out for a nurse. 'In a minute!' she shouted from afar. But she arrived too late: I was violently ill all over the scant bedding, screens and floor. She came skidding across the tiles, muttering, 'God help him. Poor thing.'

Too unwell to travel on to the weekend of lectures I'd been booked to take, I was hospitalised for the night, next to a suicide attempt on my left and a drugs overdose case on my right.

But as soon as dawn filtered across the watery sky, I'd had quite enough. I signed myself out, and by seven o'clock that night I'd travelled the extra thirty miles and took my public meeting — weakly, but nevertheless I'd kept my appointment with the invisible world.

I was determined not to let them down.

Unfortunately the illness took its toll and the following morning I had a gushing nosebleed and was rushed to another hospital to cauterise the wound. My God, I remember thinking, this hasn't been my week at all.

For years I'd been travelling the highways and byways of Great Britain, much of my time spent either on a train or in a trance!

Countryside had flown past; there were so many destinations: large cities, smaller towns, villages and hamlets — each one welcoming a wanderer like me.

I loathe travelling and train journeys are often boring and seem such a waste of precious time. They're lengthened by complicated connections, and on boiling-hot summer days they're unbearable. The incessant *clickety-click, clickety-clack* lulls me to sleep, when other passengers aren't being noisy or obtrusive.

But travelling isn't the only problem I've encountered in the course of spreading the news of an eternal life. I've endured humiliation, too, because of my beliefs.

During one séance in Huddersfield, held for a Paranormal Research Group, two hostile sceptics were present among the forty people who'd gathered for a table-tilt experiment. We had to wait an agonising forty-five minutes before the spirit power built up sufficiently to lift and dance the table.

But our two aggressive guests were woefully unimpressed and accused everyone of manipulating the phenomena.

How dreadful to sit through a tirade of allegations like that. I countered, 'If we were pushing the table, don't you think we'd have moved it ages ago?'

They eventually retracted their claims, but what was more unbelievable: the people around the table were their friends.

I've been heckled too. I recall one man who sat arrogantly in the stalls, legs apart, lips folded in a thin line and his beady eyes stabbing me in the face from thirty yards away. People forget that mediums are sensitive beings and I'd spotted him the moment I took the stage. I'd only just started my talk — I wasn't even into the communications — when suddenly he yelled out in a booming voice, '*Rubbish!*'

His repeated interruptions were so abusive that the entire audience railed on him and ordered him to '*Shut up!*' He made quite a fool of himself; and when I continued speaking in calm tones without the slightest trace of retaliation the crowd burst into spontaneous applause.

It'll be a long time before that man disrupts another meeting like that.

But I sat down afterwards and thought to myself: Why on Earth do you put up with it, Stephen? The gruelling tours, the sniggering from the sceptics: why?

And then I remembered.

I'd been relaxing in an armchair when I instantly left my body and was standing in the Spirit Spheres upon a plateau at the top of a mountain. The air was crisp and clear, the heavens were brilliant blue. On the horizon I saw a speck of distant colour: it was a human form, gliding towards me at incredible speed.

Wrapped in silence, I fixed my gaze on the approaching man. As he drew nearer a great peace enfolded my spirit. And there he stood tall: my 'friend' of long ago, White Owl.

I searched his face. How could he look so young and yet emanate this feeling of being so wise and ancient?

But more surprises lay in store. With an outstretched hand he touched my breast and instantly my skin parted, revealing my beating heart. These were only powerful symbolic visions and I was not afraid.

His soundless voice said, 'Open your heart' — and I knew he meant: be compassionate. 'There are thousands who need your help.'

Then I found myself floating up some huge sandstone steps, heat rising from them under the sun's hot rays. Together we glided upwards to the top of what looked like an Aztec temple.

Then I became aware of lying flat-out on a sacrificial altar, my face toward the golden sky: giant birds cried out and wheeled high above me. My companion stood over me with a symbolic ceremonial knife raised high above my form. In an instant he plunged the blade deep into my breast and blackness engulfed me; and I heard the word 'sacrifice'.

The scene shifted again and I stood upon a platform inside a modern building before thousands of people all awaiting my efforts to deliver a message of peace and hope. There were seas of expectant faces and others were queuing outside to get in.

Why am I here? I wondered.

And the answer was granted:

'This is a shadow of things to come. It is the future.'

The words 'Serve whenever you can, wherever you can,' sailed through my mind.

The symbolic meaning was clear: a life dedicated to the service of others involves great personal sacrifices.

Then my guide's deep tones broke into my consciousness again. 'Give of yourself and do not count the cost.'

In that moment I saw him standing close to me as I viewed the waiting crowds.

'You will be given what is needed to complete the task. Trust and I will guide,' he said.

As swiftly as a thought, a swirling grey mist enveloped these pictures: the ground fell away from underneath my feet and I was dropping down through space and time — and I awoke in my armchair to the sights of Mother Earth once more.

But in my heart a life-changing realisation was pounding: I had been born to accomplish something: to point out a spiritual way perhaps? I knew I'd often fallen short of these great ideals, but now this should change.

All those years ago when this vision of another world was granted to me I knew I was setting out my future path. In my mind, the road ahead was being framed and born. I knew too that it would be a way strewn with hardships and tears, as well as with laughter and joy. But nevertheless, with characteristic determination, I was going to walk it. I had promised my 'friend'. We were an inseparable pair; a two worlds team.

It was quite a while before I realised I'd joined the ranks of the 'recognised', so to speak. In fact, it was only when a young man said, 'Thank you for your advice. It's not often famous mediums take time to give that,' that I was startled.

'But I'm not famous,' I replied with a raised eyebrow.

But when I sat down and thought about it, people from all walks of life had travelled from different parts of the world to attend the conferences at which I'd taught, from America, South Africa, Iceland, France, Holland, Australia and other countries.

I remembered being stopped in the streets and spoken to by complete strangers. They would smile and ask how I was. 'Fine,' I'd say. But when they'd gone I'd wonder who on earth they were.

This kind of attention has never sat well with me.

After one television appearance I was out shopping, unshaven and with my woolly hat pulled firmly down on my head to combat the cold, and as I passed a checkout I overheard three sales girls saying, 'He's a medium. I saw him on the telly last night.' I walked behind a fixture and straightened my hat. (I can't imagine why; no amount of straightening would have improved it!)

I quickly left the store through the nearest exit.

Having now joined the ranks of 'celebrities', whom the public mistakenly believes it knows so well, I found coping with recognition stressful.

I'm a very private individual, almost living the life of a recluse, and it took a long time for me to accept with a modicum of grace the attention my work generates.

I was helped in this process by the touching letters that started arriving from all over the kingdom, and was immensely moved when reading them. Such as the letter from an eighty-three-year-old widow who wrote, 'I was very impressed and greatly helped by your meeting last night. You told us we should count our blessings and that's what I've been doing all day. It's thirty-three years since my husband died and left me alone. You have no idea how important your work is to the many thousands like me. So may God bless you and all your efforts. And may the years ahead be very happy. My constant prayer is that you will be richly blessed.'

There was another touching note from a family whose daughter enclosed a gift of a tie, saying, 'My thanks to you for the happiness you radiated not only to me but to everyone who needs your help.' Her father wrote, 'I expect this is one of many letters you receive but I don't think any are written with more sincerity. May the Divine Spirit guide you in your wonderful work.'

Another couple penned, 'You are prayed for each evening, that you may be kept well to go forward to greater heights, giving out compassion to so many who need you' — and they enclosed a donation for a Handicapped Children's Society and the NSPCC, two of the charities I was supporting.

Personal gifts were often sent to me; people were so kind, especially the poorest of the poor, who exhibited the most thoughtfulness of them all.

Gifts would often come with poignant notes saying how much a small contact from a loved one had changed the whole course of people's lives and given them new hope to struggle on.

After meetings, people gathered around the stage or waited in corridors just to get my autograph or have their pictures taken with me; something I've never condoned or fully understood.

In the end, organisers placed stewards at strategic points backstage to protect my privacy; and these 'bodyguards' had quite a task preventing fervent admirers the access they demanded.

Once, there was so much bother removing an insistent crowd from outside my locked dressing-room that I considered clambering through a high window to go to my hotel in peace.

Some people have gone so far as to want their children blessed. 'Just hold him,' they'd say; and people pressed around me simply to touch me. I guess they thought this would heal them; but such 'adoration' has always made me feel most uncomfortable.

One woman confided she'd often called upon my name when under stress and that she'd been helped many times in this way.

'Please,' I reminded these people, 'don't treat me like this. I'm just an ordinary person. Please don't make me into something I'm not.'

But some people just don't want to listen it seems, for at other times I was asked to bless jewellery and even rosary beads. 'Say a prayer over them and I know they'll carry some of your power to help me through my life,' said a gentle lady.

I'm never amazed any more.

But other requests were most welcome, such as the invitation to open and speak at a peace rally to remember the 80,000 people killed in Hiroshima and Nagasaki in the Second World War. Prayers were delivered in the hope that this travesty caused by the misuse of nuclear power would never happen again; then lighted candles were floated down a river in memory of those lost.

Being in the public eye did bring some compensations though: I got to meet fascinating people I never would have known otherwise; and none were more intriguing than a holy man called Guru Sagar Swami. The neighbours had a real treat when he and his attendant came to call: he floated up the garden path in his long orange silk shift, his head shaved and his bright eyes shining with happiness. They were such a mystical sight.

For over two hours we discussed the vital issues of life and its meaning, each gaining knowledge from the other and challenging one another's viewpoint. At the finish he said, 'I give you an open invitation to my temple, day or night; and I bless you with the name of Lotus-Mouth — he who speaks wisdom.'

For once in my life I was speechless; and Swami and his faithful attendant floated away again down the garden path.

Another visitor gave me an even greater surprise, especially as she wasn't of this world. One sunny afternoon while I was listening to classical music, I caught sight of something happening in the corner of the room and when I turned my head, there before me stood the actress Judy Garland. I could hardly believe my eyes. She was petite and wore a black skirt and jacket, and red button earrings; her hair was cropped short on the sides and swept up on to the top of her head.

Miss Garland had died in London in June 1969 and the pathologist, Dr Derek Pocock, gave the post mortem verdict as 'accidental death by an incautious dose of barbiturates'. It was noted that she'd been taking sleeping pills for several years, and when she passed over she was such a frail and tired human being.

But here she was now, standing in my living-room as large as life: a radiant picture of health, full of smiles and obviously pleased to be seen. But suddenly her face darkened and she spoke.

'I'm worried about one of my daughters, Liza Minnelli. I'm concerned she might take the same path I went along myself,' she said.

Before I could question her — she vanished.

But why had she appeared to me in the first place? I'd enjoyed her films but didn't know any of her family, so what on earth was the purpose of this contact with me?

However, the spirit people had been quietly at work, not only to amaze me with her presence but also to drive home a spiritual truth.

Two years after this manifestation, Liza Minnelli's personal struggles at the Betty Ford Clinic in California came to light and became public knowledge in Britain, confirming Judy's concerns.

The Betty Ford Clinic helped many people come to terms with drug and drink related problems, difficulties which Judy Garland herself had encountered in her lifetime.

This clever spirit prediction reinforced my conviction that people on the other side of life can have access to knowledge that is out of our present awareness.

Anyway, it was great to see Judy Garland at such close quarters, glowing with health.

I've had to learn to mix with rich and famous people, but that certainly doesn't mean I belong to their income bracket. Some people think all mediums are wealthy, yet nothing could be further from the truth. Hundreds drag themselves out through rain and snow each week to serve the public and they barely cover their expenses. In my own case, I usually lost out because the profits from my meetings were donated to registered charities, struggling to survive in today's expensive world.

On one occasion Lord Northampton (known by some in the House of Lords as the Mystic Marquis because of his interest in the paranormal) opened a seminar at a five-star hotel where I was to teach over a hundred students. We dined opposite each other; me with barely a penny to my name, and he'd just sold a family masterpiece for eight million pounds!

What a staggering thought.

But my spirit teachers have often told me, 'What counts are the treasures of the heart, not earthly wealth.'

And I agree with them.

I've also been invited to appear all over the globe but too many commitments (plus my reticence to travel) prevented me from accepting. 'Perhaps one day, I'll come,' I told disappointed organisers. Even the world-renowned psychic artist Coral Polge received a polite refusal when she asked me to join her in South America. I declined by saying, 'Perhaps you can bring me back some nuts from Brazil, Coral!' And we smiled good-heartedly about it.

Coral Polge is the world's foremost psychic

artist and we've worked together on many occasions. Coral's highly acclaimed drawings of spirit communicators are projected up onto a huge screen, I then supply evidence to place them with audience members.

I recall one of her sketches was of an elderly man in the spirit world, whom I spoke with. I informed the recipient, 'He was a farmer, and he's your husband's grandfather.'

I went on to describe his house in Poland with the yard outside, and the place where logs had been stacked ready to combat a bitter winter.

Coral's drawing showed a dignified but rugged face of an elderly man with a white beard and moustache. The recipient, Mrs Wojciechowska, was amazed at the resemblance it bore to her husband, who wasn't present at the séance, and whom Coral had never seen.

However, she couldn't verify any of the details. 'I'll have to take everything home and check it out,' she promised.

A few weeks later she said, 'I showed the picture to my husband and he instantly recognised his grandfather, who'd died when my husband was quite young. "Just to make sure," he said to me, "we'll send a copy to Poland, to my sister, Stefania. She's older than me and she'll remember him better than I do."

'So the drawing was sent on a round trip of 1,500 miles by airmail, where it was immediately verified by Stefania, along with the evidence as perfectly correct. *"Where on earth did you get this picture of grandfather?"* she wanted to know!'

I smiled, because another soul had been touched by the power of the spirit.

Coral Polge and I first appeared together before a sell-out audience of 650 people; she's a lovely lady who has much credibility, integrity and professionalism.

An interesting snippet from this meeting revolves around the drawing of a beautiful six-year-old spirit girl with bobbed, blonde hair. I gave her name as 'Mary' and conveyed a relevant surname, then connected her with her brother in the crowd. 'She tells me that she was one of eight children,' I said pointedly.

'*No*,' he disagreed with conviction, 'that's where you're wrong, Mr O'Brien, because there were only seven children.' The auditorium fell silent, but I stayed true to the child's voice and quietly repeated her evidence.

After a pause he suddenly cried out, 'No, *wait*! There are seven children left — she's the *eighth*!' The crowd gasped at the spirit girl's tenacity.

After sending love to her mother, the young child delivered the clinching evidence about 'dying in water' and her brother told the hundreds, 'She drowned in the bath.'

What a happy man he was, after that contact.

Appearances on radio and television have always brought a good response from the public: many said they'd been comforted or their minds had been stimulated into new areas of thought.

One amusing incident with the television people always sticks in my mind. It occurred at a large demonstration and video cameras had been set up all around the City Hall, including one at the side of the stage to view recipients' expressions as their messages came through.

I sat at a table while being introduced to the audience: my eyes were closed and mentally I asked my inspirers for help, when suddenly I heard a crystal-clear voice whispering, 'Keep to the centre of the stage.'

Good God, I thought, the psychic power's fantastic tonight: that voice was as clear as a bell. But when I opened my eyes I came face to face with the cameraman giving me his instructions!

Sometimes when appearing at theatres, radio stations invited me to speak, and the spirit people lost no time in touching souls through this medium.

During one interview a listener felt impelled to ring the station to express her gratitude for the comments I'd made. She said she was terminally ill but my words had brought her peace and comfort. I felt proud of my spirit friends, for without them, none of my spiritual experiences would have occurred.

Meeting followed meeting.

Audiences flocked to city halls and theatres, leisure complexes, spiritual churches and conference centres. Many were turned away for lack of room as others gathered in their hundreds to hear a Message of Hope delivered by a World of Light.

I always instructed organisers to pack in as

many investigators as possible and to refuse no one the opportunity to hear the Message of the Spirit. I've even had my own seat taken from underneath me and given to someone in the hall.

Some demonstrations aroused so much interest that all the tickets were snapped up long before the event. One thousand-seater venue sold-out faster than for the world renowned singing group *The Three Degrees*, who appeared there the following evening.

A thousand people is sometimes a difficult number to handle: there are faces everywhere — banked up all around me, to either side of me and sometimes even behind me. Stalls and galleries blur under the powerful lights and it's not easy to see where hands are raising to claim connections.

So many people, so many needs, thousands of hopes and expectations. I pray that I'm given the strength and inspiration to meet some of them successfully.

At one particularly large theatre, when I finished my clairvoyance the crowd burst into enthusiastic applause. I sat down amid the noise, but they just kept on clapping wildly and cheering, and I had to stand up and take another bow.

The warmth of their love washed over me from the stalls and poured down on me from the circle.

As the wall of sound raised around me I gazed out at the smiling hundreds and immediately felt the presence of my unseen friend close by. Mentally I thanked him, for his promises of long ago had all been kept. Here we were, standing together, touching souls and moving minds.

As loud applause echoed around the theatre a kaleidoscope of emotional images clouded my thoughts: the tragic illness and early death of my mother and her startling spirit return; that thrilling but nervous moment when I took my first public meeting. I saw countless 'thank you' letters and felt once more the desolation and loneliness of my wilderness years when I didn't know my pathway. TV camera crews and journalists appeared clutching their notepads; followed by the rich and famous, standing beside the destitute and poor.

Another cheer from the crowd brought me back into the theatre.

And there, standing silently at the side of the stage, I saw a spirit woman surrounded by glimmering golden light and dressed in shining white robes — and my heart leapt within me as I beheld the smiling face of my mother... and in her hands she carried one deep red rose.

Then White Owl's voice reverberated in my silent mind again.

'Together we serve,' he said.

As a team we've travelled many thousands of miles. I've met thousands of people and despite all the hardships and sacrifices involved, I wouldn't change it all for anything. Someone once worked out that, so far, over 30,000 communicators have returned through my mediumship to get even a small word of hope to those who love and miss them. And millions more through press features, television and radio appearances — however briefly — have heard the wonderful news that whatever else may happen to them in their daily lives, they cannot die.

And it has been my immense privilege, in some small way, to have helped that Great Truth to reach them.

The Beginning...

20

The Beginning

The pattern is set and the work keeps flooding in. The telephone rings and promoters show great interest in bringing the Message of the Spirit through my mediumship to a much wider public day by day.

Glancing forward I can see television programme researchers getting in touch, nationwide media networks requesting interviews, and hundreds of organisations wanting me to appear for them to demonstrate that what the prophets of old taught is still true today: man is an immortal being and the Kingdom of Heaven is very close at hand — within us.

This morning's mail sits awaiting me. It'll take about two hours to answer it, I guess. Requests, thanks, expressions of gratitude for having shed a little light into darkened lives — all these will need a reply.

I see there's one letter from the General Secretary of the PDSA: 'I know that our Patron,

Her Royal Highness Princess Alexandra would like me to thank you on her behalf for all the goodwill and support you have given to the PDSA.'

But the pleasure was all mine.

Wherever I go I'm greeted by the same grief-stricken cry for help. The features and circumstances are different but the plea is always the same: 'Please Mr O'Brien, I've lost someone who meant the world to me. My whole life is in pieces and I don't think I can go on. Can you help me?'

I will try, of course: but how can I possibly accommodate so many demands upon my time and strength?

The answer is simple: I'll do what I can in the time God has given me.

I am a voice crying out a message of hope from a world of light. I've been called by the spirit to serve; and I know, therefore, that my pathway will not be easy. But I pray God will give me the strength to complete what I was born to do.

Thinking back, I've come a long way since those spirit hands hammered on our front door in the early hours when I was just ten years old. Only now, in retrospect, can I truly see the weaving of the pattern: how each thread has slipped into its rightful place, how each colour of the design has added depth and growth to the whole.

There's been heartache, sorrow, grief and tears.

There was a stirring search for love.

There was the sacrifice of personal happiness in order to help others.

But there's also been joy and laughter; and above all else, service. The great work of service has brought lasting friendships and a sense of purpose into my life.

I've had to learn humility, too, and the spiritual grace to accept what I could not possibly have changed.

I have done what was asked of me; I've endured what was meant for me.

And through it all I've kept my promise to the other world, and emerged with my sense of humour intact, and with a smile on my face, thank God.

What White Owl told me all those years ago when we first became a team has come to pass:

If together we can lift only one who lies fallen by the wayside, if we can touch only *one* soul and stir it into thinking, then our work will not have been in vain.

We can give solace to the lonely, knowledge to the ignorant and comfort to the bereaved through the great truth that sets man free.

When spirit truths touch the hearts of men and women everywhere with the knowledge that might is not right and that materialism and selfishness are not the only ways, then the Great Spirit's Children will slowly realign their thinking and bring out from within them the love that is there, and give it freely to all those in need.

When this happens and peace reigns in your world, we in the spirit realms shall sing for joy.

In a quiet moment, I asked him why he'd undertaken this great mission and he said he did it:

Out of love for my brothers and sisters still encased in the flesh.

I have walked your way. I know its sorrows and its trials well.

When I was at my lowest ebb, when all seemed dark around me in my life, from somewhere someone came and held out a torch for me to find my way again.

I have never forgotten those who gave up their time to help a humble 'uneducated' man towards inner happiness through the food of the spirit, which they gave me so freely.

When I knew the opportunity was open for me to do likewise for others, I grasped it in both hands and approached the grey earth again.

Did I not say when we first united under the banner of co-operation that the way would not be easy?

It never is for those who travel the path of service. But life is about growth: learning, discovering; a journey through time and space, overflowing with human experiences that help the soul to find itself and wake up to its infinite possibilities.

Together we have helped many towards the light of knowledge. I promised that we would; and what a great joy it is to know that we have played our parts.

But I could not have done it without you; you have been my voice, my eyes and ears, my hands.

In the time you have left to exist on earth I sincerely pray that our partnership will continue, my friend.

There is still much work to do and few to do it. But on behalf of all the spirits linked together in our band of helpers here with me, we give you our undying thanks and tell you, without any doubt, that we love you.

*

I went back to my hills and valleys of Wales just recently, thinking about this book and the events that led me to where I am today. The old house where I was born no longer exists: it's just a distant dream now, and in its place stands a smart estate where my father lives in one of the new houses in Lion Street. Dad and I are now friends: those old disagreements are dead and gone and we're both older and, thank God, wiser.

Someone once said that time is a great healer; and I think they're right.

'How are you getting on?' Dad asked.

'Fine thanks. How about you?'

'Oh, mustn't grumble.'

'No point,' I said. 'Tomorrow's the first day of the rest of our lives.'

Then we walked to the front door and I glanced over my shoulder and looked up at the top of the landing, and saw the place where my mother appeared to me in a blaze of golden light, three months after her death, all those years ago. And I wondered if she was with us both as we talked.

We parted company at the top of our steps.

'Take care of yourself, Stephen. You live so far away now; but don't forget, if there's ever anything I can do to help you, I will. You're my son.'

'Thanks Dad... and make sure you keep well.'

'Aye... I'll do my best.'

And for the first time in my life I leaned across and kissed my father on the cheek. Our eyes met and I think he realised that despite all our differences a respect was growing between us.

'Goodbye then, Dad. I'll come and see you again soon.'

'Goodbye, son.'

For old time's sake I went strolling around my boyhood haunts: the school where my mother met me in bad weather, the park where I played as a lad — they're all still there.

Standing in the parkland I recalled my youth; and as the sun beat down upon me the memories flooded in, and I recalled the woman whose love had started it all. The loss of my mother and her remarkable spirit-return changed the course of my life. Her urgent voice calling to me from beyond death, her glowing form appearing at the top of our staircase, the gentle kiss she gave me, the many proofs of her survival and continuing care... all these thoughts filled my mind.

Standing in the sunshine I watched a group of children, laughing and playing tag down on the grassy slopes below me, chasing each other in circles, arms flying and bright heads ringed with sunlight. In my mind's eye I could see myself there in my green years, running wild and free.

How young and full of joy they were.

Pictures of my childhood came unbidden: those days when I didn't have a clue about what my adult years would bring me, or the great responsibilities they would place upon shoulders.

I remembered, too, who had been the centre of our lives then: my mother. I recalled what a kind person she had been; and I knew beyond doubt that one day, when my life here is over, she will meet me at the gateway and we'll be together again.

Just then, I felt her welcome presence drawing close to me. And as faint as a whisper, I heard her voice say, 'What have you learned, Stephen?'

Without hesitation I replied, 'Many lessons. But for me, just one stands out in my mind. Only one single thought, just one code of conduct means more than anything else now.'

'And what's that, son?' she asked.

And breathing in the scented summer air I replied, 'Without love we are nothing.'

'Stephen,' my mother's voice whispered, 'the adventure is just beginning…'

And
when we stand
on the Shores of Eternity
and look back
upon our Experiences
in Earthlife,
we will notice
how all the things we did
happened
in just the right places,
at just the right times:

and
we shall say to Ourselves:

It is Good.

*   *   *

Stephen O'Brien moved back to Swansea,
South Wales, in late 1987.
The original edition of this book was then accepted
for publication and it became an immediate psychic
bestseller, which rocketed him to fame in the field of
mediumship and spiritual writings.

In the following years he swept through
the United Kingdom on mammoth nationwide tours,
delivering to thousands of people the message of
survival and the importance of enthroning
in their lives the power of unconditional love.
Through media appearances and a series of books,
educational cassettes, and Internet web sites his
spiritual work reached many millions of souls
across the world.

The publication of this revised edition
was released in 2000 to celebrate
Stephen O'Brien's first 25 years as a visionary,
spiritual healer, medium and poet;
and also to welcome in the first year
of the third millennium.

More great books and tapes by Stephen O'Brien →

*If you enjoyed
Stephen O'Brien's Autobiography,
then you must read his other psychic books:*

ANGELS BY MY SIDE
BY STEPHEN O'BRIEN:

'We are not alone in this Universe...'

Stephen O'Brien's extraordinary spiritual and psychic
gifts have comforted millions of people and have
silenced sceptics around the world.
In *Angels By My Side* Stephen reveals through his
acclaimed powers:

- ◆ Timeless Wisdom from the 'Silent Sentinels'
  and Angel Beings who watch over us.
- ◆ Fascinating glimpses into Mankind's Future.
- ◆ The secret Psychic Powers of Light and Colour
  that enhance Well-being and Self-healing.
- ◆ A compelling view of 'The One Living God'.
- ◆ What kind of life awaits us all after death,
  and the secrets of the Next World.
- ◆ Irrefutable evidence of survival.

He also shares with his countless readers
more of his amazing Out-of-the-Body excursions
into the Spirit World itself.

A Voices Paperback (384 pages; illustrated)
ISBN: 0-9536620-0-4

IN TOUCH WITH ETERNITY
BY STEPHEN O'BRIEN:

> *'As the hazy shape materialised*
> *there was revealed to us an Angel of Light,*
> *a beautiful woman with golden hair,*
> *whose eyes were deep blue-green like*
> *unfathomed ocean waters.*
> *"Peace," she said...'*

Make incredible journeys into the World of the Spirit
with Stephen O'Brien's remarkable
True-Life Psychic Experiences:

Go behind the scenes at Séances and discover how
Guardian Angels strive to contact us through the
Psychic Power we unknowingly provide.
Read stunning Survival Evidence of human and animal
souls after death, including children's messages to their
parents and a communication from
Dr Martin Luther King.

- ♦ Unveil the truth about Reincarnation,
  Telepathy, Life Before Life, Out-of-the-Body
  Experiences, Soul Powers, and how to Heal with
  Psychic Sound.
- ♦ Encounter *'The Shining Ones'* deep within the
  Spiritual Spheres of Light, and learn of their
  concern for the human family and our planet.
- ♦ Meet the Nature Spirits, and some amazing
  Animals that can communicate with us.

Fascinating Spiritual Experiences from
Britain's Renowned Visionary, Medium and Healer.

A Voices Paperback (352 pages; illustrated)
ISBN: 0-9536620-2-0

A GIFT OF GOLDEN LIGHT
BY STEPHEN O'BRIEN:

The Press described this remarkable book as
'un-put-downable'.

Follow Stephen as he recalls his exciting 20-year
psychic apprenticeship and strives to perfect the
extraordinary paranormal skills which have brought
happiness, comfort and hope to millions of people.
With warmth and candour he:

♦ Shares his thrilling encounters with apparitions,
  hauntings, spiritual healing and telepathic
  powers.
♦ Reveals the mystical Gift of Golden Light which
  illuminates everyone's spiritual journey through
  life.
♦ Presents a compelling array of survival evidence
  of human and animal souls after death.

A Voices Paperback (384 pages; illustrated)
ISBN: 0-9536620-1-2

'The epitome of mediumistic excellence' –
Psychic News

*Available from our worldwide Mail Order
service, or you may order these titles through
good book stores and libraries everywhere,
or Online through Internet outlets. Signed copies are
available from the Voices Online Shop at:*
www.stephenobrien.co.uk

*Keep in touch with our mail order department
for news of new titles and other products
originated by Stephen.*

The Spoken Word:
Six Recordings by the Same Author.

High quality digitally-recorded stereo audio cassettes,
running-time 60 minutes each, containing a wealth of
information and education that all seekers, healers,
mediums and psychic readers should know.

Stephen O'Brien's gentle voice can speak in your home
or private development class, teaching and explaining
each subject in easy-to-understand terms.

Develop your Mediumship & Psychic Powers:
*A step-by-step guide to the unfoldment and
safe practice of your psychic & mediumistic skills.*

Heal Yourself:
*Gain peace of mind & freedom from stress.
The way to spiritual, physical, emotional and mental
self-healing and well-being; includes meditations.*

4 Meditations:
*Obtain peace & tranquillity; health & strength;
guidance & inspiration; sensitivity & awareness.*

Develop your Healing Powers:
*Everyone's guide to success as a healer:
'We all have the power to heal.'*

4 Visualisations:
*Relax your body; calm your mind;
quieten your spirit; refresh your soul.*

Life After Death:
*What awaits the soul after its transition.
Life in the world of spirit is revealed.*

Available from the Voices Online Shop at
www.stephenobrien.co.uk

*More titles will be released.
For details of our world-wide
Mail Order Catalogue Service, see page 384.*

For further information on all aspects of the
life and work of visionary, spiritual healer,
medium and poet, Stephen O'Brien,
including how to obtain by Mail Order
his best-selling books, educational cassettes,
spiritual healing crystals, and a full range of
other quality products (or to contact him directly)
please write, enclosing a large SAE, to:

VOICES MANAGEMENT
(Dept VB1)
PO Box 8
SWANSEA
SA1 1BL
UK

Or search the Internet for 'Stephen O'Brien'.
Visit our Online Shop where you may order signed
copies of all of the Stephen O'Brien products at:
www.stephenobrien.co.uk

Voices Management regrets it cannot reply
without a large stamped self-addressed envelope
and correspondents are respectfully advised
not to mail irreplaceable items to the author,
for neither Voices, nor Mr O'Brien,
can accept responsibility for the loss or damage
of any unsolicited manuscripts, poems,
sentimental objects, photographs, or cassettes etc.,
which are often posted by the public.

Your letters are always welcome,
but please keep them brief and to the point —
and be patient when awaiting your replies,
for Stephen receives vast quantities of mail
from around the world.

Thank you.